The Economist

POCKET WORLD IN FIGURES

The
Economist

=== POCKET ===
WORLD IN
FIGURES

THE ECONOMIST IN ASSOCIATION WITH
PROFILE BOOKS LTD

Published by Profile Books Ltd,
58A Hatton Garden, London EC1N 8LX

First published by The Economist Books Ltd 1991

Material researched and compiled by
Robert Eves, Andrew Gilbert, Steven Higgins, Carol Howard,
Stella Jones, Dianne Martin, David McKelvey, Henrietta Nelder,
Nic Wiseman, Simon Wright

Typeset in Univers by MacGuru
macguru@pavilion.co.uk

Printed in Italy by
LEGO S.p.a. – Vicenza – Italy

A CIP catalogue record for this book is available
from the British Library

ISBN 1 86197 110 9

Contents

9 Notes
10 Abbreviations

11 Part I World Rankings

12 Countries: *natural facts*
Countries: the largest   Mountains: the highest
Rivers: the longest   Waterfalls: the highest

14 Population: *explosions revealed*
Largest 1996   Largest 2015   Fastest growing 1990–2000
Slowest growing 1990–2000   Fastest growing 2000–2015
Slowest growing 2000–2015

16 Population density
Highest population density   Lowest population density

17 City living
Biggest cities   Quality of life index
Highest urban population   Lowest urban population

18 Population: *age and sex*
Youngest populations   Oldest populations
Most male populations   Most female populations

20 Population: *matters of breeding*
Highest crude birth rates   Highest fertility rates
Lowest crude birth rates   Lowest fertility rates   Abortion rates

22 The world economy
Biggest economies   Biggest economies by purchasing power
Regional GDP   Regional purchasing power   Regions by population
Regional international trade

24 Living standards
Highest GDP per head   Lowest GDP per head
Highest purchasing power   Lowest purchasing power

26 The quality of life
Human development index   Economic freedom index

28 Economic growth
Fastest economic growth 1990–96   Slowest economic growth 1990–96
Fastest economic growth 1980–90   Slowest economic growth 1980–90
Highest industrial growth 1990–96   Highest services growth 1990–96
Highest agricultural growth 1990–96

30 Trading places
Biggest traders   Most trade dependent   Least trade dependent
Biggest visible traders   Biggest invisible traders

32 Current account
Largest surpluses   Largest deficits
Largest surpluses as % of GDP   Largest deficits as % of GDP

34 Inflation
Highest inflation 1996–97   Highest inflation 1990–97
Lowest inflation 1996–97   Lowest inflation 1990–97

36 Debt
Highest foreign debt   Highest debt service
Highest foreign debt burden   Highest debt service ratios

CONTENTS

38 Aid
Largest donors   Largest recipients
Largest donors, % of GDP   Largest recipients per head
40 Industry and services
Largest industrial output   Highest growth in industrial output
Lowest growth in industrial output   Largest manufacturing output
Largest services output
42 Agriculture
Most economically dependent on agriculture
Least economically dependent on agriculture   Fastest growth
Slowest growth   Biggest producers: cereals, meat, fruit, vegetables
44 Commodities
Leading producers and consumers of: wheat, rice, sugar, coarse
grains, tea, coffee, cocoa, copper, lead, zinc, tin, nickel, aluminium,
precious metals, rubber, raw wool, cotton, major oil seeds, oil, natural
gas, coal
50 Energy
Largest producers   Largest consumers   Energy efficiency
Largest exporters   Largest importers   Largest consumption per head
52 Workers of the world
Highest % of population in labour force   Most male workforce
Most female workforce   Lowest % of population in labour force
Highest rate of unemployment
54 The business world
Global competitiveness   The business environment
56 Businesses and banks
Largest businesses   Largest banks
58 Stockmarkets
Largest market capitalisation
Highest growth in market capitalisation
Highest growth in value traded
Highest growth in number of listed companies
60 Transport: *roads and cars*
Longest road networks   Densest road networks   Most crowded road
networks   Most used road networks   Highest car ownership
Lowest car ownership   Most accidents   Most deaths
62 Transport: *planes and trains*
Most air passenger-km   Busiest airports
Busiest international airports   Longest railway networks
Most rail passengers   Most rail freight
66 Transport: *sail away*
Largest merchant fleets
67 Tourism
Most tourist arrivals   Biggest tourist spending
Largest tourist receipts
68 Education
Highest primary enrolment   Lowest primary enrolment
Highest tertiary enrolment   Least literate
Highest education spending   Lowest education spending

70 Life: *the chances*

Highest life expectancy Highest male life expectancy
Highest female life expectancy Lowest life expectancy
Lowest male life expectancy Lowest female life expectancy

72 Death: *the chances*

Highest death rates Highest infant mortality
Lowest death rates Lowest infant mortality

74 Death and diseases

Cancer Heart attack Infectious disease Motor accident
Tuberculosis Malaria AIDS

76 Health

Highest health spending Lowest health spending
Highest population per doctor Most hospital beds
Lowest population per doctor

78 Till death us do part

Highest marriage rates Lowest marriage rates
Highest divorce rates Lowest divorce rates

80 Households and prices

Biggest households Highest cost of living
Smallest households Lowest cost of living

82 Consumer goods: *ownership*

TV Telephone Computer Video cassette recorder
Mobile telephone

84 Books and newspapers

Book sales Daily newspapers

85 Music and the Internet

Music sales Internet hosts

86 Prizes and medals

Nobel prize winners Olympic medal winners

88 Drinking and smoking

Beer drinkers Wine drinkers Pure alcohol Smokers

89 Crime and punishment

Serious assault Theft Prisoners

90 Environment: *trees and disasters*

Top deforesters Top reafforesters Fastest forest depletion
Most forested countries Oil tanker spills Industrial disasters

92 Environment: *pollution and waste*

Carbon dioxide emissions Nitrogen oxide emissions
Sulphur dioxide emissions Solid hazardous waste generated
Industrial waste generated Solid municipal waste generated

94 Environment: *recycling and water*

Glass recycling Paper recycling Freshwater resources Water use

CONTENTS

95 Part II Country Profiles

96 Algeria
98 Argentina
100 Australia
102 Austria
104 Bangladesh
106 Belgium
108 Brazil
110 Bulgaria
112 Cameroon
114 Canada
116 Chile
118 China
120 Colombia
122 Côte d'Ivoire
124 Czech Republic
126 Denmark
128 Egypt
130 Finland
132 France
134 Germany
136 Greece
138 Hong Kong
140 Hungary
142 India
144 Indonesia
146 Iran
148 Iraq
150 Ireland
152 Israel
154 Italy
156 Japan
158 Kenya

160 Malaysia
162 Mexico
164 Morocco
166 Netherlands
168 New Zealand
170 Nigeria
172 Norway
174 Pakistan
176 Peru
178 Philippines
180 Poland
182 Portugal
184 Romania
186 Russia
188 Saudi Arabia
190 Singapore
192 Slovakia
194 South Africa
196 South Korea
198 Spain
200 Sweden
202 Switzerland
204 Taiwan
206 Thailand
208 Turkey
210 Ukraine
211 Ex-Soviet Republics
212 United Kingdom
214 United States
216 Venezuela
218 Zimbabwe

220 Glossary
222 Sources
223 List of countries

Notes

This edition of the annual *Economist Pocket World in Figures*
has been expanded to include a larger number of countries.
The country profiles cover some 62 major countries, including
Russia and Ukraine, and a selection of statistics for the other
ex-Soviet republics. The world rankings consider 171: all
those with a population of at least 1m or a GDP of at least
$1bn; they are listed on page 223. The extent and quality of
the statistics available varies from country to country. Every
care has been taken to specify the broad definitions on
which the data are based and to indicate cases where data
quality or technical difficulties are such that interpretation of
the figures is likely to be seriously affected. Nevertheless,
figures from individual countries will often differ from
standard international statistical definitions.

In ex-Yugoslavia, Serbia and Montenegro now constitute
the Federal Republic of Yugoslavia, and Macedonia is officially
known as the Former Yugoslav Republic of Macedonia. Data
for Cyprus normally refer to Greek Cyprus only. Data for
China do not include Hong Kong. For other countries such as
Morocco they exclude disputed areas. Congo refers to the
Democratic Republic of Congo, formerly known as Zaire.
Congo-Brazzaville refers to the other Congo. Data for the EU
refer to its 15 members following the enlargement of the
Union on January 1 1995.

Statistical basis

The all-important factor in a book of this kind is to be able to
make reliable comparisons between countries. Although this
is never quite possible for the reasons stated above, the best
route, which this book takes, is to compare data for the same
year or period and to use actual, not estimated, figures
wherever possible. The research for this edition of *The
Economist Pocket World in Figures* was carried out in 1998
using the latest available sources that present data on an
internationally comparable basis. Data, therefore, unless
otherwise indicated, refers to the year ending December 31 1996.

In the country profiles, life expectancy, crude birth, death
and fertility rates are based on 1995–2000 averages; human
development indices are for 1994 and energy data refer to
1995; household data are latest available and marriage and
divorce data refer to the latest year with available figures,

1990–96. In a number of cases, data are shown for the latest year within a range.

Other definitions
Data shown on country profiles may not always be consistent with those shown on the world rankings because the definitions or years covered can differ. Data may also differ between two different rankings.

Most countries' national accounts are now compiled on a GDP basis so, for simplicity, the term GDP has been used interchangeably with GNP. GDP figures in this book come from the World Bank. It bases its rouble conversions on purchasing power parities.

Statistics for principal exports and principal imports are normally based on customs statistics. These are generally compiled on different definitions to the visible exports and imports figures shown in the balance of payments section.

Definitions of the statistics shown are given on the relevant page or in the glossary at the end of the book. Figures may not add exactly to totals, or percentages to 100, because of rounding or, in the case of GDP, statistical adjustment. Sums of money have generally been converted to US dollars at the official exchange rate ruling at the time to which the figures refer.

Energy consumption data are not always reliable, particularly for the major oil producing countries. Consumption per head data may therefore be higher than in reality. Energy exports can exceed production and imports can exceed consumption if transit operations distort trade data or oil is imported for refining and re-exported.

Abbreviations

bn	billion (one thousand million)	GNP	Gross national product
CIS	Commonwealth of Independent States	GRT	Gross tonnage
		m	million
EU	European Union	NDP	Net domestic product
kg	kilogram	NMP	Net material product
km	kilometre	PPP	Purchasing power parity
GDP	Gross domestic product	...	not available

Part I
WORLD RANKINGS

Countries: *natural facts*

Countries: *the largest[a]*
'000 sq km

1	Russia	17,075	31	Nigeria	924
2	Canada	9,971	32	Venezuela	912
3	China	9,561	33	Namibia	824
4	United States	9,373	34	Pakistan	804
5	Brazil	8,512	35	Mozambique	799
6	Australia	7,682	36	Turkey	779
7	India	3,287	37	Chile	757
8	Argentina	2,767	38	Zambia	753
9	Kazakhstan	2,717	39	Myanmar	677
10	Sudan	2,506	40	Afghanistan	652
11	Algeria	2,382	41	Somalia	638
12	Congo	2,345	42	Central African Rep	622
13	Saudi Arabia	2,200	43	Ukraine	604
14	Mexico	1,973	44	Madagascar	587
15	Indonesia	1,919	45	Kenya	584
16	Libya	1,760	46	Botswana	581
17	Iran	1,648	47	France	544
18	Mongolia	1,565	48	Yemen	528
19	Peru	1,285	49	Thailand	513
20	Chad	1,284	50	Spain	505
21	Niger	1,267	51	Turkmenistan	488
22	Angola	1,247	52	Cameroon	475
23	Mali	1,240	53	Papua New Guinea	463
24	South Africa	1,226	54	Sweden	450
25	Colombia	1,142	55	Morocco	447
26	Ethiopia	1,134		Uzbekistan	447
27	Bolivia	1,099	57	Iraq	438
28	Mauritania	1,031	58	Paraguay	407
29	Egypt	1,000	59	Zimbabwe	391
30	Tanzania	945	60	Japan	378

Mountains: *the highest[b]*

	Name	Location	Height (m)
1	Everest	Nepal-China	8,848
2	K2 (Godwin Austen)	Pakistan	8,611
3	Kangchenjunga	Nepal-Sikkim	8,586
4	Lhotse	Nepal-China	8,516
5	Makalu	Nepal-China	8,463
6	Cho Oyu	Nepal-China	8,201
7	Dhaulagiri	Nepal	8,167
8	Manaslu	Nepal	8,163
9	Nanga Parbat	Pakistan	8,125
10	Annapurna I	Nepal	8,091
11	Gasherbrum I	Pakistan-China	8,068
12	Broad Peak	Pakistan-China	8,047
13	Xixabangma (Gosainthan)	China	8,046
14	Gasherbrum II	Pakistan-China	8,035

a Includes freshwater.
b Includes separate peaks which are part of the same massif.

Rivers: *the longest*

Name	Location	Length (km)
1 Nile	Africa	6,695
2 Amazon	South America	6,516
3 Yangtze	Asia	6,380
4 Mississippi-Missouri	North America	6,019
5 Ob'-Irtysh	Asia	5,570
6 Yenisey-Angara	Asia	5,550
7 Hwang He (Yellow)	Asia	5,464
8 Congo	Africa	4,667
9 Parana	South America	4,500
10 Mekong	Asia	4,425
11 Amur	Asia	4,416
12 Lena	Asia	4,400
13 Mackenzie	North America	4,250
14 Niger	Africa	4,030
15 Missouri	North America	3,969
16 Mississippi	North America	3,779
17 Murray-Darling	Australia	3,750
18 Volga	Europe	3,688
19 Kolyma	Asia	3,513
20 Madeira	South America	3,200
21 Yukon	North America	3,185
22 Indus	Asia	3,180
23 Syrdar'ya	Asia	3,078
24 Salween	Asia	3,060
25 Sao Francisco	South America	2,900
26 Rio Grande	North America	2,870
27 Danube	Europe	2,850
28 Brahmaputra	Asia	2,840
29 Euphrates	Asia	2,815
30 Para-Tocantis	South America	2,750

Waterfalls: *the highest*

Name	Location	Height (m)
1 Angel	Venezuela	979
2 Tugela	South Africa	948
3 Utigard	Norway	800
4 Mongefossen	Norway	774
5 Yosemite	California, USA	739
6 Mardalsfossen	Norway	656
7 Tyssestrengane	Norway	646
8 Cuquenan	Venezuela	609
9 Ribbon	California, USA	491
10 Della	Canada	440

Notes: Estimates of the lengths of different rivers vary widely according to the rules adopted concerning the selection of tributaries to be followed, the path to take through a delta, where different hydrological systems begin and end etc. The Nile is normally taken as the world's longest river but some estimates put the Amazon as longer if a southerly path through its delta leading to the River Para is followed. Likewise, difficulties in waterfall measurements exist depending on which breaks in the fall are counted. The more famous waterfalls, Niagara and Victoria, are surprisingly small, 50m and 108m respectively; their notoriety evolving from their width and accessibility.

Population: *explosions revealed*

Largest populations, 1996
Millions

1	China	1,232.1		31	Argentina	35.2
2	India	944.6		32	Tanzania	30.8
3	United States	269.4		33	Canada	29.7
4	Indonesia	200.5		34	Algeria	28.8
5	Brazil	161.1		35	Kenya	27.8
6	Russia	148.1		36	Sudan	27.3
7	Pakistan	140.0		37	Morocco	27.0
8	Japan	125.4		38	Peru	23.9
9	Bangladesh	120.1		39	Uzbekistan	23.2
10	Nigeria	115.0		40	Romania	22.7
11	Mexico	92.7		41	North Korea	22.5
12	Germany	81.9		42	Venezuela	22.3
13	Vietnam	75.2		43	Nepal	22.0
14	Iran	70.0		44	Taiwan	21.5
15	Philippines	69.3		45	Afghanistan	20.9
16	Egypt	63.3		46	Iraq	20.6
17	Turkey	61.8		46	Malaysia	20.6
18	Thailand	58.7		48	Uganda	20.3
19	France	58.3		49	Saudi Arabia	18.8
20	Ethiopia	58.2		50	Australia	18.1
21	United Kingdom	58.1		50	Sri Lanka	18.1
22	Italy	57.2		52	Ghana	17.8
23	Ukraine	51.6		52	Mozambique	17.8
24	Congo	46.8		54	Kazakhstan	16.8
25	Myanmar	45.9		55	Yemen	15.7
26	South Korea	45.3		56	Netherlands	15.6
27	South Africa	42.4		57	Madagascar	15.4
28	Spain	39.7		58	Syria	14.6
29	Poland	38.6		59	Chile	14.4
30	Colombia	36.4		60	Côte d'Ivoire	14.0

Largest populations, 2015
Millions

1	China	1,409.1		16	Egypt	85.4
2	India	1,211.7		17	Germany	82.1
3	United States	310.8		18	Congo	80.9
4	Indonesia	251.8		19	Turkey	78.6
5	Pakistan	224.5		20	Thailand	66.3
6	Brazil	199.6		21	South Africa	61.8
7	Nigeria	190.9		22	Myanmar	61.1
8	Bangladesh	162.7		23	France	60.2
9	Russia	138.1		24	United Kingdom	59.0
10	Japan	125.8		25	Italy	54.6
11	Mexico	119.2		26	South Korea	51.1
12	Iran	109.5		27	Tanzania	49.9
13	Ethiopia	103.6		28	Ukraine	48.1
14	Vietnam	98.1		29	Colombia	47.6
15	Philippines	94.9		30	Argentina	43.5

Fastest growing populations, 1990–2000
Average annual growth, %

1	Afghanistan	5.51	11	Ethiopia	3.19
2	Yemen	4.47	11	Madagascar	3.19
3	West Bank and Gaza	4.41	13	Guinea	3.12
4	Oman	4.20	14	Mali	3.10
5	Jordan	3.97	15	Laos	3.04
6	Libya	3.40	16	Gambia, The	3.01
7	Niger	3.35	17	Saudi Arabia	3.00
8	Angola	3.26	18	Uganda	2.99
9	Congo	3.25	19	Nigeria	2.92
10	Mozambique	3.22	20	Somalia	2.91

Slowest growing populations, 1990–2000
Average annual growth, %

1	Latvia	-1.13	11	Portugal	-0.09
2	Estonia	-1.03	12	Croatia	-0.08
3	Kuwait	-0.87		Georgia	-0.08
4	Hungary	-0.55	14	Slovenia	-0.02
5	Bulgaria	-0.49	15	Belarus	0.03
6	Romania	-0.31		Italy	0.03
7	Ukraine	-0.21	17	Bosnia	0.07
8	Russia	-0.15	18	Kazakhstan	0.11
9	Lithuania	-0.13	19	Spain	0.14
10	Czech Republic	-0.11		United Kingdom	0.14

Fastest growing populations, 2000–2015
Average annual growth, %

1	West Bank and Gaza	3.87	11	Angola	2.91
2	Oman	3.73		Uganda	2.91
3	Yemen	3.31	13	Saudi Arabia	2.90
4	Niger	3.06	14	Benin	2.89
5	Somalia	3.04	15	Mali	2.82
6	Libya	3.02	16	Guinea	2.79
7	Ethiopia	2.99	17	Burkina Faso	2.77
8	Congo	2.98	18	Jordan	2.76
	Liberia	2.98	19	Congo-Brazzaville	2.70
10	Madagascar	2.93	20	Cameroon	2.66

Slowest growing populations, 2000–2015
Average annual growth, %

1	Latvia	-0.56	11	Croatia	-0.19
2	Hungary	-0.50	12	Lithuania	-0.17
3	Estonia	-0.47	13	Czech Republic	-0.16
4	Bulgaria	-0.43	14	Spain	-0.14
5	Russia	-0.38	15	Greece	-0.11
6	Ukraine	-0.36	15	Portugal	-0.11
7	Italy	-0.30	17	Germany	-0.05
8	Slovenia	-0.29	18	Japan	-0.03
9	Belarus	-0.22	19	Belgium	0.04
9	Romania	-0.22	20	Denmark	0.05

Population density

Highest population density
Population per sq km

1	Macau	24,468		21	El Salvador	275
2	Hong Kong	5,924		22	Israel	269
3	Singapore	5,476		23	Réunion	265
4	West Bank and Gaza	2,189		24	Haiti	262
5	Bermuda	1,200		25	Guadeloupe	253
6	Malta	1,168		25	Trinidad & Tobago	253
7	Bahrain	840		27	Netherlands Antilles	244
8	Bangladesh	834		28	United Kingdom	238
9	Barbados	608		29	Philippines	231
10	Taiwan	596		30	Germany	230
11	Mauritius	553		31	Jamaica	227
12	South Korea	458			Vietnam	227
13	Puerto Rico	420		33	Burundi	224
14	Netherlands	381		34	Rwanda	205
15	Martinique	348		35	Italy	190
16	Belgium	333		36	North Korea	186
17	Japan	332		37	Pakistan	176
18	Lebanon	297		38	Switzerland	175
19	India	287		39	Dominican Republic	163
20	Sri Lanka	276		40	Luxembourg	160

Lowest population density
Population per sq km

1	Australia	2			Turkmenistan	9
	Mauritania	2		22	Papua New Guinea	10
	Mongolia	2		23	Oman	11
	Namibia	2			Sudan	11
5	Botswana	3			Zambia	11
	Canada	3		26	Algeria	12
	Iceland	3		27	Paraguay	12
	Libya	3		28	Argentina	13
	Suriname	3			New Zealand	13
10	Gabon	4			Norway	13
11	Central African Rep	5		31	Finland	15
	Chad	5			Somalia	15
13	Kazakhstan	6		33	Uruguay	18
14	Bolivia	7		34	Brazil	19
	Niger	7			Chile	19
16	Congo-Brazzaville	8			Peru	19
17	Angola	9		37	Bahamas	20
	Mali	9			Congo	20
	Russia	9			Liberia	20
	Saudi Arabia	9			Sweden	20

Note: Estimates of population density refer to the total land area of a country. In countries such as Japan and Canada, where much of the land area is virtually uninhabitable, the effective population densities of the habitable areas are much greater than the figures suggest.

City living

Biggest cities[a]
Population millions

1	Tokyo	27.2
2	Mexico city	16.9
3	Sao Paulo	16.8
4	New York	16.4
5	Mumbai (Bombay)	15.7
6	Shanghai	13.7
7	Los Angeles	12.6
8	Calcutta	12.1
9	Buenos Aires	11.9
10	Seoul	11.8
11	Beijing	11.4
12	Lagos	10.9
13	Osaka	10.6
14	Delhi	10.3
	Rio de Janeiro	10.3
16	Karachi	10.1
17	Cairo	9.9
18	Manila	9.6
	Paris	9.6
	Tianjin	9.6
21	Moscow	9.3
22	Dhaka	9.0
23	Jakarta	8.8
24	Istanbul	8.2
25	London	7.6
26	Chicago	6.9
	Tehran	6.9
28	Lima	6.8
29	Bangkok	6.7
30	Essen	6.5

Quality of life index[b]
New York=100, November 1997

1	Vancouver	105.47
2	Auckland	104.79
2	Toronto	104.79
4	Zurich	104.59
5	Geneva	104.56
6	Melbourne	104.22
7	Sydney	104.20
8	Helsinki	103.95
9	Vienna	103.83
10	Brussels	103.45
11	Perth	103.43
12	Copenhagen	103.39
13	Amsterdam	103.27
14	Berne	103.01
15	Montreal	102.42
16	Munich	102.29
17	Dusseldorf	102.09
18	Stockholm	102.05
19	Oslo	101.91
20	Brisbane	101.90
21	Frankfurt	101.86
22	Luxembourg	101.83
23	Hamburg	101.53
24	Singapore	101.45
25	Wellington	101.03
26	Atlanta	100.98
27	San Francisco	100.94
28	Paris	100.91
29	Calgary	100.76
30	Tokyo	100.63

Highest urban pop.
% pop. living in urban areas, latest year

1	Bermuda	100
	Singapore	100
3	Guadeloupe	99
	Macau	99
5	Belgium	97
	Kuwait	97
7	Hong Kong	95
8	West Bank and Gaza	94
9	Martinique	93
	Venezuela	93

Lowest urban pop.
% pop. living in urban areas, latest year

1	Bhutan	6
	Rwanda	6
3	Burundi	8
4	Ethiopia	13
	Oman	13
	Uganda	13
7	Malawi	14
	Nepal	14
9	Papua New Guinea	16
10	Eritrea	17

a Urban agglomerations. Estimates of cities' populations vary according to where geographical boundaries are defined.
b Based on 42 factors as diverse as personal security and political stability.

Population: *age and sex*

Youngest populations
% aged under 15, 1996

1	West Bank and Gaza	51.7		Togo	45.9
2	Uganda	48.6	22	Congo-Brazzaville	45.7
3	Benin	48.4	23	Nigeria	45.5
	Niger	48.4	24	Libya	45.3
5	Zambia	48.2	25	Mozambique	44.9
6	Angola	47.7	26	Côte d'Ivoire	44.8
7	Somalia	47.5		Ghana	44.8
	Yemen	47.5		Laos	44.8
9	Burkina Faso	47.4		Syria	44.8
	Mali	47.4	30	Senegal	44.5
11	Congo	47.2	31	Iran	44.4
	Oman	47.2	32	Guatemala	44.3
13	Guinea	47.1	33	Zimbabwe	44.3
14	Madagascar	46.9	34	Cameroon	44.2
	Malawi	46.9	35	Sierra Leone	44.1
16	Rwanda	46.7	36	Eritrea	44.0
17	Burundi	46.6	37	Honduras	43.8
18	Ethiopia	46.2	38	Chad	43.6
19	Kenya	46.0	39	Nicaragua	43.6
20	Tanzania	45.9	40	Botswana	43.4

Oldest populations
% aged over 65, 1996

1	Sweden	17.3	22	Estonia	12.9
2	Italy	16.1	23	Croatia	12.8
3	Greece	15.9	24	Czech Republic	12.6
	Norway	15.9		United States	12.6
5	Belgium	15.8	26	Belarus	12.5
	United Kingdom	15.8	27	Slovenia	12.5
7	France	15.2	28	Uruguay	12.3
	Germany	15.2	29	Lithuania	12.2
9	Denmark	15.1	30	Canada	12.0
10	Spain	15.0	31	Russia	12.0
11	Portugal	14.8	32	Barbados	11.9
12	Austria	14.7	33	Romania	11.8
13	Bulgaria	14.5	34	Australia	11.7
14	Switzerland	14.3	35	Georgia	11.4
15	Japan	14.2		New Zealand	11.4
16	Finland	14.1		Serbia, Montenegro	11.4
17	Hungary	14.0	38	Ireland	11.3
	Ukraine	14.0	39	Iceland	11.1
19	Luxembourg	13.8	40	Malta	11.0
20	Latvia	13.3		Poland	11.0
21	Netherlands	13.2			

Most male populations
Number of men per 100 women[a], 1997

1	Qatar	193.3		Jordan	104.8
2	United Arab Emirates	176.4	22	Côte d'Ivoire	104.0
3	Bahrain	133.7	23	Iraq	103.6
4	Saudi Arabia	125.1	24	Iran	103.5
5	Oman	113.4	25	Dominican Republic	103.4
6	Trinidad & Tobago	111.3	26	Fiji	103.3
7	Brunei	110.3	27	Egypt	103.1
8	Tunisia	109.8	28	Algeria	102.5
9	Libya	108.2		Nepal	102.5
10	Hong Kong	107.6	30	Costa Rica	102.3
11	Pakistan	106.9		Turkey	102.3
12	India	106.8	32	Syria	102.2
13	Papua New Guinea	106.4	33	Panama	102.1
14	China	106.2	34	Guatemala	101.9
15	Taiwan	105.8		Malaysia	101.9
16	Kuwait	105.6	36	Honduras	101.6
17	Bangladesh	105.4		Macedonia, FYR	101.6
18	Afghanistan	105.1		Paraguay	101.6
19	West Bank and Gaza	105.0		Singapore	101.6
20	Albania	104.8		South Korea	101.6

Most female populations
Number of men per 100 women, 1997

1	Latvia	84.3	22	Kazakhstan	94.7
2	Ukraine	86.8	23	Poland	94.8
3	Russia	88.0	24	Slovakia	94.9
4	Estonia	88.7	25	France	95.0
5	Belarus	88.8		Uruguay	95.0
6	Lithuania	89.7	27	Finland	95.1
7	Georgia	91.4	28	Burundi	95.3
8	Hungary	91.6	29	Bulgaria	95.4
	Moldova	91.6		Lebanon	95.4
10	Swaziland	92.4	31	Congo-Brazzaville	95.5
11	Portugal	92.9	32	Czech Republic	95.6
12	Netherlands Antilles	93.1		Réunion	95.6
13	Cambodia	93.6	34	Germany	95.9
	Puerto Rico	93.6	35	Guadeloupe	96.0
15	Croatia	93.7	36	Belgium	96.1
16	Central African Rep	93.9		Kirgizstan	96.1
	Slovenia	93.9		Macau	96.1
18	Martinique	94.0	39	Azerbaijan	96.2
19	Barbados	94.1		Sierra Leone	96.2
20	Armenia	94.6		United Kingdom	96.2
	Italy	94.6			

a Large numbers of immigrant workers, mostly men, result in the high male ratios of several Middle East countries.

Population: *matters of breeding*

Highest crude birth rates

No. of live births per 1,000 population, 1995–2000

1	Afghanistan	53.4		Mozambique	42.5
2	Uganda	51.1	22	Zambia	42.4
3	Niger	50.2	23	Nigeria	42.3
4	Somalia	50.0	24	Benin	42.0
5	Ethiopia	48.2	25	Togo	41.9
	Guinea	48.2	26	Chad	41.6
7	Angola	47.7	27	Bhutan	41.3
	Malawi	47.7	28	Tanzania	41.2
	Yemen	47.7	29	Madagascar	41.1
10	Liberia	47.5		Senegal	41.1
11	Mali	47.4	31	Guinea-Bissau	40.3
12	West Bank and Gaza	46.7	32	Libya	40.0
13	Sierra Leone	46.5	33	Gambia, The	39.9
14	Burkina Faso	45.9	34	Eritrea	39.8
15	Congo	44.9	35	Cameroon	39.3
16	Laos	44.2		Mauritania	38.3
17	Oman	44.1	37	Ghana	38.2
18	Rwanda	42.8	38	Central African Rep	37.6
19	Burundi	42.5		Gabon	37.6
	Congo-Brazzaville	42.5	40	Jordan	37.5

Highest fertility rates

Average no. of children per woman, 1995–2000

1	West Bank and Gaza	8.00	21	Rwanda	6.00
2	Yemen	7.60	22	Nigeria	5.97
3	Oman	7.20	23	Libya	5.92
4	Niger	7.10	24	Saudi Arabia	5.90
	Uganda	7.10	25	Bhutan	5.89
6	Ethiopia	7.00	26	Congo-Brazzaville	5.87
	Somalia	7.00	27	Benin	5.83
8	Afghanistan	6.90	28	Madagascar	5.65
9	Angola	6.69	29	Senegal	5.62
	Laos	6.69	30	Chad	5.51
	Malawi	6.69	31	Zambia	5.49
12	Guinea	6.61	32	Tanzania	5.48
13	Mali	6.60	33	Guinea-Bissau	5.42
14	Burkina Faso	6.57	34	Gabon	5.40
15	Liberia	6.33	35	Eritrea	5.34
16	Burundi	6.28	36	Cameroon	5.30
17	Zaire	6.24	37	Ghana	5.28
18	Togo	6.08	38	Iraq	5.25
19	Mozambique	6.06	39	Gambia, The	5.20
	Sierra Leone	6.06	40	Jordan	5.13

Notes: The crude birth rate is the number of live births in one year per 1,000 population. In addition to the fertility rate (see below) it depends on the population's age structure and will tend to be higher if there is a large proportion of women of childbearing age.

The fertility rate is the average number of children born to a woman who completes her childbearing years.

Lowest crude birth rates
Number of live births per 1,000 population, 1995–2000

1	Estonia	9.0	22	Belgium	11.2
2	Italy	9.1		Portugal	11.2
3	Germany	9.3	24	France	11.6
4	Slovenia	9.5	25	Slovakia	11.7
5	Russia	9.6	26	Canada	11.9
6	Spain	9.7		Netherlands	11.9
	Ukraine	9.7		Poland	11.9
8	Latvia	9.8		Sweden	11.9
9	Belarus	10.0		United Kingdom	11.9
	Greece	10.0	31	Finland	12.0
11	Hungary	10.2	32	Serbia, Montenegro	12.6
12	Austria	10.3	33	Luxembourg	12.7
	Bulgaria	10.3	34	Denmark	13.0
	Japan	10.3		Ireland	13.0
15	Hong Kong	10.6	36	Cuba	13.1
16	Czech Republic	10.7	37	Armenia	13.3
17	Bosnia	10.8	38	Norway	13.4
	Croatia	10.8	39	Moldova	13.6
	Lithuania	10.8	40	Georgia	13.8
20	Switzerland	10.9		United States	13.8
21	Romania	11.0			

Lowest fertility rates
Average number of children per woman, 1995–2000

1	Italy	1.19
2	Spain	1.22
3	Estonia	1.30
	Germany	1.30
	Slovenia	1.30
6	Hong Kong	1.32
7	Russia	1.35
8	Greece	1.38
	Ukraine	1.38
10	Belarus	1.40
	Bosnia	1.40
	Czech Republic	1.40
	Hungary	1.40
	Latvia	1.40
	Romania	1.40
16	Austria	1.42
17	Bulgaria	1.45
18	Switzerland	1.46
19	Japan	1.48
	Portugal	1.48

Abortion rates
Abortions per 1,000 women aged 15–44, latest year

1	Vietnam	100.1
2	Romania[a]	99.6
3	Russia	80.8
4	Ukraine	71.5
5	Estonia	70.3
6	Bosnia	65.2
7	Moldova	56.7
8	Cuba	54.5
9	Serbia, Montenegro	52.9
10	Bulgaria	52.4
11	Peru[b]	51.8
12	Latvia	50.2
13	Macedonia, FYR	46.7
14	Chile[b]	45.4
15	Albania	45.1
16	Dominican Republic[b]	43.7
17	Brazil[b]	38.1
18	Lithuania	37.0
19	South Korea[c]	36.4
20	China	35.8

a Official statistics that are incomplete.
b Indirect estimates based on hospital data. Rate is per 1,000 women aged 15–49.
  Includes safe and unsafe abortions.
c Estimates based on surveys or other data.

The world economy

Biggest economies
GDP, $bn

1	United States	7,434	27	Hong Kong	153
2	Japan	5,149	28	Norway	151
3	Germany	2,365	29	Saudi Arabia	137
4	France	1,534	30	South Africa	133
5	United Kingdom	1,152	31	Poland	125
6	Italy	1,141	32	Greece	120
7	China	906	33	Finland	119
8	Brazil	710	34	Portugal	101
9	Canada	570	35	Singapore	93
10	Spain	563	36	Israel	90
11	South Korea	483		Malaysia	90
12	Netherlands	403	38	Philippines	83
13	Australia	368	39	Iran	82
14	India	358	40	Colombia	80
15	Russia	356	41	Chile	70
16	Mexico	342	42	Venezuela	67
17	Switzerland	314	43	Egypt	64
18	Argentina	295		Pakistan	64
19	Taiwan	275	45	Ireland	62
20	Belgium	269	46	Ukraine	61
21	Austria	227	47	Peru	59
	Sweden	227	48	New Zealand	57
23	Indonesia	213	49	Czech Republic	49
24	Thailand	178	50	Algeria	44
	Turkey	178		Hungary	44
26	Denmark	169			

Biggest economies by purchasing power
GDP PPP, $bn

1	United States	7,433	16	Thailand	402
2	China	4,047	17	Turkey	380
3	Japan	2,945	18	Taiwan	378
4	Germany	1,729	19	Australia	364
5	India	1,493	20	Argentina	336
6	France	1,256	21	Iran	335
7	United Kingdom	1,173	22	Netherlands	324
8	Italy	1,141	23	South Africa	280
9	Brazil	1,023	24	Philippines	255
10	Mexico	714	25	Colombia	252
11	Indonesia	652	26	Poland	232
12	Canada	641	27	Belgium	228
13	Russia	619	28	Malaysia	214
14	Spain	600		Pakistan	214
15	South Korea	596	30	Saudi Arabia	188

For list of all countries with their GDP see pages 223–4.

Regional GDP

$bn		*% growth 1989–96*	
World	29,510	World	3.0
Advanced economies	23,614	Advanced economies	2.2
G7	19,343	G7	1.9
EU15	8,469	EU15	1.7
Asia[a]	2,106	Asia[a]	8.3
Latin America	1,754	Latin America	3.0
Eastern Europe[b]	850	Eastern Europe[b]	-5.6
Middle East and Europe[c]	682	Middle East and Europe[c]	4.1
Africa	376	Africa	2.3

Regional purchasing power

GDP in PPP, % of total		*$*	
Advanced economies	56.6	World	5,129
G7	45.4	Advanced economies	25,876
EU15	20.4	G7	28,441
Asia[a]	22.5	EU15	22,729
Latin America	8.8	Asia[a]	704
Eastern Europe[b]	4.2	Latin America	3,758
Middle East and Europe[c]	4.6	Eastern Europe[b]	2,088
Africa	3.4	Middle East and Europe[c]	2,375
		Africa	652

Regions by population

% of total		*No. of countries[d]*	
Advanced economies	15.8	Advanced economies	28
G7	11.8	G7	7
EU15	6.5	EU15	15
Asia[a]	52.3	Asia[a]	26
Latin America	8.3	Latin America	33
Eastern Europe[b]	7.1	Eastern Europe[b]	28
Middle East and Europe[c]	5.1	Middle East and Europe[c]	17
Africa	11.4	Africa	51

Regional international trade

Exports of goods and services, % of tot.		*Current account balances, $bn*	
Advanced economies	78.5	Advanced economies	20
G7	48.8	G7	-34
EU15	40.0	EU15	91
Asia[a]	7.4	Asia[a]	-38
Latin America	4.1	Latin America	-39
Eastern Europe[b]	4.2	Eastern Europe[b]	-19
Middle East and Europe[c]	3.8	Middle East and Europe[c]	8
Africa	1.9	Africa	-6

a Excludes Hong Kong, Japan, Singapore, South Korea and Taiwan.
b Includes Russia and other CIS.
c Includes Turkey.
d IMF definition.

Living standards

Highest GDP per head
$

1	Luxembourg	45,750	36	Macau[a]	9,910
2	Switzerland	43,420	37	Slovenia	9,560
3	Japan	41,080	38	Bahrain	9,420
4	Norway	34,780	39	Malta	9,240
5	Bermuda	32,550	40	Argentina	8,380
6	Denmark	32,250	41	Puerto Rico	8,100
7	Germany	28,860	42	Barbados	7,640
8	Austria	27,940	43	Saudi Arabia	7,240
9	United States	27,590	44	Liberia[b]	7,010
10	Singapore	27,480	45	Netherlands Antilles[b]	6,740
11	Iceland	26,480	46	Oman	6,610
12	Belgium	26,440	47	Uruguay	5,770
13	France	26,290	48	Guadeloupe[b]	4,880
14	Netherlands	25,850	49	Chile	4,860
15	Sweden	25,770	50	Czech Republic	4,770
16	Hong Kong	24,760	51	Brazil	4,410
17	Finland	23,230		Hungary	4,410
18	Australia	20,370	53	Malaysia	4,360
19	Italy	19,930	54	Croatia	4,020
20	United Kingdom	19,810	55	Gabon	3,980
21	United Arab Emirates	19,740	56	Lebanon	3,920
22	Canada	19,200	57	Trinidad & Tobago	3,860
23	Kuwait	18,370	58	Libya	3,790
24	Ireland	17,450	59	Mauritius	3,720
25	Brunei	16,620	60	Mexico	3,690
26	Israel	15,940	61	Slovakia	3,400
27	New Zealand	15,850	62	Poland	3,230
28	Qatar	15,020	63	South Africa	3,130
29	Spain	14,200	64	Estonia	3,060
30	Cyprus	13,230		Panama	3,060
31	Taiwan	12,800	66	Thailand	3,020
32	Bahamas	12,480		Venezuela	3,020
33	Greece	11,440	68	Botswana	2,930
34	South Korea	10,660	69	Turkey	2,870
35	Portugal	10,290	70	Costa Rica	2,600

Lowest GDP per head
$

1	Mozambique	84	11	Nepal	213
2	Ethiopia	103	12	Mali	216
3	Congo	122	13	Madagascar	221
4	Chad	153	14	Burkina Faso	223
5	Bhutan	156	15	Nigeria	240
6	Tanzania	169	16	Rwanda	241
7	Burundi	177	17	Bangladesh	260
8	Malawi	183	18	Angola	268
9	Niger	201	19	Guinea-Bissau	275
10	Sierra Leone	209	20	Uganda	286

a 1993.
b Estimate.

Highest purchasing power
GDP per head in PPP (USA = 100)

1	Luxembourg	126.1	36	Czech Republic	39.6
2	United States	100.0	37	Barbados	38.6
3	Switzerland	93.5	38	Malaysia	37.6
4	Hong Kong	89.6	39	Bahamas	36.9
5	Singapore	87.7	40	Saudi Arabia	36.2
6	Kuwait[a]	86.2	41	Argentina	34.5
7	Japan	85.2	42	Mauritius	32.7
8	Norway	84.8	43	Oman	29.8
9	Belgium	81.2	44	Venezuela	29.5
10	Denmark	80.6	45	Lebanon	29.0
11	Iceland	78.9	46	Uruguay	28.2
12	Canada	78.2	47	Mexico	27.9
13	Austria	78.0	48	Slovakia	27.0
	France	78.0	49	Botswana	26.6
15	Germany	76.5	50	Panama	25.6
16	Netherlands	75.3	51	Colombia	25.0
17	Australia	73.1	52	Thailand	24.8
	United Kingdom	73.1	53	Hungary	24.7
19	Italy	72.3	54	South Africa	24.0
20	Qatar	69.8	55	Gabon	23.3
21	Sweden	68.2	56	Costa Rica	23.1
22	Finland	66.2	57	Brazil	23.0
23	Israel	65.9	58	Turkey	22.3
24	Taiwan	64.0	59	Trinidad & Tobago	22.1
25	Ireland	61.9	60	Poland	21.8
26	New Zealand	60.4	61	Namibia	19.6
27	United Arab Emirates[a]	59.7	62	Iran	17.4
28	Spain	54.8	63	Ecuador	17.1
29	Bahrain	53.2	64	Estonia	16.8
30	Malta	51.1	65	Algeria	16.7
31	Portugal	49.4	66	Romania	16.6
32	South Korea	47.7	67	Croatia	16.5
33	Greece	46.1	68	Tunisia	16.4
34	Slovenia	45.4	69	Peru	16.2
35	Chile	42.4	70	Dominican Republic	15.9

Lowest purchasing power
GDP per head in PPP (USA = 100)

1	Ethiopia	1.8		Madagascar	2.9
2	Mozambique	1.8	11	Nigeria	3.1
3	Sierra Leone	2.0	12	Chad	3.2
4	Burundi	2.2		Tajikistan	3.2
5	Mali	2.3	14	Niger	3.3
6	Tanzania[a]	2.4	15	Burkina Faso	3.4
7	Malawi	2.5		Gambia, The[a]	3.4
8	Congo	2.8		Haiti[a]	3.4
	Rwanda	2.8	18	Zambia	3.5
9	Yemen	2.9	19	Uganda	3.6

a 1995.
Note: for definition of purchasing power parity see page 221.

The quality of life

Human development index

1	Canada	96.0	41	Bahrain	87.0
2	France	94.6	42	United Arab Emirates	86.6
3	Norway	94.3	43	Panama	86.4
4	Iceland	94.2	44	Fiji	86.3
	United States	94.2	45	Venezuela	86.1
6	Finland	94.0	46	Hungary	85.7
	Japan	94.0	47	Mexico	85.3
	Netherlands	94.0	48	Colombia	84.8
9	New Zealand	93.7	49	Kuwait	84.4
10	Sweden	93.6	50	Qatar	84.0
11	Spain	93.4	51	Poland	83.4
12	Austria	93.2	52	Thailand	83.3
	Belgium	93.2	53	Malaysia	83.2
14	Australia	93.1	54	Mauritius	83.1
	United Kingdom	93.1	55	Belarus	80.6
16	Switzerland	93.0	56	Libya	80.1
17	Ireland	92.9	57	Lebanon	79.4
18	Denmark	92.7	58	Russia	79.2
19	Germany	92.4		Suriname	79.2
20	Greece	92.3	60	Brazil	78.3
21	Italy	92.1	61	Bulgaria	78.0
22	Hong Kong	91.4		Iran	78.0
23	Israel	91.3	63	Estonia	77.6
24	Barbados	90.7	64	Ecuador	77.5
	Cyprus	90.7	65	Saudi Arabia	77.4
26	Singapore	90.0	66	Turkey	77.2
27	Luxembourg	89.9	67	North Korea	76.5
28	Bahamas	89.4	68	Lithuania	76.2
29	Chile	89.1	69	Croatia	76.0
30	Portugal	89.0	70	Syria	75.5
	South Korea	89.0	71	Macedonia, FYR	74.8
32	Costa Rica	88.9		Romania	74.8
33	Malta	88.7		Tunisia	74.8
34	Slovenia	88.6	74	Algeria	73.7
35	Argentina	88.4	75	Jamaica	73.6
36	Uruguay	88.3	76	Jordan	73.0
37	Brunei	88.2	77	Cuba	72.3
	Czech Republic	88.2		Turkmenistan	72.3
39	Trinidad & Tobago	88.0	79	Dominican Republic	71.8
40	Slovakia	87.3		Oman	71.8

Notes: GDP or GDP per head is often taken as a measure of how developed a country is but its usefuless is limited as it refers only to economic welfare. In 1990 the UN Development Programme published its first estimate of a Human Development Index, which combined statistics on two other indicators – adult literacy and life expectancy – with income levels to give a better, though still far from perfect, indicator of human development. In 1991 average years of schooling was combined with adult literacy to give a knowledge variable. The index is shown here scaled from 0 to 100; countries scoring over 80 are considered to have high human development, those scoring from 50 to 79 medium human development and those under 50 have low human development.

Economic freedom index

1	Hong Kong	1.25		Portugal	2.60
2	Singapore	1.30	44	Bolivia	2.65
3	Bahrain	1.70		Oman	2.65
4	New Zealand	1.75		Philippines	2.65
5	Switzerland	1.90	47	Swaziland	2.70
	United States	1.90		Uruguay	2.70
7	Luxembourg	1.95	49	Botswana	2.75
	Taiwan	1.95		Jordan	2.75
	United Kingdom	1.95		Namibia	2.75
10	Bahamas	2.00		Tunisia	2.75
	Ireland	2.00	53	Costa Rica	2.80
12	Australia	2.05		Guatemala	2.80
	Japan	2.05		Israel	2.80
14	Belgium	2.10		Peru	2.80
	Canada	2.10		Saudi Arabia	2.80
	United Arab Emirates	2.10		Turkey	2.80
17	Austria	2.15		Uganda	2.80
	Chile	2.15	60	Indonesia	2.85
	Estonia	2.15		Latvia	2.85
20	Czech Republic	2.20		Malta	2.85
	Netherlands	2.20		Paraguay	2.85
22	Denmark	2.25	64	Greece	2.90
	Finland	2.25		Hungary	2.90
24	Germany	2.30		South Africa	2.90
	Iceland	2.30	67	Benin	2.95
	South Korea	2.30		Ecuador	2.95
27	Norway	2.35		Gabon	2.95
28	Kuwait	2.40		Morocco	2.95
	Malaysia	2.40		Poland	2.95
	Panama	2.40	72	Colombia	3.00
	Thailand	2.40		Ghana	3.00
32	El Salvador	2.45		Lithuania	3.00
	Sri Lanka	2.45	75	Kenya	3.05
	Sweden	2.45		Slovakia	3.05
35	France	2.50		Zambia	3.05
	Italy	2.50	78	Mali	3.10
	Spain	2.50		Mongolia	3.10
38	Trinidad & Tobago	2.55		Slovenia	3.10
39	Argentina	2.60	81	Honduras	3.15
	Barbados	2.60		Papua New Guinea	3.15
	Cyprus	2.60	83	Fiji	3.20
	Jamaica	2.60		Pakistan	3.20

Notes: The index of economic freedom, published by the Heritage Foundation, ranks countries on the basis of ten indicators of how government intervention can restrict the economic relations between individuals. The economic indicators are trade policy, taxation, monetary policy, the banking system, foreign-investment rules, property rights, the amount of economic output consumed by the government, regulation policy, the size of the black market and the extent of wage and price controls. A country can score between 1 and 5 in each category, 1 being the most free and 5 being the least free.

Economic growth

Fastest economic growth, 1990–96
Average annual % increase in real GDP

1	China	12.3	21	Israel	6.4
2	Kuwait	12.2	22	Ireland	6.1
3	Lebanon	9.3	23	Oman	6.0
4	Malaysia	8.7		Peru	6.0
	Singapore	8.7	25	El Salvador	5.8
6	Vietnam	8.5		India	5.8
7	Thailand	8.3	27	Hong Kong	5.5
8	Indonesia	7.7	28	Nepal	5.1
9	Jordan	7.6	29	Mauritius	5.0
	Papua New Guinea	7.6	30	Argentina	4.9
11	Syria	7.4	31	Panama	4.8
12	South Korea	7.3		Sri Lanka	4.8
13	Chile	7.2	33	Dominican Republic	4.7
	Uganda	7.2	34	Pakistan	4.6
15	Mozambique	7.1	35	Colombia	4.5
16	Myanmar	6.8	36	Benin	4.4
	Sudan	6.8		Ghana	4.4
18	Laos	6.7	38	Bangladesh	4.3
	Lesotho	6.7		Costa Rica	4.3
20	Cambodia	6.5		Slovenia	4.3

Slowest economic growth, 1990–96
Average annual % increase in real GDP

1	Georgia	-26.1	21	Sierra Leone	-3.3
2	Armenia	-21.2	22	Zambia	-1.1
3	Azerbaijan	-17.7	23	Cameroon	-1.0
4	Moldova	-16.7		Croatia	-1.0
5	Ukraine	-13.6		Czech Republic	-1.0
6	Kirgizstan	-12.3		Slovakia	-1.0
7	Latvia	-10.7	27	Angola	-0.9
8	Kazakhstan	-10.5	28	Togo	-0.6
9	Rwanda	-9.7	29	Hungary	-0.4
10	Turkmenistan	-9.6	30	Switzerland	-0.1
11	Macedonia, FYR	-9.1	31	Romania	0.0
12	Russia	-9.0	32	Congo-Brazzaville	0.1
13	Belarus	-8.3	33	Finland	0.3
14	Congo	-6.6	34	Madagascar	0.4
15	Estonia	-6.5	35	Algeria	0.6
16	Lithuania	-6.0		Sweden	0.6
17	Haiti	-5.0	37	Central African Rep	0.7
18	Burundi	-3.8	38	Jamaica	0.8
19	Bulgaria	-3.5	39	Italy	1.0
20	Uzbekistan	-3.5		Niger	1.0

Fastest economic growth, 1980–90
Average annual % increase in real GDP

1	Botswana	10.3	12	India	5.8
2	China	10.2	13	Mongolia	5.5
3	South Korea	9.4	14	Turkey	5.3
4	Oman	8.3	15	Malaysia	5.2
5	Thailand	7.6	16	Egypt	5.0
6	Hong Kong	6.9	17	Nepal	4.6
7	Singapore	6.4	18	Guinea-Bissau	4.5
8	Chad	6.3	19	Burundi	4.4
	Pakistan	6.3	20	Bangladesh	4.3
10	Mauritius	6.2		Lesotho	4.3
11	Indonesia	6.1			

Slowest economic growth, 1980–90
Average annual % increase in real GDP

1	Trinidad & Tobago	-2.5	11	Bolivia	0.0
2	Nicaragua	-2.0	12	Côte d'Ivoire	0.1
	United Arab Emirates	-2.0	13	El Salvador	0.2
4	Jordan	-1.5	14	Panama	0.3
5	Saudi Arabia	-1.2	15	Uruguay	0.4
6	Niger	-1.1	16	Gabon	0.5
7	Argentina	-0.3		Georgia	0.5
8	Haiti	-0.2		Romania	0.5
	Mozambique	-0.2	19	Guadeloupe	0.8
	Peru	-0.2		Zambia	0.8

Highest industrial growth, 1990–96
Average annual % increase in real terms

1	China	17.3	6	Laos	12.1
2	Papua New Guinea	13.6	7	Cambodia	11.3
3	Vietnam	13.3	8	Malaysia	11.2
4	Lesotho	12.5	9	Jordan	10.9
5	Uganda	12.2	10	Myanmar	10.7

Highest services growth, 1990–96
Average annual % increase in real terms

1	Mozambique	11.9		Vietnam	8.5
2	China	9.6	7	Cambodia	8.4
3	Uganda	8.6	8	Chile	8.2
4	Malaysia	8.5	9	Laos	8.0
	Singapore	8.5		South Korea	8.0

Highest agricultural growth, 1990–96
Average annual % increase in real terms

1	United Arab Emirates	9.3	7	Chile	5.5
2	Lithuania	8.7	8	Chad	5.2
3	Albania	8.2		Vietnam	5.2
4	Jamaica	6.7	10	Benin	5.1
5	Myanmar	6.2		Malawi	5.1
6	Peru	5.6			

Trading places

Biggest traders
% of total world exports (visible & invisible)

1	United States	14.22	21	Malaysia	1.20
2	Japan	9.34	22	Australia	1.14
3	Germany	9.17	23	Thailand	1.02
4	United Kingdom	6.59	24	Norway	0.92
5	France	5.56	25	Saudi Arabia	0.89
6	Italy	4.86	26	Ireland	0.80
7	Netherlands	3.52	27	Brazil	0.79
8	Canada	3.41	28	Indonesia	0.78
9	Belgium	3.39	29	Finland	0.68
10	China	2.41	30	Turkey	0.63
11	Spain	2.16	31	India	0.58
12	South Korea	2.13	32	Philippines	0.53
13	Switzerland	2.07	33	Poland	0.52
14	Taiwan	1.87	34	Portugal	0.50
15	Singapore	1.56	35	South Africa	0.46
	Sweden	1.56	36	Argentina	0.43
17	Mexico	1.49	37	Czech Republic	0.42
18	Russia	1.44	38	Israel	0.41
19	Austria	1.41	39	Hong Kong	0.37
	Denmark	1.41	40	Venezuela	0.36

Most trade dependent
Trade as % of GDP[a]

1	Malaysia	131.1
2	Congo-Brazzaville	122.2
3	Swaziland	122.0
4	Singapore	121.9
5	Suriname	119.7
6	Bahrain	115.9
7	Panama	111.6
8	Ireland	105.1
9	Malta	94.1
10	Mongolia[b]	86.6
11	United Arab Emirates	85.4
12	Belgium-Luxembourg	84.5
13	Gabon[b]	82.3
14	Macedonia, FYR	81.5
15	Estonia	80.6
16	Slovakia	79.0
17	Netherlands Antilles[b]	76.7
18	Bulgaria	72.9
19	Czech Republic	72.6
20	Yemen[a]	72.0

Least trade dependent
Trade as % of GDP[a]

1	Myanmar	2.3
2	Burundi	9.0
3	Somalia[b]	9.8
4	Brazil	10.5
5	Japan	10.8
6	Iraq	10.9
7	Argentina	11.8
8	Sudan	12.1
9	Guinea-Bissau	12.2
10	Rwanda	13.1
11	United States	13.7
12	Greece	13.8
13	Congo	14.1
14	Haiti	14.5
	India	14.5
16	Georgia	16.7
17	Peru	16.8
18	Sierra Leone	16.9
19	Ethiopia	17.3
20	Egypt	17.7

Notes: The figures are drawn from balance of payment statistics and, therefore, have differing technical definitions from trade statistics taken from customs or similar sources. The invisible trade figures do not show some countries, notably ex-Soviet republics, due to unavailable data. For Hong Kong and Singapore, domestic exports and retained imports only are used.

Biggest visible traders
% of world visible exports

1	United States	12.10	21	Saudi Arabia	1.12
2	Germany	10.24	22	Austria	1.10
3	Japan	7.89	23	Thailand	1.07
4	France	5.56	24	Denmark	1.00
5	United Kingdom	5.16	25	Indonesia	0.98
6	Italy	4.94		Norway	0.98
7	Canada	4.06	27	Ireland	0.96
8	Netherlands	3.47	28	Brazil	0.94
9	Belgium-Luxembourg	3.04	29	Finland	0.80
10	China	2.98	30	India	0.65
11	South Korea	2.53	31	Turkey	0.64
12	Taiwan	2.26	32	South Africa	0.57
13	Spain	2.01	33	Hong Kong	0.54
14	Mexico	1.89		Poland	0.54
15	Switzerland	1.88	35	United Arab Emirates	0.51
16	Russia	1.78	36	Portugal	0.50
17	Sweden	1.67	37	Argentina	0.47
18	Malaysia	1.55		Venezuela	0.47
19	Singapore	1.45	39	Iran	0.44
20	Australia	1.18	40	Czech Republic	0.43

Biggest invisible traders
% of world invisible exports

1	United States	18.71	21	Philippines	0.81
2	Japan	12.41	22	Norway	0.79
3	United Kingdom	9.73	23	Russia	0.70
4	Germany	6.84	24	Mexico	0.63
5	France	5.56	25	Turkey	0.62
6	Italy	4.67	26	Portugal	0.50
7	Belgium	4.13	27	Poland	0.48
8	Netherlands	3.62	28	Brazil	0.47
9	Spain	2.48		Egypt	0.47
10	Switzerland	2.46		Ireland	0.47
11	Denmark	2.30		Malaysia	0.47
12	Austria	2.05	32	Greece	0.45
13	Canada	2.02	33	India	0.44
14	Singapore	1.78	34	Finland	0.43
15	Sweden	1.33	35	Israel	0.41
16	South Korea	1.25	36	Czech Republic	0.40
17	China	1.18	37	Saudi Arabia	0.39
18	Australia	1.03	38	Argentina	0.33
	Taiwan	1.03		Indonesia	0.33
20	Thailand	0.89	40	Kuwait	0.32

a Average of imports and exports of goods as % of GDP.
b 1995

Current account

Largest surpluses
$m

1	Japan	65,884	21	Ireland	1,406
2	Italy	41,040	22	Algeria	1,400
3	Netherlands	25,258	23	Botswana	609
4	France	20,561	24	Bahrain[a]	557
5	Switzerland	20,470	25	Papua New Guinea	313
6	Singapore	14,283	26	Trinidad & Tobago[a]	294
7	Belgium-Luxembourg	13,999	27	Syria	285
8	Russia	11,598	28	Saudi Arabia	215
9	Norway	11,246	29	Yemen[a]	183
10	Taiwan	10,481	30	Libya	127
11	Venezuela	8,824	31	Ecuador	111
12	China	7,243	32	Lesotho[b]	108
13	Kuwait	6,773	33	Barbados	103
14	Sweden	5,892	34	Gabon[a]	100
15	Iran	5,232	35	Cameroon[a]	90
16	Finland	4,787	36	Netherlands Antilles[a]	87
17	Nigeria	3,092	37	Namibia	84
18	Denmark	2,865	38	Suriname[a]	73
19	Canada	2,808	39	Iceland[a]	51
20	Spain	1,756	40	Mongolia[a]	39

Largest deficits
$m

1	United States	-148,726	21	Chile	-2,921
2	Brazil	-24,300	22	United Kingdom	-2,890
3	South Korea	-23,061	23	Hong Kong	-2,600
4	Australia	-15,857	24	Romania	-2,579
5	Thailand	-14,692	25	Slovakia	-2,090
6	Germany	-13,072	26	South Africa	-2,033
7	Indonesia	-8,000	27	Mexico	-1,923
8	Israel	-7,057	28	Hungary	-1,689
9	India	-5,299	29	Portugal	-1,491
10	Colombia	-4,754	30	Croatia	-1,452
11	Malaysia	-4,700	31	Turkey	-1,450
12	Greece	-4,554	32	Ukraine	-1,186
13	Czech Republic	-4,299	33	Uzbekistan	-1,075
14	Austria	-3,990	34	Congo-Brazzaville	-1,034
15	New Zealand	-3,948	35	Bangladesh	-959
16	Philippines	-3,900	36	Belarus	-909
17	Argentina	-3,787	37	Sudan	-827
18	Peru	-3,607	38	Azerbaijan	-811
19	Pakistan[a]	-3,333	39	Kazakhstan	-752
20	Poland	-3,264	40	Paraguay[b]	-749

Largest surpluses as % of GDP
%

1	Kuwait	21.86		21	Taiwan	3.84
2	Suriname[a]	20.28		22	Italy	3.60
3	Singapore	15.36		23	Russia	3.26
4	Venezuela	13.11		24	Algeria	3.20
5	Botswana	12.40		25	Gabon[a]	2.66
6	Bahrain[a]	12.31		26	Sweden	2.59
7	Nigeria	11.20		27	Namibia	2.33
8	Lesotho[b]	7.73		28	Ireland	2.27
9	Norway	7.44		29	Mauritania[a]	2.10
10	Netherlands Antilles[a]	6.59		30	Benin[b]	1.84
11	Switzerland	6.53		31	Denmark	1.70
12	Netherlands	6.27			Syria	1.70
13	Papua New Guinea	6.26		33	France	1.34
14	Trinidad & Tobago[a]	6.06		34	Japan	1.28
15	Belgium-Luxembourg	5.21		35	Cameroon[a]	1.04
16	Barbados	5.17		36	China	0.80
17	Mongolia[a]	5.08			Swaziland	0.80
18	Yemen[a]	4.53		38	Iceland[a]	0.76
19	Finland	4.02		39	Ecuador	0.63
20	Iran	3.94		40	Libya	0.55

Largest deficits as % of GDP
%

1	Congo-Brazzaville	-57.44		21	Sierra Leone[a]	-8.86
2	Mozambique[a]	-32.89		22	Czech Republic	-8.79
3	Nicaragua	-29.24		23	Moldova	-8.56
4	Malawi[b]	-28.85		24	Madagascar	-8.56
5	Bosnia	-22.94		25	Lithuania	-8.51
6	Azerbaijan	-22.53		26	Thailand	-8.28
7	Laos	-19.21		27	Croatia	-8.02
8	Kirgizstan	-16.84		28	Angola[b]	-7.91
9	Guinea-Bissau[a]	-15.47		29	Israel	-7.82
10	Zambia	-14.44		30	Sudan	-7.76
11	Macedonia, FYR	-14.40		31	Niger[a]	-7.75
12	Gambia, The	-13.56		32	Romania	-7.12
13	Armenia	-12.13		33	Nepal	-6.96
14	Slovakia	-11.48		34	Bahamas	-6.93
15	Malta	-10.74		35	New Zealand	-6.91
16	Paraguay[b]	-9.85		36	Mali[b]	-6.77
17	Tanzania	-9.83		37	Peru	-6.14
18	Cambodia	-9.61		38	Haiti	-6.00
19	Estonia	-9.40		39	Jamaica	-5.98
20	Congo	-9.14		40	Colombia	-5.93

a 1995
b 1994

Inflation

Highest inflation, 1996–97

% consumer price inflation

1	Bulgaria	1,082.6	31	Colombia	18.5
2	Congo	176.0	32	Hungary	18.3
3	Angola	160.0	33	Kazakhstan	17.4
4	Romania	154.8	34	Iran	17.2
5	Tajikistan	90.0	35	Myanmar[a]	16.3
6	Turkmenistan	87.0	36	Tanzania	16.1
7	Turkey	85.7	37	Poland	15.9
8	Belarus	63.9		Ukraine	15.9
9	Uzbekistan	58.8	39	Russia	14.6
10	Guinea-Bissau[a]	50.7	40	Armenia	13.9
11	Venezuela	50.0	41	Costa Rica	13.2
12	Zambia[a]	46.3	42	Laos[a]	13.0
13	Mongolia[a]	45.8	43	Swaziland[a]	12.5
14	Mozambique[a]	45.0	44	Chad[a]	12.4
15	Malawi[a]	37.6	45	Kenya	12.0
16	Albania	33.2	46	Nicaragua[a]	11.6
17	Burundi	31.1		Papua New Guinea[a]	11.6
18	Ecuador	30.6	48	Rwanda	11.5
19	Nigeria[a]	29.3	49	Pakistan	11.4
20	Ghana	27.9	50	Estonia	11.2
21	Jamaica[a]	26.4	51	Moldova	11.0
22	Kirgizstan	26.0	52	Sri Lanka	9.6
23	Sierra Leone[a]	23.2	53	Nepal[a]	9.4
24	Algeria[a]	21.6	54	Lesotho[a]	9.3
25	Zimbabwe[a]	21.4	55	Guatemala	9.2
26	Serbia, Montenegro	21.2	56	Slovenia	9.1
27	Haiti	20.6	57	India[a]	9.0
	Mexico	20.6		Israel	9.0
29	Honduras	20.2	59	Botswana	8.9
30	Uruguay	19.8		Lithuania	8.9

Highest inflation, 1990–97

% average annual consumer price inflation

1	Congo	1,258.4	16	Bulgaria	191.0
2	Turkmenistan[b]	756.8	17	Peru	153.1
3	Georgia	715.7	18	Croatia[b]	148.2
4	Angola[f]	520.1	19	Serbia[f]	147.6
5	Tajikistan[b]	465.9	20	Mongolia[d]	125.9
6	Ukraine[b]	454.7	21	Kazakhstan[e]	116.6
7	Belarus[b]	425.9	22	Romania	108.0
8	Armenia[b]	375.7	23	Estonia[f]	96.8
9	Kazakhstan[b]	365.4	24	Zambia[c]	91.8
10	Uzbekistan[b]	310.6	25	Turkey	77.3
11	Azerbaijan[b]	302.5	26	Suriname	75.5
12	Macedonia	278.8	27	Poland	64.7
13	Russia[b]	244.9	28	Venezuela[c]	59.2
14	Brazil	234.3	29	Uruguay	56.1
15	Nicaragua[c]	231.3	30	Albania[b]	50.2

Lowest inflation, 1996–97
% consumer price inflation

1	Ethiopia[a]	-5.1		Singapore	2.0
2	Bahrain[a]	-0.2		Spain	2.0
	Congo-Brazzaville[a]	-0.2	28	Burkina Faso	2.2
4	Australia	0.3		Denmark	2.2
5	Argentina	0.5		Netherlands	2.2
	Bahamas	0.5		Portugal	2.2
	Sweden	0.5	32	United States	2.3
	Switzerland	0.5	33	Côte d'Ivoire[a]	2.5
9	Taiwan	0.9	34	Norway	2.6
10	Morocco	1.0	35	Malaysia	2.7
11	Finland	1.2	36	China	2.8
	France	1.2		Gambia, The	2.8
	New Zealand	1.2		Senegal[a]	2.8
	Saudi Arabia[a]	1.2	39	Jordan	3.0
15	Austria	1.3	40	United Kingdom	3.1
	Panama	1.3	41	Azerbaijan	3.2
17	Ireland	1.4	42	Malta	3.3
	Luxembourg	1.4		Netherlands Antilles	3.3
19	Belgium	1.6	44	Fiji	3.4
	Canada	1.6		Trinidad & Tobago[a]	3.4
21	Iceland	1.7	46	Kuwait[a]	3.5
	Japan	1.7	47	Cyprus	3.6
23	Germany	1.8		Macedonia, FYR	3.6
24	Syria	1.9		Tunisia	3.6
25	Italy	2.0	50	Central African Rep[a]	3.7

Lowest inflation, 1990–97
% average annual consumer price inflation

1	Bahrain[c]	1.0		Norway	2.5
2	Panama	1.1	17	Luxembourg	2.6
3	Japan	1.5	18	Kuwait[c]	2.7
4	Saudi Arabia	1.8	19	Australia	2.8
5	Denmark	2.1		Austria	2.8
6	France	2.2		Netherlands Antilles	2.8
7	Finland	2.3		Switzerland	2.8
	Oman[c]	2.3	23	Cambodia	2.9
9	Belgium	2.4	24	Qatar[c]	3.0
	Canada	2.4	25	Malta	3.1
	Ireland	2.4	26	Bahamas	3.2
	Singapore	2.4	27	United States	3.3
13	Germany	2.5	28	Barbados	3.5
	Netherlands	2.5	29	Malaysia	3.8
	New Zealand	2.5	30	Sweden	3.9

a	1995–96		d	1992–96
b	1991–97		e	1993–97
c	1990–96		f	1992–97

Notes: Inflation is measured as the % increase in the consumer price index between two dates. The figures shown are based on the average level of the index during the relevant years.

Debt

Highest foreign debt[a]

$m

1	Brazil	179,047	21	Hungary	26,958
2	Mexico	157,125	22	Vietnam	26,764
3	Indonesia	129,033	23	South Africa	23,590
4	China	128,817	24	Morocco	21,767
5	Russia	124,785	25	Syria	21,420
6	Argentina	93,841	26	Iran	21,183
7	Thailand	90,824	27	Czech Republic	20,094
8	India	89,827	28	Côte d'Ivoire	19,713
9	Turkey	79,789	29	Sudan	16,972
10	Philippines	41,214	30	Bangladesh	16,083
11	Poland	40,895	31	Ecuador	14,491
12	Malaysia	39,777	32	Serbia, Montenegro	13,439
13	Venezuela	35,344	33	Congo	12,826
14	Algeria	33,260	34	Angola	10,612
15	Egypt	31,407	35	Ethiopia	10,077
	Nigeria	31,407	36	Tunisia	9,887
17	Pakistan	29,901	37	Bulgaria	9,819
18	Peru	29,176	38	Cameroon	9,515
19	Colombia	28,859	39	Ukraine	9,335
20	Chile	27,411	40	Romania	8,291

Highest debt service[b]

$m

1	Mexico	35,350	21	Poland	2,547
2	Brazil	23,157	22	Peru	2,534
3	Indonesia	19,926	23	Nigeria	2,461
4	China	14,944	24	Czech Republic	2,402
5	Argentina	12,649	25	Egypt	2,088
6	India	11,342	26	Tunisia	1,381
7	Turkey	9,711	27	Côte d'Ivoire	1,285
8	Hungary	7,961	28	Ecuador	1,192
9	Malaysia	7,171	29	Ukraine	1,161
10	Thailand	6,449	30	Bulgaria	995
11	Russia	6,010	31	Slovakia	980
12	Chile	5,862	32	Slovenia	945
13	Colombia	5,087	33	Panama	803
14	Philippines	4,972	34	Romania	769
15	Algeria	3,991	35	Kenya	747
16	Venezuela	3,751	36	Oman	720
17	South Africa	3,692	37	Kazakhstan	663
18	Iran	3,123	38	Angola	645
19	Morocco	3,107	39	Zimbabwe	600
20	Pakistan	2,672	40	Bangladesh	595

a Foreign debt is debt owed to non-residents and repayable in foreign currency; the figures shown include liabilities of government, public and private sectors. Developed countries have been excluded.

b External debt for the former Yugoslavia had not been entirely allocated to the newly independent republics.

Highest foreign debt burden
Foreign debt as % of GDP

1	Mozambique	432	21	Madagascar	127
2	Somalia	406	22	Jordan	126
3	Nicaragua	395	23	Togo	125
4	Guinea-Bissau	376	24	Cameroon	124
5	Angola	368	25	Gambia, The	122
6	Congo-Brazzaville	309	26	Nigeria	121
7	Sudan	282	27	Honduras	118
8	Mauritania	234	28	Ghana	107
9	Côte d'Ivoire	230		Yemen	107
10	Zambia	225	30	Jamaica	102
11	Ethiopia	187	31	Chad	101
12	Tanzania	152	32	Burundi	100
13	Malawi	145	33	Gabon	98
14	Congo	140	34	Rwanda	95
15	Sierra Leone	138	35	Bulgaria	94
16	Syria	136	36	Central African Rep	92
	Vietnam	136		Guinea	92
18	Mali	133	38	Panama	91
19	Laos	132	39	Bolivia	89
20	Liberia	130	40	Ecuador	88

Highest debt service ratios[c]
%

1	Burundi	54.6	21	Ghana	26.4
2	Sierra Leone	52.6	22	Côte d'Ivoire	26.2
3	Guinea-Bissau	48.6	23	Zambia	24.6
4	Argentina	44.2	24	Nicaragua	24.2
5	Ethiopia	42.2	25	India	24.1
6	Brazil	41.1	26	Cameroon	23.6
7	Hungary	41.0	27	Ecuador	22.6
8	Indonesia	36.8	28	Mauritania	21.7
9	Mexico	35.4	29	Turkey	21.7
10	Peru	35.4	30	Congo	21.3
11	Colombia	34.6	31	Bulgaria	20.5
12	Chile	32.3	32	Rwanda	20.4
13	Mozambique	32.2	33	Uganda	20.0
14	Bolivia	30.9	34	Tanzania	18.7
15	Iran[d]	29.3	35	Malawi	18.6
16	Honduras	28.8	36	Iraq	18.0
17	Algeria	27.7	37	Jamaica	18.0
18	Morocco	27.7	38	Mali	17.9
19	Kenya	27.5	39	Niger	17.3
20	Pakistan	27.4	40	Venezuela	16.8

c Debt service is the sum of interest and principal repayments (amortization) due on
   outstanding foreign debt. The debt service ratio is debt service expressed as a
   percentage of the country's exports of goods and services.
d 1995

Aid

Largest bilateral and multilateral donors
$m

1	Japan	9,439	13	Australia	1,121
2	United States	9,377	14	Switzerland	1,026
3	Germany	7,601	15	Belgium	913
4	France	7,451	16	Austria	557
5	Netherlands	3,246	17	Kuwait	412
6	United Kingdom	3,199	18	Finland	408
7	Italy	2,416	19	Saudi Arabia	306
8	Sweden	1,999	20	Portugal	218
9	Canada	1,795	21	Greece	184
10	Denmark	1,772	22	Ireland	179
11	Norway	1,311	23	South Korea	159
12	Spain	1,251	24	New Zealand	122

Largest recipients of bilateral and multilateral aid
$m

1	China	2,617	36	Brazil	408
2	Israel	2,217	37	Nepal	401
3	Egypt	2,212	38	Iraq	387
4	India	1,936	39	Papua New Guinea	385
5	Bangladesh	1,255	40	Haiti	375
6	Indonesia	1,121	41	Zimbabwe	374
7	Côte d'Ivoire	968	42	Honduras	367
8	Nicaragua	954	43	Malawi	364
9	Vietnam	927	44	South Africa	361
10	Mozambique	923	45	Laos	339
11	Tanzania	894	46	Georgia	318
12	Philippines	883	47	El Salvador	317
13	Pakistan	877	48	Algeria	309
14	Bolivia	850	49	Chad	305
15	Ethiopia	849	50	Armenia	295
16	Thailand	832		Guinea	295
17	Bosnia	812	52	Benin	293
18	Uganda	684	53	Mexico	289
19	Rwanda	674	54	Argentina	277
20	Ghana	654	55	Mauritius	274
21	Morocco	651	56	Ecuador	261
22	Zambia	614	57	Yemen	260
23	Kenya	606	58	Niger	259
24	West Bank and Gaza	593	59	Colombia	251
25	Senegal	582	60	Lebanon	233
26	Angola	544	61	Turkey	233
27	Jordan	514	62	Kirgizstan	232
28	Mauritania	505	63	Sudan	230
29	Mali	501	64	Afghanistan	228
30	Sri Lanka	494	65	Syria	225
31	Cambodia	453	66	Albania	222
32	Congo	430	67	Guatemala	216
33	Burkina Faso	418	68	Madagascar	207
34	Cameroon	413	69	Burundi	204
35	Peru	410	70	Chile	203

Largest bilateral and multilateral donors
% of GDP

1	Denmark	1.04		13	Australia	0.30
2	Norway	0.85		14	United Kingdom	0.27
3	Sweden	0.84		15	Austria	0.24
4	Netherlands	0.81		16	Saudi Arabia	0.22
5	France[a]	0.48			Spain	0.22
6	Luxembourg	0.44		18	New Zealand	0.21
7	Belgium	0.34			Portugal	0.21
	Finland	0.34		20	Italy	0.20
	Switzerland	0.34			Japan	0.20
10	Germany	0.33		22	Greece	0.16
11	Canada	0.32		23	United States	0.12
12	Ireland	0.31		24	United Arab Emirates	0.07

Largest recipients of bilateral and multilateral aid
$ per head

1	Netherlands Antilles	621		35	Angola	49
2	Israel	391		36	Eritrea	48
3	Suriname	257			Liberia	48
4	Mauritius	243			Macedonia, FYR	48
5	Nicaragua	225		39	Chad	47
6	Bosnia	224		40	Mali	45
7	Mauritania	216			Sierra Leone	45
8	Malta	195		42	Cambodia	44
9	Guinea-Bissau	165		43	Slovenia	43
10	Rwanda	125		44	Cyprus	40
11	Namibia	120			Togo	40
12	Gabon	115		46	Burkina Faso	39
13	Bolivia	112			Guinea	39
14	Jordan	92		48	Ghana	37
15	Papua New Guinea	88			Malawi	37
16	Armenia	81		50	Egypt	35
	Mongolia	81			Swaziland	35
18	Lebanon	76		52	Bhutan	34
19	Zambia	74			Panama	34
20	Côte d'Ivoire	69			Uganda	34
21	Senegal	68		55	Burundi	33
22	Laos	67			Gambia, The	33
23	Albania	65			Zimbabwe	33
24	Congo-Brazzaville	63		58	Cameroon	30
	Honduras	63			Croatia	30
26	Georgia	58		60	Tanzania	29
27	Fiji	56		61	Niger	27
28	Botswana	55			Oman	27
	El Salvador	55			Sri Lanka	27
30	Benin	53		64	Jamaica	24
31	Haiti	52			Morocco	24
	Kirgizstan	52		66	Ecuador	22
	Mozambique	52			Kenya	22
34	Central African Rep	50		68	Guatemala	20

a Including overseas territories.

Industry and services

Largest industrial output
$bn, 1995

1	Japan	1,941	22	Saudi Arabia	67
2	United States	1,808		Thailand	67
3	Germany	780	24	Mexico	65
4	France	415	25	Turkey	51
5	United Kingdom	354	26	Denmark	50
6	Italy	337	27	Finland	46
7	China	335		Poland	46
8	Brazil	255	29	Norway	44
9	South Korea	196	30	Malaysia	37
10	Spain	187		Portugal	37
11	Canada	174	32	Ukraine	34
12	Russia	131	33	Greece	33
13	Netherlands	107	34	Singapore	30
14	Australia	98	35	Venezuela	29
15	Switzerland	96	36	Israel	28
16	India	94	37	Chile	24
17	Argentina	87		Colombia	24
18	Belgium	83		Hong Kong	24
	Indonesia	83		Philippines	24
20	Austria	79		South Africa	24
21	Sweden	73			

Highest growth in industrial output
Average annual real % growth, 1990–96

1	China	17.3	11	Thailand	10.3
2	Papua New Guinea	13.6	12	Indonesia	10.2
3	Vietnam	13.3	13	Singapore	9.1
4	Lesotho	12.5	14	Nepal	8.5
5	Uganda	12.2	15	Panama	7.9
6	Laos	12.1	16	South Korea	7.5
7	Cambodia	11.3	17	Bangladesh	7.2
8	Malaysia	11.2	18	India	6.8
9	Jordan	10.9	19	Sri Lanka	6.6
10	Myanmar	10.7	20	Peru	6.5

Lowest growth in industrial output
Average annual real % growth, 1990–96

1	Armenia	-28.7	11	Albania	-11.0
2	Moldova	-23.7		Russia	-11.0
3	Kirgizstan	-21.7	13	Azerbaijan	-10.8
4	Latvia	-20.2	14	Lithuania	-10.4
5	Ukraine	-20.0	15	Belarus	-10.0
6	Congo	-15.9	16	Burundi	-8.3
7	Kazakhstan	-15.7	17	Croatia	-8.2
8	Rwanda	-14.9	18	Slovakia	-7.2
9	Haiti	-13.7	19	Sierra Leone	-6.4
10	Estonia	-11.6	20	Uzbekistan	-6.0

Largest manufacturing output
$bn, 1995

1	United States	1,251		21	Denmark	36
2	Japan	1,226		22	Finland	35
3	France	292			Turkey	35
4	China	265		24	Poland	31
5	United Kingdom	232		25	Ukraine	30
6	Italy	228		26	Malaysia	28
7	Brazil	165		27	Singapore	23
8	South Korea	123		28	Israel	20
9	Canada	121		29	Greece	19
10	Russia	107			South Africa	19
11	Netherlands	71		31	Philippines	17
12	Belgium	62		32	Colombia	14
	India	62			Peru	14
14	Argentina	56		34	Hong Kong	13
	Austria	56			Venezuela	13
16	Sweden	53		36	Chile	12
17	Australia	52			Saudi Arabia	12
18	Indonesia	48		38	New Zealand	11
	Mexico	48		39	Hungary	10
	Thailand	48			Pakistan	10

Largest services output
$bn, 1995

1	United States	5,005		21	India	133
2	Japan	3,065		22	Hong Kong	119
3	Germany	1,611		23	Denmark	115
4	France	1,091		24	Norway	99
5	United Kingdom	730		25	Turkey	87
6	Italy	717		26	Thailand	82
7	Canada	381		27	Indonesia	81
8	Spain	351		28	Finland	71
9	Brazil	337		29	Poland	64
10	Netherlands	277		30	Israel	62
11	Australia	244		31	Portugal	61
12	South Korea	228		32	Singapore	54
13	China	216		33	Saudi Arabia	51
14	Switzerland	196		34	South Africa	50
15	Russia	190		35	Venezuela	42
16	Belgium	183		36	Colombia	41
17	Argentina	177		37	Greece	39
18	Mexico	168		38	Chile	38
19	Sweden	151			Malaysia	38
20	Austria	147			New Zealand	38

Agriculture

Most economically dependent on agriculture
% of GDP from agriculture

1	Georgia	67		Sierra Leone	42
2	Somalia	66	23	Cameroon	39
3	Tanzania	58		Niger	39
4	Ethiopia	57	25	Togo	38
5	Albania	56	26	Rwanda	37
	Burundi	56	27	Benin	34
7	Afghanistan	53		Burkino Faso	34
8	Laos	52		Madagascar	34
9	Cambodia	51	30	Mozambique	33
10	Moldova	50		Nicaragua	33
	Uganda	50		Uzbekistan	33
12	Ghana	46	33	Bangladesh	31
	Guinea-Bissau	46		Côte d'Ivoire	31
	Mali	46	35	India	29
15	Armenia	44		Kenya	29
	Central African Republic	44	37	Gambia	28
	Chad	44		Nigeria	28
	Haiti	44		Vietnam	28
	Kirgizstan	44	40	Azerbaijan	27
20	Malawi	42		Mauritania	27
	Nepal	42			

Least economically dependent on agriculture
% of GDP from agriculture

1	Hong Kong	0		Spain	4
	Kuwait	0	24	Botswana	5
	Singapore	0		Slovenia	5
4	Germany	1		South Africa	5
5	Austria	2		Venezuela	5
	Belgium	2	28	Argentina	6
	France	2		Czech Republic	6
	Israel	2		Finland	6
	Japan	2		Poland	6
	Norway	2		Saudi Arabia	6
	Sweden	2		Slovakia	6
	United Arab Emirates	2	34	Chile	7
	United Kingdom	2		Lebanon	7
	United States	2		Peru	7
15	Australia	3		Russia	7
	Canada	3		South Korea	7
	Italy	3	39	Estonia	8
	Netherlands	3		Hungary	8
	Switzerland	3		Ireland	8
	Trinidad & Tobago	3		Jordan	8
21	Denmark	4		Mexico	8
	Portugal	4		New Zealand	8

Fastest growth
Average annual real % growth, 1990–96

1	United Arab Emirates	9.3		Vietnam	5.2
2	Lithuania	8.7	10	Benin	5.1
3	Albania	8.2		Malawi	5.1
4	Jamaica	6.7	12	Guinea-Bissau	4.8
5	Myanmar	6.2		Iran	4.8
6	Peru	5.6		Papua New Guinea	4.8
7	Chile	5.5	15	Mauritania	4.7
8	Chad	5.2			

Slowest growth
Average annual real % growth, 1990–96

1	Ukraine	-26.1		Russia	-8.2
2	Kazakhstan	-15.3	10	Estonia	-6.5
3	Moldova	-14.7	11	Azerbaijan	-6.0
4	Latvia	-13.0	12	Hungary	-5.0
5	Belarus	-9.8	13	Spain	-4.8
6	Angola	-9.5	14	Kirgizstan	-4.6
7	Rwanda	-8.4	15	Croatia	-4.4
8	Czech Republic	-8.2			

Biggest producers
'000 tonnes

Cereals

1	China	435,654	6	Indonesia	60,090
2	United States	337,667	7	Canada	59,407
3	India	214,082	8	Brazil	46,101
4	Russia	68,030	9	Germany	42,102
5	France	62,488	10	Australia	34,602

Meat

1	China	60,095	6	Russia	5,272
2	United States	34,564	7	India	4,295
3	Brazil	10,965	8	Italy	4,072
4	France	6,326	9	Spain	3,800
5	Germany	5,840	10	Mexico	3,682

Fruit

1	China	45,462	6	Mexico	12,179
2	India	39,197	7	Spain	12,095
3	Brazil	35,928	8	France	11,211
4	United States	28,841	9	Uganda	10,189
5	Italy	17,182	10	Iran	9,774

Vegetables

1	China	202,155	6	Italy	13,555
2	India	64,672	7	Russia	11,099
3	United States	34,393	8	South Korea	10,562
4	Turkey	20,796	9	Spain	10,524
5	Japan	13,589	10	Egypt	9,377

Commodities

Wheat

Top 10 producers '000 tonnes		Top 10 consumers '000 tonnes	
1 China	110,600	1 China	115,000
2 EU 15	99,800	2 EU 15	83,500
3 India	62,600	3 India	67,800
4 United States	62,100	4 Russia	37,400
5 Russia	34,900	5 United States	35,600
6 Canada	29,800	6 Pakistan	19,600
7 Australia	23,700	7 Turkey	16,600
8 Pakistan	16,900	8 Iran	16,000
9 Turkey	16,200	9 Ukraine	15,300
10 Argentina	15,900	10 Egypt	12,600

Rice

Top 10 producers[a] '000 tonnes		Top 10 consumers[b] '000 tonnes	
1 China	195,100	1 China	132,070
2 India	120,822	2 India	79,250
3 Indonesia	48,500	3 Indonesia	33,410
4 Bangladesh	27,633	4 Bangladesh	18,520
5 Vietnam	27,273	5 Vietnam	14,500
6 Thailand	20,758	6 Japan	9,250
7 Myanmar	15,517	7 Myanmar	9,010
8 Japan	12,930	8 Thailand	8,536
9 Philippines	11,177	9 Philippines	7,965
10 Brazil	9,747	10 Brazil	7,950

Sugar[c]

Top 10 producers '000 tonnes		Top 10 consumers '000 tonnes	
1 EU 15	17,692	1 India	14,600
2 India	17,058	2 EU 15	14,517
3 Brazil	14,718	3 United States	8,701
4 China	7,091	4 Brazil	8,490
5 United States	6,593	5 China	8,250
6 Thailand	6,154	6 Russia	5,400
7 Australia	5,618	7 Mexico	4,229
8 Mexico	4,784	8 Indonesia	3,074
9 Cuba	4,400	9 Pakistan	2,800
10 Ukraine	2,935	10 Japan	2,579

Coarse grains[d]

Top 5 producers '000 tonnes		Top 5 consumers '000 tonnes	
1 United States	267,600	1 United States	206,400
2 China	141,600	2 China	130,000
3 EU 15	105,000	3 EU 15	95,000
4 Brazil	36,900	4 Brazil	37,000
5 India	34,000	5 Russia	33,000

Tea

Top 10 producers		*Top 10 consumers*	
'000 tonnes		*'000 tonnes*	
1 India	780	1 India	618
2 China	593	2 China	428
3 Sri Lanka	259	3 United Kingdom	148
4 Kenya	257	4 Japan	137
5 Indonesia	144	5 Russia	119
6 Turkey	115	6 Turkey	113
7 Japan	89	7 Pakistan	111
8 Bangladesh	55	8 United States	89
9 Iran	50	9 Iran	76
10 Argentina	43	10 Egypt	72

Coffee

Top 10 producers		*Top 10 consumers*	
'000 tonnes		*'000 tonnes*	
1 Brazil	1,655	1 United States	1,108
2 Colombia	646	2 Brazil	660
3 Indonesia	493	3 Germany	617
4 Vietnam	342	4 Japan	385
5 Mexico	322	5 France	338
6 Guatemala	270	6 Italy	291
7 Uganda	255	7 Spain	188
8 India	207	8 Netherlands	147
9 Ethiopia	196	9 United Kingdom	142
10 Côte d'Ivoire	192	10 Indonesia	108

Cocoa

Top 10 producers		*Top 10 consumers*	
'000 tonnes		*'000 tonnes*	
1 Côte d'Ivoire	1,200	1 United States	552
2 Ghana	404	2 Germany	232
3 Indonesia	285	3 United Kingdom	201
4 Brazil	231	4 France	178
5 Nigeria	158	5 Russia	158
6 Cameroon	135	6 Japan	139
7 Malaysia	115	7 Brazil	119
8 Ecuador	103	8 Italy	84
9 Dominican Republic	55	9 Canada	65
10 Colombia	50	10 Belgium	60

a   Paddy (unmilled rice, in the husk).
b   Milled rice.
c   Raw.
d   Includes: maize (corn), barley, sorghum, rye, oats and millet.

Copper

Top 10 producers[a] '000 tonnes		Top 10 consumers[b] '000 tonnes	
1 Chile	3,116	1 United States	2,621
2 United States	1,918	2 Japan	1,480
3 Canada	688	3 China	1,161
4 Australia	548	4 Germany	1,055
5 Indonesia	526	5 South Korea	588
6 Russia	480	6 Taiwan	544
7 Peru	479	7 France	518
8 China	439	8 Italy	504
9 Poland	422	9 United Kingdom	396
10 Mexico	341	10 Belgium	359

Lead

Top 10 producers[a] '000 tonnes		Top 10 consumers[b] '000 tonnes	
1 China	643	1 United States	1,631
2 Australia	522	2 China	464
3 United States	444	3 Japan	330
4 Canada	257	4 Germany	303
5 Peru	249	5 United Kingdom	273
6 Mexico	167	6 Italy	268
7 Sweden	99	7 France	255
8 South Africa	88	8 South Korea	231
9 Morocco	72	9 Spain	149
10 Poland	54	10 Mexico	141

Zinc

Top 10 producers[a] '000 tonnes		Top 10 consumers[c] '000 tonnes	
1 Canada	1,235	1 United States	1,210
2 China	1,121	2 China	977
3 Australia	1,071	3 Japan	736
4 Peru	761	4 Germany	468
5 United States	600	5 South Korea	350
6 Mexico	348	6 Italy	336
7 Ireland	164	7 Belgium	253
8 Sweden	160	8 France	248
9 Kazakhstan	158	9 India	199
Poland	158	10 Taiwan	196

Tin

Top 5 producers[a] '000 tonnes		Top 5 consumers[b] '000 tonnes	
1 China	69.6	1 China	42.8
2 Indonesia	51.0	2 United States	36.4
3 Peru	27.0	3 Japan	26.9
4 Brazil	20.3	4 Germany	19.3
5 Bolivia	14.8	5 South Korea	11.2

Nickel

Top 10 producers[a] '000 tonnes		*Top 10 consumers*[b] '000 tonnes	
1 Russia	224.0	**1** Japan	187.1
2 Canada	193.1	**2** United States	143.1
3 New Caledonia	124.8	**3** Germany	86.0
4 Australia	113.1	**4** South Korea	50.3
5 Indonesia	87.9	**5** Taiwan	50.0
6 Cuba	53.6	**6** China	46.3
7 China	43.8	**7** Italy	44.0
8 South Africa	33.6	**8** France	43.4
9 Dominican Republic	30.4	**9** United Kingdom	42.2
10 Colombia	22.9	**10** Russia	32.1

Aluminium

Top 10 producers[d] '000 tonnes		*Top 10 consumers*[e] '000 tonnes	
1 United States	3,577	**1** United States	5,300
2 Russia	2,870	**2** Japan	2,474
3 Canada	2,283	**3** China	2,033
4 China	1,901	**4** Germany	1,394
5 Australia	1,370	**5** South Korea	698
6 Brazil	1,197	**6** France	693
7 Norway	862	**7** Canada	620
8 Venezuela	635	**8** United Kingdom	600
9 South Africa	617	**9** Italy	585
10 Germany	577	**10** India	576

Precious metals

Gold [a] *Top 10 producers* tonnes		*Silver* [a] *Top 10 producers* tonnes	
1 South Africa	494.6	**1** Mexico	2,499
2 United States	312.0	**2** United States	1,430
3 Australia	289.5	**3** Peru	1,949
4 Canada	166.4	**4** Canada	1,309
5 Russia	123.4	**5** Chile	1,130
6 China	120.6	**6** Australia	1,020
7 Indonesia	83.6	**7** Poland	933
8 Uzbekistan	80.0	**8** China	918
9 Brazil	76.8	**9** Kazakhstan	414
10 Peru	65.1	**10** Bolivia	384

a   Mine production.
b   Refined consumption.
c   Slab consumption.
d   Primary refined production.
e   Primary refined consumption.

Rubber (natural and synthetic)

Top 10 producers		*Top 10 consumers*	
'000 tonnes		*'000 tonnes*	
1 United States	2,486	**1** United States	3,189
2 Thailand	1,978	**2** Japan	1,839
3 Indonesia	1,543	**3** China	1,670
4 Japan	1,520	**4** South Korea	804
5 Malaysia	1,083	**5** India	700
6 China	983	**6** France	618
7 Russia	775	**7** Germany	609
8 India	603	**8** Russia	454
9 France	582	**9** Brazil	445
10 South Korea	516	**10** Malaysia	427

Raw wool

Top 10 producers [a]		*Top 10 consumers* [b]	
'000 tonnes		*'000 tonnes*	
1 Australia	704	**1** China	359
2 China	300	**2** Italy	157
3 New Zealand	275	**3** Ex-Soviet Union	76
4 Ex-Soviet Union	193	**4** Turkey	70
5 Uruguay	85	United Kingdom	70
6 Argentina	78	**6** Japan	66
7 Turkey	72	**7** India	55
8 South Africa	62	**8** South Korea	47
United Kingdom	62	**9** United States	46
10 Pakistan	54	**10** Germany	34

Cotton

Top 10 producers		*Top 10 consumers*	
'000 tonnes		*'000 tonnes*	
1 China	4,203	**1** China	4,700
2 United States	4,124	**2** India	2,795
3 India	3,000	**3** United States	2,422
4 Pakistan	1,615	**4** Pakistan	1,520
5 Uzbekistan	1,062	**5** Turkey	991
6 Turkey	784	**6** Brazil	800
7 Australia	613	**7** Indonesia	475
8 Egypt	346	**8** Italy	349
9 Argentina	330	**9** Thailand	345
10 Brazil	305	**10** Mexico	344

Major oil seeds [c]

Top 5 producers		*Top 5 consumers*	
'000 tonnes		*'000 tonnes*	
1 United States	74,414	**1** United States	51,703
2 China	38,301	**2** China	39,897
3 Brazil	27,618	**3** EU 15	32,166
4 India	22,890	**4** Brazil	22,160
5 Argentina	17,164	**5** India	21,795

Oil[d]

Top 15 producers *'000 barrels per day*		*Top 15 consumers* *'000 barrels per day*	
1 Saudi Arabia[e]	8,920	1 United States	17,400
2 United States	8,300	2 Japan	5,830
3 Russia	6,075	3 China	3,615
4 Iran[e]	3,715	4 Germany	2,920
5 Norway	3,315	5 Russia	2,565
6 Mexico	3,280	6 South Korea	2,145
7 China	3,170	7 Italy	1,955
8 Venezuela[e]	3,145	8 France	1,930
9 United Kingdom	2,735	9 United Kingdom	1,790
10 United Arab Emirates[e]	2,600	10 Canada	1,735
11 Canada	2,460	11 India	1,630
12 Kuwait[e]	2,155	12 Mexico	1,605
13 Nigeria[e]	2,150	13 Brazil	1,600
14 Indonesia[e]	1,640	14 Spain	1,220
15 Libya[e]	1,440	15 Iran	1,170

Natural gas

Top 10 producers *Billion cubic metres*		*Top 10 consumers* *Billion cubic metres*	
1 Russia	561.1	1 United States	632.4
2 United States	546.9	2 Russia	352.2
3 Canada	153.0	3 United Kingdom	85.2
4 United Kingdom	84.6	4 Germany	83.6
5 Netherlands	75.8	5 Ukraine	78.2
6 Indonesia	66.5	6 Canada	73.7
7 Algeria	65.9	7 Japan	66.1
8 Uzbekistan	45.7	8 Italy	52.1
9 Saudi Arabia	41.3	9 Uzbekistan	44.4
10 Iran	38.1	10 Netherlands	41.7

Coal

Top 10 producers *Million tonnes*		*Top 10 consumers* *Million tonnes*	
1 China	1,300.0	1 China	666.0
2 United States	562.2	2 United States	516.0
3 India	283.0	3 India	140.3
4 Australia	199.8	4 Russia	119.0
5 Russia	172.0	5 Germany	88.9
6 South Africa	207.0	6 Japan	88.3
7 Poland	136.2	7 South Africa	81.7
8 Germany	47.9	8 Poland	72.0
9 Kazakhstan	73.2	9 United Kingdom	44.9
10 Ukraine	68.1	10 Ukraine	30.5

a   Greasy basis.
b   Clean basis.
c   Soybeans, sunflower seed, cottonseed, groundnuts and rapeseed.
d   Includes crude oil, shale oil, oil sands and natural gas liquids.
e   Opec members.

Energy

Largest producers

Million tonnnes coal equivalent, 1995

1	United States	2,444.2	16	Algeria	170.5
2	Russia	1,512.0	17	South Africa	168.2
3	China	1,237.3	18	France	166.0
4	Saudi Arabia	660.7	19	Kuwait	162.6
5	Canada	496.0	20	Nigeria	138.3
6	United Kingdom	364.2	21	Poland	135.5
7	Iran	323.1	22	Japan	132.6
8	India	311.0	23	Ukraine	118.9
9	Venezuela	284.5	24	Kazakhstan	108.9
10	Mexico	282.8	25	Libya	106.8
11	Indonesia	266.7	26	Netherlands	102.6
12	Australia	261.0	27	Argentina	95.4
13	Norway	258.3	28	Brazil	93.5
14	Germany	200.0	29	North Korea	89.4
15	United Arab Emirates	196.4	30	Malaysia	89.1

Largest consumers

Million tonnes coal equivalent, 1995

1	United States	3,021.6	16	Poland	136.7
2	China	1,170.7	17	Iran	130.0
3	Russia	1,004.7	18	Spain	125.1
4	Japan	638.5	19	South Africa	124.8
5	Germany	461.0	20	Netherlands	114.9
6	India	358.7	21	Saudi Arabia	113.7
7	Canada	320.9	22	Indonesia	109.7
8	United Kingdom	309.9	23	North Korea	97.9
9	France	308.6	24	Venezuela	97.6
10	Ukraine	237.3	25	Kazakhstan	94.4
11	Italy	235.6	26	Argentina	77.0
12	Mexico	186.7	27	Thailand	73.2
13	South Korea	186.0	28	Turkey	72.7
14	Brazil	145.0	29	Belgium	69.4
15	Australia	140.8	30	Uzbekistan	60.3

Energy efficiency

Most efficient
GDP per kg of energy, 1995, $

1	Uganda	24.8
2	Benin	18.4
3	Bhutan[a]	16.9
4	Burkina Faso	16.4
5	Central African Rep	13.6
6	Mali	12.1
	Sudan	12.1
8	Chad	10.7
9	Laos	9.6
10	Macau[a]	9.2

Least efficient
GDP per kg of energy, 1995, $

1	Azerbaijan	0.2
	Ukraine	0.2
3	Kazakhstan	0.3
	Uzbekistan	0.3
5	Kirgizstan	0.5
	Russia	0.5
	Tajikistan	0.5
8	Armenia	0.6
9	Belarus	0.7
	China	0.7
	Georgia[a]	0.7
	Poland	0.7
	Romania	0.7

Largest exporters
Million tonnes coal equivalent, 1995

1	Saudi Arabia	501.5		14	Algeria	119.5
2	Russia	499.9		15	Netherlands	114.4
3	Canada	239.9		16	Mexico	105.6
4	Norway	228.5		17	Libya	86.3
5	Iran	192.2		18	China	60.1
6	Venezuela	185.9		19	Singapore	58.7
7	United Arab Emirates	154.1		20	Oman	58.2
8	Australia	150.7		21	South Africa	54.2
9	United Kingdom	146.5		22	Malaysia	50.1
10	Indonesia	135.9		23	Egypt	36.6
11	Kuwait	130.2		24	Angola	35.9
12	United States	128.7		25	Kazakhstan	33.0
13	Nigeria	120.0				

Largest importers
Million tonnes coal equivalent, 1995

1	United States	748.5		14	Brazil	65.3
2	Japan	560.0		15	Canada	59.4
3	Germany	305.8		16	Turkey	52.5
4	Italy	218.2		17	Thailand	48.0
5	South Korea	201.5		18	China	44.0
6	France	193.7		19	Russia	43.3
7	Netherlands	136.1		20	Sweden	40.2
8	Ukraine	127.1		21	Belarus	35.2
9	Spain	115.5		22	Poland	33.4
10	Singapore	105.1		23	Greece	31.6
11	United Kingdom	100.3		24	Hong Kong	31.0
12	Belgium	90.2		25	Australia	28.1
13	India	73.9				

Largest consumption per head
Kg coal equivalent, 1995

1	Qatar	35,117		16	Russia	6,767
2	United Arab Emirates	18,718		17	Sweden	6,736
3	Bahrain	17,724		18	Iceland	6,491
4	Brunei	17,334		19	Netherlands Antilles	6,258
5	Kuwait	12,902		20	Saudi Arabia	6,226
6	Luxembourg	12,214		21	New Zealand	5,839
7	United States	11,312		22	Germany	5,650
8	Canada	10,913		23	Kazakhstan	5,614
9	Singapore	8,612		24	United Kingdom	5,315
10	Australia	7,879		25	France	5,309
11	Trinidad & Tobago	7,503		26	Japan	5,105
12	Netherlands	7,421		27	Czech Republic	4,959
13	Finland	7,203		28	Denmark	4,820
14	Norway	7,131		29	Estonia	4,702
15	Belgium	6,857		30	Ukraine	4,585

a 1994
Note: Consumption data for small countries, especially oil producers, can be
unreliable, often leading to unrealistically high consumption per head rates.

Workers of the world

Highest % of population in labour force
1996–97 or latest

1	Singapore	57.0		26	Brazil	48.7
2	Denmark	55.8		27	Central African Rep	48.2
3	Iceland	55.6			Germany	48.2
4	Switzerland	55.4		29	Austria	48.0
5	Latvia	55.1		30	Australia	47.7
6	Lithuania	54.9		31	Burkina Faso	47.6
7	Japan	53.5		32	Moldova	47.5
8	Burundi	52.9			Panama	47.5
9	Thailand	52.6			Slovenia	47.5
10	Belarus	52.5		35	Cyprus	47.0
11	Romania	51.8		36	Uruguay	46.8
12	United States	51.3		37	Bulgaria	46.3
13	Bahamas	51.0			Rwanda	46.3
14	Czech Republic	50.4		39	Russia	46.2
15	Macau	50.3			Slovakia	46.2
16	Canada	50.1		41	Bangladesh	46.0
	New Zealand	50.1		42	Colombia	45.9
18	Hong Kong	50.0		43	Indonesia	45.8
19	Ukraine	49.9		44	France	45.3
20	Sweden	49.6		45	Poland	45.2
21	Finland	49.4		46	Bahrain	44.6
	Norway	49.4			Paraguay	44.6
23	United Kingdom	49.3		48	Ecuador	44.5
24	Estonia	49.2		49	South Korea	44.4
25	Portugal	48.8		50	Mauritius	44.1

Most male workforce
Highest % men in workforce

1	Iran	90
2	Pakistan	87
3	Bahrain	82
	Syria	82
5	Guatemala	81
6	Tunisia	79
7	Egypt	78
8	Morocco	74
	Senegal	74
10	Argentina	72
	Malta	72
12	India	71
	Nicaragua	71
14	Costa Rica	70
	Turkey	70
16	Chile	68
	Côte d'Ivoire	68
	Sri Lanka	68
19	Mauritius	67
	Mexico	67
	Nigeria	67
	Venezuela	67

Most female workforce
Highest % women in workforce

1	Cambodia	56
2	Burundi	53
	Rwanda	53
4	Malawi	51
5	Lithuania	50
	Ukraine	50
7	Barbados	49
	Belarus	49
	Burkina Faso	49
10	Bulgaria	48
	Estonia	48
	Sudan	48
	Sweden	48
	Zimbabwe	48
15	Bahamas	47
	Central African Rep	47
	Finland	47
	Iceland	47
	Jamaica	47
	Latvia	47
	Netherlands Antilles	47
	Russia	47

Lowest % of population in labour force

1996–97 or latest

1	Iran	26.0	26	El Salvador		38.5
2	Peru	27.2	27	Costa Rica		38.7
3	Pakistan	27.5	28	Azerbaijan		38.9
4	Syria	27.8		Kuwait		38.9
5	Guatemala	29.7	30	Malaysia		39.2
6	Tunisia	29.8	31	Venezuela		39.3
7	Egypt	29.9	32	Côte d'Ivoire		39.4
8	Sudan	30.5		Malta		39.4
9	Nigeria	31.1	34	Mexico		39.7
10	Puerto Rico	32.4		Nepal		39.7
11	Morocco	32.5	36	Hungary		40.1
12	Nicaragua	33.2	37	Italy		40.3
13	Botswana	33.3	38	Sri Lanka		40.4
	Gambia, The	33.3	39	Trinidad & Tobago		40.5
	Suriname	33.3	40	Barbados		40.6
16	Saudi Arabia	34.0	41	Philippines		40.8
	Senegal	34.0		Spain		40.8
18	Zimbabwe	34.6	43	Ireland		41.3
19	Honduras	35.0	44	Argentina		41.5
20	Fiji	35.2		Greece		41.5
21	Turkey	35.3	46	Luxembourg		41.8
22	Israel	36.9	47	Netherlands		41.9
23	India	37.5	48	Belgium		42.1
	South Africa	37.5	49	Bolivia		42.2
25	Chile	37.8	50	Croatia		42.6

Highest rate of unemployment

% of labour force

1	Macedonia, FYR	38.8	21	Italy	12.1
2	Réunion[a]	34.4	22	Ireland	11.9
3	Algeria[b]	23.8	23	Egypt[e]	11.3
4	Spain	22.2		Sri Lanka	11.3
5	Guadeloupe[c]	19.9	25	Colombia	11.2
6	Latvia	18.3	26	Ecuador	10.4
7	Argentina	16.3	27	Venezuela[e]	10.3
	Trinidad & Tobago	16.3	28	Uruguay[e]	10.2
9	Finland	16.1	29	Greece[e]	10.0
10	Morocco[b]	16.0	30	Hungary	9.9
11	Jamaica[b]	15.9	31	Mauritius[e]	9.8
12	Barbados	15.6	32	Canada	9.7
13	Netherlands Antilles	14.0	33	Belgium	9.6
	Nicaragua[c]	14.0	34	Russia	9.3
15	Panama	13.9	35	Germany	8.8
16	Puerto Rico	13.4	36	Australia	8.6
17	Bahamas[d]	13.3	37	Suriname[e]	8.4
18	Slovakia	12.6	38	United Kingdom	8.2
19	France	12.4	39	Sweden	8.0
20	Poland	12.3	40	El Salvador	7.7

a 1993 b 1992 c 1991 d 1994 e 1995

The business world

Global competitiveness

Overall	Government	Internationalisation
1 United States	Singapore	United States
2 Singapore	Hong Kong	Singapore
3 Hong Kong	Malaysia	Hong Kong
4 Netherlands	New Zealand	Luxembourg
5 Finland	China	United Kingdom
6 Norway	Ireland	Netherlands
7 Switzerland	Canada	Ireland
8 Denmark	Switzerland	Germany
9 Luxembourg	Australia	Belgium
10 Canada	United Kingdom	France
11 Ireland	Luxembourg	Finland
12 United Kingdom	Norway	Denmark
13 New Zealand	United States	Portugal
14 Germany	Taiwan	Sweden
15 Australia	Finland	Norway
16 Taiwan	Chile	New Zealand
17 Sweden	Netherlands	Switzerland
18 Japan	Iceland	Spain
19 Iceland	Philippines	Italy
20 Malaysia	Denmark	China
21 France	Brazil	Argentina
22 Austria	Thailand	Canada
23 Belgium	Spain	Chile
24 China	Indonesia	Malaysia
25 Israel	Mexico	Austria
26 Chile	Hungary	Hungary
27 Spain	Japan	Australia
28 Hungary	India	Philippines
29 Portugal	Portugal	Czech Republic
30 Italy	Argentina	Russia
31 Argentina	South Africa	Turkey
32 Philippines	Austria	Taiwan
33 Turkey	Israel	Israel
34 Mexico	South Korea	Japan
35 South Korea	Sweden	Greece
36 Greece	Germany	Indonesia
37 Brazil	Russia	Thailand
38 Czech Republic	Turkey	Iceland
39 Thailand	Venezuela	Brazil
40 Indonesia	Czech Republic	Mexico
41 India	Colombia	Venezuela
42 South Africa	France	India
43 Venezuela	Greece	Poland

Notes: Rankings reflect assessments for the ability of a country to achieve sustained high rates of GDP growth per head. Column 1 is based on 259 criteria covering: the openness of an economy, the role of the government, the development of financial markets, the quality of infrastructure, technology, business management and judicial and political institutions and labour-market flexibility. Column 2 looks at the extent to which government policies are conducive to competitiveness. Column 3 is based on the extent to which a country participates in international trade and investment flows.

The business environment

		1997 score	1996 score	1996 Ranking
1	Netherlands	8.78	8.57	3
2	United Kingdom	8.74	8.59	2
3	United States	8.64	8.44	5
4	Canada	8.61	8.42	6
5	Singapore	8.56	8.52	4
6	Denmark	8.43	8.06	8
7	Switzerland	8.42	7.99	9
8	New Zealand	8.29	8.18	7
9	Ireland	8.28	7.94	10
10	Sweden	8.24	7.77	13
11	Germany	8.23	7.88	12
12	France	8.21	7.73	15
13	Australia	8.20	7.93	11
14	Finland	8.17	7.71	16
15	Belgium	8.13	7.59	17
16	Norway	8.12	7.75	14
17	Hong Kong	8.11	8.84	1
18	Austria	7.89	7.56	18
	Spain	7.89	6.92	22
20	Chile	7.82	7.47	19
21	Portugal	7.75	6.74	23
22	Japan	7.68	6.74	23
23	Taiwan	7.61	7.27	20
24	Italy	7.53	6.38	28
25	South Korea	7.26	6.38	28
26	Argentina	7.18	6.67	25
27	Hungary	7.14	5.71	35
28	Malaysia	7.11	7.25	21
29	Israel	6.98	6.50	27
30	Philippines	6.88	5.80	33
31	Poland	6.84	5.51	36
32	Thailand	6.79	6.52	26
33	Czech Republic	6.74	6.22	30
34	Greece	6.64	5.88	32
35	Mexico	6.58	5.45	39
36	Brazil	6.38	5.08	46
	Peru	6.38	5.38	41
38	South Africa	6.23	5.46	38
39	Indonesia	6.20	6.15	31
40	Colombia	6.04	5.74	34
41	Turkey	5.97	5.47	37
42	Egypt	5.92	5.36	42
43	Saudi Arabia	5.90	5.12	45
	Slovakia	5.90	5.42	40
	Sri Lanka	5.90	5.27	43
46	India	5.77	5.15	44
	Romania	5.77	4.20	52

Note: Scores reflect the opportunities for, and hindrances to, the conduct of business, measured by countries' rankings in ten categories including market potential, tax and labour-market policies, infrastructure, skills and the political environment.

Businesses and banks

Largest businesses

By sales, $bn

1	General Motors	United States	168.4
2	Ford Motor	United States	147.0
3	Mitsui[a]	Japan	144.9
4	Mitsubishi[a]	Japan	140.2
5	Itochu[a]	Japan	135.5
6	Royal Dutch/Shell Group	United Kingdom/Netherlands	128.2
7	Marubeni[a]	Japan	124.0
8	Exxon	United States	119.4
9	Sumitomo[a]	Japan	119.3
10	Toyota Motor[a]	Japan	108.7
11	Wal-Mart Stores[b]	United States	106.1
12	General Electric	United States	79.2
13	Nissho Iwai[a]	Japan	78.9
14	Nippon Telegraph and Telephone[ac]	Japan	78.3
15	Intl. Business Machines	United States	75.9
16	Hitachi[a]	Japan	75.7
17	AT&T	United States	74.5
18	Nippon Life Insurance[a]	Japan	72.6
19	Mobil	United States	72.3
20	Daimler-Benz	Germany	71.6
21	British Petroleum	United Kingdom	69.9
22	Matsushita Electric Industrial[a]	Japan	68.1
23	Volkswagen	Germany	66.5
24	Daewoo	South Korea	65.2
25	Siemens[d]	Germany	63.7
26	Chrysler	United States	61.4
27	Nissan Motor[a]	Japan	59.1
28	Allianz	Germany	56.6
29	U.S. Postal Service[cd]	United States	56.4
30	Philip Morris	United States	54.5
31	Unilever	United Kingdom/Netherlands	52.1
32	Fiat	Italy	50.5
33	Sony[a]	Japan	50.3
34	Dai-Ichi Mutual Life Insurance[a]	Japan	49.1
	IRI[c]	Italy	49.1
36	Nestlé	Switzerland	48.9
37	Toshiba[a]	Japan	48.4
38	Honda Motor[a]	Japan	47.0
39	Elf Aquitaine	France	46.8
40	Tomen[a]	Japan	46.5

a Year ended March 31, 1997.
b Year ended January 31, 1997.
c Government owned.
d Year ended September 30, 1996.

Notes: Industrial and service corporations. Figures refer to the year ended December 31, 1996, except where specified. They include sales of consolidated subsidiaries but exclude excise taxes, thus differing, in some instances, from figures published by the companies themselves.

Largest banks
By capital, $m

1	HSBC Holdings	United Kingdom	25,716
2	Bank of Tokyo-Mitsubishi	Japan	24,323
3	Crédit Agricole	France	22,235
4	Chase Manhattan Corp	United States	21,095
5	Citicorp	United States	20,109
6	Deutsche Bank	Germany	18,517
7	BankAmerica Corp	United States	17,181
8	ABN-Amro Bank	Netherlands	16,098
9	Sumitomo Bank	Japan	15,994
10	Union Bank of Switzerland	Switzerland	15,743
11	Fuji Bank	Japan	15,724
12	Dai-Ichi Kangyo Bank	Japan	15,162
13	Sanwa Bank	Japan	15,161
14	Sakura Bank	Japan	14,772
15	Bank of China	China	13,737
16	NationsBank	United States	12,662
17	Barclays Bank	United Kingdom	12,635
18	Industrial Bank of Japan	Japan	12,384
19	Groupe Caisse d'Epargne	France	12,368
20	National Westminster Bank	United Kingdom	11,914
21	Banque Nationale de Paris	France	11,612
22	Credit Suisse Group	Switzerland	11,611
23	J.P. Morgan & Co.	United States	11,469
24	Rabobank Nederland	Netherlands	11,423
25	Industrial & Commercial Bank of China	China	11,172
26	Companie Financière de Paribas	France	10,765
27	Société Générale	France	10,735
28	Swiss Bank Corp	Switzerland	10,264
29	Dresdner Bank	Germany	9,325
30	First Chicago NBD Corporation	United States	9,318
31	Lloyds TSB Group	United Kingdom	8,937
32	Long-Term Credit Bank of Japan	Japan	8,489
33	Tokai Bank	Japan	8,487
34	Westdeutsche Landesbank Girozentrale	Germany	8,320
35	Commerzbank	Germany	8,157
36	Banc One Corp	United States	8,107
37	Crédit Mutuel	France	8,065
38	National Australia Bank	Australia	8,042
39	Asahi Bank	Japan	7,871
40	First Union Corp	United States	7,790

Notes: Capital is essentially equity and reserves.
Figures for Japanese banks refer to the year ended March 31, 1997. Figures for all
other countries refer to the year ended December 31, 1996.

Stockmarkets

Largest market capitalisation
$m, end 1996

1	United States	8,484,433		26	Philippines	80,649
2	Japan	3,088,850		27	Denmark	71,688
3	United Kingdom	1,740,246		28	Chile	65,940
4	Germany	670,997		29	Finland	63,078
5	France	591,123		30	Norway	57,423
6	Canada	486,268		31	Argentina	44,679
7	Hong Kong	449,381		32	New Zealand	38,288
8	Switzerland	402,104		33	Russia	37,230
9	Netherlands	378,721		34	Israel	35,934
10	Australia	311,988		35	Austria	33,953
11	Malaysia	307,179		36	Luxembourg	32,692
12	Taiwan	273,608		37	Turkey	30,020
13	Italy	258,160		38	Portugal	24,660
14	Sweden	247,217		39	Greece	24,178
15	Spain	242,779		40	Czech Republic	18,077
16	South Africa	241,571		41	Colombia	17,137
17	Brazil	216,990		42	Egypt	14,173
18	Singapore	150,215		43	Peru	12,291
19	South Korea	138,817		44	Pakistan	10,639
20	India	122,605		45	Venezuela	10,055
21	Belgium	119,831		46	Morocco	8,705
22	China	113,755		47	Poland	8,390
23	Mexico	106,540		48	Hungary	5,273
24	Thailand	99,828		49	Jordan	4,551
25	Indonesia	91,106		49	Bangladesh	4,551

Highest growth in market capitalisation, $ terms
% increase, 1987–96

1	Indonesia	133,747		21	Hong Kong	731
2	Russia[a]	16,978		22	India	619
3	Poland[b]	3,679		23	Uruguay	565
4	Argentina	2,841		24	Egypt	559
5	Philippines	2,636		25	Tunisia	544
6	Morocco	2,338		26	China[b]	523
7	Thailand	1,720		27	Taiwan	463
8	Ghana[b]	1,676		28	Swaziland[c]	453
9	Namibia[c]	1,589		29	Pakistan	443
10	Malaysia	1,558		30	Greece	442
11	Peru	1,379		31	Mauritius[d]	437
12	Colombia	1,265		32	Zimbabwe	406
13	Mexico	1,173		33	Norway	386
14	Bangladesh	1,024		34	Austria	358
15	Iran[b]	998		35	Venezuela	341
16	Hungary[b]	838		36	Netherlands	339
17	Turkey	832		37	Kenya	335
18	Honduras[d]	745		38	South Korea	322
19	Singapore	738		39	Nigeria	266
20	Paraguay[a]	733		40	Trinidad & Tobago	262

Highest growth in value traded, $ terms

% increase, 1987–96

1	Indonesia	1,071,300	**21**	Costa Rica	1,300
2	Turkey	31,927	**22**	Peru	1,164
3	Bangladesh	11,933	**23**	Sri Lanka	1,118
4	Morocco	5,300	**24**	Brazil	1,067
5	Tunisia	4,583	**25**	Zimbabwe	1,009
6	Malaysia	4,433	**26**	Nigeria	929
7	Namibia[c]	3,700	**27**	Thailand	858
8	Pakistan	3,637	**28**	Venezuela	761
9	Poland[b]	3,216	**29**	Netherlands	759
10	Egypt	1,902	**30**	Trinidad & Tobago	723
11	Greece	1,778	**31**	Swaziland[c]	700
12	Denmark	1,712	**32**	South Korea	611
13	Argentina	1,646	**33**	Sweden	599
14	Colombia	1,600	**34**	Spain	591
15	Ghana[b]	1,600	**35**	Russia[a]	536
16	Chile	1,582	**36**	Singapore	524
17	Philippines	1,574	**37**	Kenya	509
18	India	1,523	**38**	Kuwait	490
19	China[b]	1,432	**39**	Taiwan	459
20	Hungary[b]	1,303	**40**	Switzerland	421

Highest growth in number of listed companies

% increase, 1987–96

1	Indonesia	954	**21**	Hungary[b]	96
2	China[b]	938	**22**	South Korea	95
3	Armenia[a]	900	**23**	Greece	93
4	Paraguay[a]	567	**24**	Iran[b]	86
5	Poland[b]	419	**25**	Nigeria	83
6	Turkey	358	**26**	Singapore	76
7	Thailand	263		Tunisia	76
8	Namibia[c]	200	**28**	Costa Rica	61
	Swaziland[c]	200	**29**	India	58
10	Russia[a]	181	**30**	Philippines	57
11	Taiwan	171	**31**	Czech Republic[a]	55
12	Malaysia	168	**32**	Austria	54
13	Oman[e]	160	**33**	Egypt	50
14	Honduras[b]	152	**34**	Sweden	46
15	Israel	131	**35**	Finland	45
16	Bangladesh	119		Panama[f]	45
17	Pakistan	106	**37**	Bolivia[a]	43
18	Hong Kong	103	**38**	Ghana[b]	40
19	Mauritius[d]	100		Sri Lanka	40
20	Colombia	97	**40**	Chile	39

a 1994–96
b 1992–96
c 1993–96
d 1991–95
e 1990–96
f 1993–95

Transport: *roads and cars*

Longest road networks

Km, 1996 or latest

1	United States	6,420,000	21	Argentina	218,276
2	India	2,060,000	22	Ukraine	172,565
3	Brazil	1,980,000	23	Iran	162,000
4	China	1,526,389	24	Saudi Arabia	162,000
5	Japan	1,144,360	25	Hungary	158,633
6	Canada	1,012,200	26	Congo	157,000
7	Russia	963,000	27	Philippines	156,997
8	Australia	913,000	28	Romania	153,358
9	France	892,500	29	Belgium	143,175
10	Germany	633,000	30	Kazakhstan	141,076
11	Indonesia	393,000	31	Sweden	138,000
12	Turkey	381,631	32	Austria	129,055
13	Poland	374,990	33	Netherlands	127,000
14	United Kingdom	372,000	34	Greece	117,000
15	Spain	344,847	35	Colombia	107,000
16	South Africa	331,265	36	Algeria	104,000
17	Italy	317,000	37	Sri Lanka	99,200
18	Mexico	252,000	38	Malaysia	94,500
19	Pakistan	224,774	39	Vietnam	93,300
20	Bangladesh	223,391	40	Ireland	92,500

Densest road networks

Km of road per km^2 land area, 1996 or latest

1	Singapore	4.71	21	Sri Lanka	1.51
2	Belgium	4.69	22	Ireland	1.32
3	Bahrain	4.36	23	Poland	1.20
4	Barbados	3.84	24	Cyprus	1.13
5	Netherlands	3.06	25	Italy	1.05
6	Japan	3.03	26	Lithuania	1.00
7	Macau	2.94	27	Latvia	0.94
8	Luxembourg	2.00	28	Mauritius	0.91
9	Germany	1.77	29	Greece	0.89
10	Jamaica	1.73	30	South Korea	0.84
11	Switzerland	1.72	31	Portugal	0.77
12	Hungary	1.71	32	Slovakia	0.75
13	Denmark	1.66	33	Slovenia	0.74
14	France	1.64	34	Israel	0.73
	Hong Kong	1.64	35	Czech Republic	0.70
16	Trinidad & Tobago	1.62	35	Costa Rica	0.70
17	Puerto Rico	1.58	37	United States	0.68
18	Bangladesh	1.55	37	Spain	0.68
19	Austria	1.54	39	Romania	0.65
20	United Kingdom	1.53	40	India	0.63

Most crowded road networks
Number of vehicles per km of road network, 1996 or latest

1	Hong Kong	276	26	Netherlands	49
2	Taiwan	241	27	Luxembourg	48
3	Lebanon	205	28	El Salvador	44
4	Singapore	168		Jordan	44
5	Kuwait	156	30	Nigeria	42
6	Qatar	154	31	Peru	40
7	Brunei	145	32	Algeria	38
8	Italy	122	33	Macedonia, FYR	35
9	South Korea	106		Serbia	35
10	Israel	98	35	Croatia	34
11	Thailand	97		France	34
12	Puerto Rico	74	37	Belgium	33
13	Germany	68		Malaysia	33
14	Czech Republic	65	39	Cyprus	32
15	United Kingdom	63		Estonia	32
16	Japan	61		Slovakia	32
17	Bahrain	58		United States	32
18	Mauritius	54	43	Dominican Republic	30
	Portugal	54	44	Sweden	29
20	Bulgaria	53	45	Denmark	28
21	Mexico	52	46	Egypt	28
	Slovenia	52		Finland	28
	Spain	52		Greece	28
	United Arab Emirates	52		Sudan	28
25	Switzerland	50	50	Ukraine	27

Most used road networks
'000 vehicle-km per year per km of road network, 1996 or latest

1	Hong Kong	5,973.9	16	Denmark	579.6
2	Israel	2,061.7	17	Belgium	568.5
3	Thailand	1,546.4	18	Finland	546.7
4	Bahrain	1,544.6	19	Slovenia	539.0
5	Italy	1,429.5	20	France	523.6
6	Portugal	1,230.7	21	Macedonia, FYR	489.1
7	United Kingdom	1,173.3	22	Sweden	474.2
8	Germany	889.7	23	United States	401.5
9	Luxembourg	879.8	24	Zimbabwe	399.7
10	Netherlands	851.2	25	Oman	391.2
11	Switzerland	712.2	26	Spain	390.1
12	Czech Republic	692.2	27	El Salvador	365.4
13	South Korea	682.7	28	Ukraine	348.7
14	Japan	602.8	29	Ecuador	328.1
15	Saudi Arabia	581.1	30	Jordan	324.4

Highest car ownership

Number of cars per 1,000 people, 1996 or latest

1	Lebanon	731	26	Czech Republic	324
2	Brunei	575	27	Ireland	279
3	Italy	568	28	Estonia	278
4	Luxembourg	561	29	Portugal	257
5	United States	518	30	Bahrain	240
6	Germany	498	31	Hungary	238
7	Australia	488	32	Puerto Rico	234
8	New Zealand	470	33	Greece	223
9	Iceland	462	34	Qatar	218
10	Switzerland	462	35	Lithuania	211
11	Austria	458	36	Poland	208
12	Canada	457	37	Israel	205
13	France	438	38	Bulgaria	204
14	Belgium	424	39	Slovakia	196
15	Sweden	411	40	Taiwan	193
16	Finland	378	41	Croatia	175
17	Norway	378	42	Bahamas	161
18	Japan	373	43	Uruguay	153
19	Spain	371	44	South Korea	152
20	United Kingdom	370	45	Serbia	145
21	Slovenia	365	46	Macedonia, FYR	141
22	Netherlands	361	47	Barbados	136
23	Kuwait	359	48	Argentina	135
24	Cyprus	348	49	Latvia	133
25	Denmark	332	50	Malaysia	132

Lowest car ownership

Number of cars per 1,000 people, 1996 or latest

1	Central African Rep	0.1	16	Guinea	2.0
	Somalia	0.1	17	Malawi	2.3
	Tajikistan	0.1	18	Liberia	2.6
4	Armenia	0.3	19	Burundi	2.8
	Mozambique	0.3	20	Mali	2.9
6	Bangladesh	0.5	21	Chad	3.2
7	Iraq	0.6		China	3.2
	Myanmar	0.6	23	Laos	3.4
9	Ethiopia	0.8	24	Burkina Faso	3.6
	Tanzania	0.8	25	Niger	3.8
11	Afghanistan	1.4	26	Sierra Leone	3.9
	Rwanda	1.4	27	Madagascar	4.1
13	Eritrea	1.5	28	Cambodia	4.4
14	Cuba	1.8		Haiti	4.4
	Uganda	1.8	30	India	4.5

Most accidents
Number of people injured per 100m vehicle-km, 1996 or latest

1	Malawi	2,730	26	United Kingdom	72
2	Rwanda	1,764	27	Mexico	66
3	South Korea	725		Slovakia	66
4	Costa Rica	406	29	Italy	63
5	Kenya	363	30	Hungary	60
6	Honduras	317	31	Yemen	59
7	Turkey	255	32	Senegal	56
8	Egypt	222	33	Bahrain	55
9	Sri Lanka	205	34	New Zealand	54
10	Portugal	194	35	Colombia	53
11	Hong Kong	175	36	Iran	53
12	Morocco	167		Oman	53
13	Israel	147	38	Switzerland	50
14	Belgium	143	39	Thailand	40
15	Kirgizstan	134	40	Ireland	38
16	Japan	129	41	France	34
	South Africa	129	42	Sweden	33
18	Latvia	125	43	Zimbabwe	32
19	Czech Republic	113	44	Ecuador	31
20	Slovenia	96	45	El Salvador	28
21	Spain	92	46	Denmark	26
22	United States	89	47	Finland	22
23	Germany	85	48	Australia	14
24	Iceland	81	49	Netherlands	11
	Macedonia, FYR	81	50	Albania	9

Most deaths
Number of people killed per 100m vehicle-km, 1996 or latest

1	Malawi	1,117	16	Albania	8
2	Egypt	44		Ecuador	8
3	Kenya	41	18	Portugal	6
4	Latvia	25	19	Colombia	5
5	Kirgizstan	24		Czech Republic	5
6	Sri Lanka	23		Hungary	5
7	South Korea	21		Iran	5
8	Honduras	16		Slovenia	5
9	Morocco	15	24	Macedonia, FYR	4
10	Thailand	13		Oman	4
	Turkey	13		Senegal	4
12	Costa Rica	11		Slovakia	4
	Yemen	11		Spain	4
14	Mexico	10	29	Belgium	3
	South Africa	10		Zambia	3

Transport: *planes and trains*

Most air passenger-km
Million passenger-km[a] per year

1	United States	921,481	15	Spain	33,205
2	United Kingdom	167,493	16	Thailand	29,801
3	Japan	141,634	17	Malaysia	27,085
4	France	78,383	18	Indonesia	24,820
5	China	70,605	19	Switzerland	22,198
6	Australia	69,930	20	India	21,365
7	Germany	65,943	21	Saudi Arabia	19,342
8	Netherlands	62,610	22	Mexico	19,297
9	Canada	56,018	23	New Zealand	18,798
10	South Korea	54,520	24	South Africa	15,538
11	Singapore	53,806	25	Philippines	15,006
12	Russia	52,710	26	Argentina	12,905
13	Brazil	37,339	27	Israel	11,660
14	Italy	36,123	28	Turkey	10,862

Busiest airports
Number of passengers '000

1	Chicago	O'Hare	69,154
2	Atlanta	Hartsfield	63,303
3	Dallas	Dallas/Ft. Worth	58,035
4	Los Angeles	Los Angeles Intl.	57,975
5	London	Heathrow	56,038
6	Tokyo	Hanedo	46,631
7	San Francisco	San Francisco Intl.	39,252
8	Frankfurt	Frankfurt/Main	38,761
9	Seoul	Kimpo Intl.	34,706
10	Miami	Miami Intl.	33,505
11	Denver	Denver Intl.	32,296
12	Paris	Charles de Gaulle	31,724

Busiest international airports
Number of international passengers '000

1	London	Heathrow	48,275
2	Frankfurt	Frankfurt/Main	30,919
3	Hong Kong	Hong Kong Intl.	29,543
4	Paris	Charles de Gaulle	28,665
5	Amsterdam	Schipol	27,085
6	Singapore	Changi	23,130
7	Tokyo	New Tokyo Intl. (Narita)	22,666
8	London	Gatwick	22,029
9	New York	Kennedy	17,453
10	Bangkok	Bangkok Intl.	16,380
11	Miami	Miami Intl.	14,913
12	Zurich	Zurich	14,783

a Air passenger–km data refer to the distance travelled by each aircraft of national origin.

Longest railway networks

'000 km, 1996 or latest year

1	United States	243.3	21	Australia	10.0
2	Russia	87.1	22	Czech Republic	9.4
3	India	62.9	23	Pakistan	8.8
4	China	56.7	24	Turkey	8.6
5	Germany	40.8	25	Hungary	7.9
6	Argentina	34.2	26	Finland	5.9
7	France	31.9	27	Austria	5.7
8	Mexico	26.5	28	Iran	5.6
9	South Africa	25.9	29	Belarus	5.5
10	Poland	23.4	30	Egypt	4.9
11	Ukraine	22.6		Philippines	4.9
12	Brazil	22.1	32	Cuba	4.8
13	Japan	20.1	33	Sudan	4.6
14	United Kingdom	17.2	34	North Korea	4.5
15	Italy	16.0	35	Bulgaria	4.3
16	Spain	13.7		New Zealand	4.3
17	Canada	13.5		Serbia, Montenegro	4.3
	Kazakhstan	13.5	38	Algeria	4.2
19	Romania	11.4		Indonesia	4.2
20	Sweden	11.0	40	Congo	4.1

Most rail passengers

Km per year per person, 1996 or latest year

1	Japan	2,005		Denmark	904
2	Switzerland	1,699	12	Italy	886
3	Austria	1,202	13	Kazakhstan	855
4	Ukraine	1,152	14	Romania	812
5	Russia	1,140	15	Czech Republic	786
6	Belarus	1,138	16	Germany	761
7	France	1,020	17	Sweden	700
8	Egypt	924	18	Slovakia	697
9	Netherlands	910	19	Luxembourg	676
10	Benin	904	20	Belgium	667

Most rail freight

Million tonnes-km per year, 1996 or latest year

1	United States	1,979,686	11	Australia	26,368
2	China	1,292,185	12	Belarus	26,018
3	Russia	1,131,251	13	Japan	24,747
4	India	270,489	14	Romania	24,155
5	Ukraine	163,384	15	Czech Republic	22,239
6	Kazakhstan	108,596	16	Italy	21,212
7	South Africa	99,850	17	Uzbekistan	19,653
8	Germany	67,880	18	Sweden	17,993
9	Poland	67,413	19	Iran	13,638
10	France	49,512	20	Austria	13,122

Transport: *sail away*

Largest merchant fleets: one

Number of vessels over 100 GRT [a], mid-1997

1	Japan	9,310	21	Turkey	1,146
2	Panama	6,188	22	Germany	1,125
3	United States	5,260	23	Denmark	1,085
4	Russia	4,814	24	Ukraine	1,025
5	China	3,175	25	India	941
6	South Korea	2,441	26	Canada	852
7	Indonesia	2,383	27	Malaysia	838
8	Norway	2,274	28	France	826
9	Philippines	1,699	29	Peru	728
10	Liberia	1,697	30	Taiwan	692
11	Singapore	1,656	31	Vietnam	662
12	Cyprus	1,650	32	Mexico	637
13	Greece	1,641	33	Australia	617
14	Spain	1,606	34	Sweden	588
15	United Kingdom	1,424	35	Thailand	576
16	Malta	1,378	36	Brazil	536
17	Honduras	1,339	37	Argentina	513
18	Italy	1,324	38	Morocco	495
19	Bahamas	1,221	39	Chile	469
20	Netherlands	1,178	40	Poland	464

Largest merchant fleets: two

Gross tonnage, '000

1	Panama	91,128	21	Malaysia	4,842
2	Liberia	60,058	22	France	4,682
3	Bahamas	25,523	23	Brazil	4,372
4	Greece	25,288	24	Netherlands	3,880
5	Cyprus	23,653	25	Iran	3,553
6	Norway	22,984	26	United Kingdom	3,486
7	Singapore	18,875	27	Indonesia	3,195
8	Japan	18,516	28	Sweden	2,754
9	China	16,339	29	Ukraine	2,690
10	Russia	12,282	30	Australia	2,607
11	United States	11,789	31	Canada	2,527
12	Philippines	8,849	32	Romania	2,345
13	South Korea	7,430	33	Thailand	2,158
14	Germany	6,950	34	Kuwait	1,984
15	India	6,935	35	Poland	1,878
16	Turkey	6,567	36	Finland	1,559
17	Italy	6,194	37	Egypt	1,288
18	Taiwan	5,931	38	Saudi Arabia	1,164
19	Denmark	5,859	39	Mexico	1,145
20	Hong Kong	5,771	40	Spain	1,141

a Gross Tonnage (GRT) = total volume within the hull and above deck. 1 GRT=100 cu ft.

Tourism

Most tourist arrivals
Number of arrivals, '000

1	France	66,800	21	Malaysia	7,200
2	United States	49,038	22	Netherlands	6,674
3	Spain	43,403	23	Singapore	6,542
4	Italy	34,087	24	Belgium	5,875
5	United Kingdom	25,960	25	Ireland	5,540
6	China	23,770	26	South Africa	5,500
7	Poland	19,514	27	Indonesia	5,036
8	Mexico	18,667	28	Macao	4,915
9	Canada	17,610	29	Argentina	4,540
10	Czech Republic	17,400	30	Australia	4,286
11	Hungary	17,248	31	Tunisia	4,263
12	Austria	16,642	32	Japan	4,223
13	Germany	15,828	33	South Korea	3,908
14	Russia	15,350	34	Croatia	3,834
15	Switzerland	11,077	35	Egypt	3,657
16	Hong Kong	10,406	36	Saudi Arabia	3,594
17	Greece	10,246	37	Puerto Rico	3,332
18	Portugal	10,100	38	Morocco	3,115
19	Turkey	9,040	39	Brazil	2,995
20	Thailand	7,263	40	Romania	2,741

Biggest tourist spending
$m

1	Germany	50,812	11	Belgium	9,895
2	United States	48,739	12	Switzerland	7,479
3	Japan	37,040	13	South Korea	6,963
4	United Kingdom	25,445	14	Taiwan	6,493
5	France	17,746	15	Sweden	6,441
6	Italy	15,516	16	Poland	6,240
7	Austria	11,811	17	Singapore	6,139
8	Netherlands	11,370	18	Brazil	5,825
9	Canada	11,090	19	Australia	5,322
10	Russia	10,723	20	Spain	4,916

Largest tourist receipts
$m

1	United States	75,056	11	Canada	8,928
2	Italy	30,000	12	Poland	8,700
3	France	27,947		Thailand	8,700
4	Spain	27,190	14	Singapore	7,993
5	United Kingdom	20,569	15	Switzerland	7,960
6	Germany	16,418	16	Mexico	7,530
7	Austria	12,393	17	Russia	7,318
8	China	12,074	18	Turkey	7,000
9	Australia	9,324	19	Netherlands	6,597
10	Hong Kong	9,242	20	Indonesia	6,589

Education

Highest primary enrolment
Number enrolled as % of relevant age group, 1995

1	Gabon	142	16	Colombia	114
2	Malawi	135		Congo-Brazzaville	114
3	Namibia	133		Indonesia	114
4	Portugal	128		Vietnam	114
5	Peru	123	20	Sri Lanka	113
6	Cambodia	122	21	Brazil	112
7	China	118	22	Honduras	111
	Togo	118		Uruguay	111
9	South Africa	117	24	Libya	110
10	Philippines	116		Nepal	110
	Tunisia	116		Nicaragua	110
	Zimbabwe	116	27	Ecuador	109
13	Botswana	115		Jamaica	109
	Mexico	115		Lebanon	109
	United Kingdom	115		Paraguay	109

Lowest primary enrolment
Number enrolled as % of relevant age group, 1995

1	Bhutan[a]	26	15	Tanzania	67
2	Niger	29	16	Côte d'Ivoire	69
3	Ethiopia	31	17	Burundi	70
4	Mali	34	18	Benin	72
5	Burkina Faso	38		Congo	72
6	Guinea	48		Madagascar	72
7	Sierra Leone[b]	48		Serbia, Montenegro	72
8	Sudan	54	22	Gambia, The	73
9	Chad	55		Kuwait	73
10	Eritrea	57		Uganda	73
11	Central African Rep	58	25	Pakistan	74
12	Mozambique	60	26	Ghana	76
13	Guinea-Bissau	64	27	Uzbekistan	77
14	Senegal	65	28	Mauritania	78

Highest tertiary enrolment[c]
Number enrolled as % of relevant age group, 1995

1	Canada	103	12	United Kingdom	48
2	United States	81	13	Spain	46
3	Australia	72	14	Austria	45
4	Finland	67		Denmark	45
5	New Zealand	58	16	Germany	43
6	Norway	55		Russia	43
7	South Korea	52		Sweden	43
8	France	50	19	Israel	41
9	Armenia	49		Italy	41
	Belgium	49		Ukraine	41
	Netherlands	49			

Notes: The gross enrolment ratios shown are the actual number enrolled as a percentage of the number of children in the official primary age group. They may exceed 100 when children outside the primary age group are receiving primary education either because they have not moved on to secondary education or because they have started primary education early.

Least literate
% adult literacy rate, 1994

1	Niger	13.1	14	Cambodia	35.0
2	Burkina Faso	18.7		Oman	35.0
3	Somalia[d]	24.9	16	Benin	35.5
4	Eritrea	25.0	17	Mauritania	36.9
5	Nepal	27.0	18	Pakistan	37.1
6	Mali	29.3	19	Gambia, The	37.2
7	Afghanistan[d]	29.8	20	Bangladesh	37.3
	Liberia[d]	29.8	21	Côte d'Ivoire	39.4
9	Sierra Leone	30.3	22	Mozambique	39.5
10	Senegal	32.1	23	Namibia	40.0
11	Ethiopia	34.5	24	Bhutan	41.1
12	Burundi	34.6		Yemen	41.1
13	Guinea	34.8	26	Morocco	42.1

Highest education spending
% of GDP, 1995

1	Botswana	9.6	14	Kenya	7.4
2	Uzbekistan	9.5	15	Canada	7.3
3	Namibia	9.4	16	Kirgizstan	6.8
4	Tajikistan	8.6		South Africa	6.8
5	Zimbabwe	8.5		Swaziland[e]	6.8
6	Denmark	8.3		Tunisia	6.8
	Norway	8.3	20	New Zealand	6.7
8	Jamaica	8.2	21	Bolivia	6.6
9	Sweden	8.0		Cuba[e]	6.6
10	Ukraine	7.7		Estonia	6.6
11	Finland	7.6		Israel	6.6
12	Barbados[e]	7.5	25	Ireland	6.3
	Yemen	7.5		Jordan	6.3

Lowest education spending
% of GDP, 1995

1	Indonesia[e]	1.3		El Salvador	2.2
	Myanmar	1.3		Mali	2.2
	Nigeria[e]	1.3		Philippines	2.2
4	Haiti[e]	1.4	17	Bangladesh	2.3
5	Brazil[e]	1.6		China	2.3
6	Guatemala	1.7	19	Laos	2.4
7	United Arab Emirates	1.8	20	Pakistan[e]	2.7
	Zambia	1.8		Vietnam	2.7
9	Dominican Republic	1.9	22	Burundi	2.8
	Madagascar[e]	1.9		Central African Rep[e]	2.8
	Uganda[e]	1.9		Hong Kong	2.8
12	Lebanon	2.0		Uruguay	2.8
13	Chad	2.2			

a 1990   b 1992
c Tertiary education includes all levels of post-secondary education including courses leading to awards not equivalent to a university degree, courses leading to a first university degree and postgraduate courses.
d 1993   e 1993–94

Life: *the chances*

Highest life expectancy
Years, 1995–2000

1	Japan	80.0		Netherlands Antilles	76.4
2	Iceland	79.3	33	Cuba	76.0
3	Canada	78.9		Kuwait	76.0
4	France	78.8	35	Denmark	75.6
	Hong Kong	78.8	36	Brunei	75.5
6	Switzerland	78.6		Guadeloupe	75.5
7	Sweden	78.5	38	Portugal	75.4
8	Australia	78.3	39	Chile	75.3
	Italy	78.3		Réunion	75.3
10	Greece	78.1	41	United Arab Emirates	74.8
11	Spain	78.0	42	Jamaica	74.6
12	Netherlands	77.9	43	Panama	73.9
13	Israel	77.7	44	Bahamas	73.8
14	Cyprus	77.6	45	Trinidad & Tobago	73.7
	Macau	77.6	46	Slovenia	73.5
	Norway	77.6	47	Argentina	73.2
17	Belgium	77.3		Bosnia	73.2
	Singapore	77.3	49	Sri Lanka	73.1
19	New Zealand	77.2	50	Bahrain	72.9
20	Martinique	77.1		Czech Republic	72.9
	United Kingdom	77.1		Uruguay	72.9
22	Austria	77.0	53	Venezuela	72.8
23	Malta	76.9	54	Georgia	72.7
24	Costa Rica	76.8	55	Fiji	72.6
25	Germany	76.7	56	Macedonia, FYR	72.5
	United States	76.7		Mexico	72.5
27	Finland	76.6		Serbia, Montenegro	72.5
	Ireland	76.6	59	South Korea	72.4
29	Puerto Rico	76.5	60	Croatia	72.2
30	Barbados	76.4		North Korea	72.2
	Luxembourg	76.4			

Highest male life expectancy
Years, 1995–2000

1	Iceland	77.4	6	Israel	75.7
2	Japan	76.9	7	Greece	75.5
3	Sweden	76.2	8	Australia	75.4
4	Canada	76.1		Cyprus	75.4
	Hong Kong	76.1	10	Switzerland	75.3

Highest female life expectancy
Years, 1995–2000

1	France	82.9	6	Spain	81.5
	Japan	82.9	7	Italy	81.4
3	Canada	81.8	8	Australia	81.2
	Hong Kong	81.8		Iceland	81.2
	Switzerland	81.8	10	Sweden	80.8

Lowest life expectancy
Years, 1995–2000

1	Sierra Leone	37.5	31	Bhutan	53.2
2	Malawi	40.7	32	Laos	53.5
3	Uganda	41.4		Mauritania	53.5
4	Rwanda	42.1	34	Cambodia	54.1
5	Zambia	43.0	35	Haiti	54.4
6	Guinea-Bissau	43.8	36	Kenya	54.5
7	Afghanistan	45.5	37	Benin	54.8
8	Burkina Faso	46.0	38	Sudan	55.0
9	Angola	46.5	39	Gabon	55.5
	Guinea	46.5		Namibia	55.5
11	Mozambique	46.9	41	Cameroon	55.9
12	Gambia, The	47.0	42	Nepal	57.3
13	Burundi	47.2	43	Papua New Guinea	57.9
14	Chad	47.7	44	Ghana	58.0
15	Mali	48.0		Yemen	58.0
16	Niger	48.5	46	Bangladesh	58.1
	Zimbabwe	48.5	47	Madagascar	58.5
18	Central African Rep	48.6	48	Lesotho	58.6
19	Somalia	49.0	49	Swaziland	60.0
20	Ethiopia	49.9	50	Myanmar	60.1
21	Togo	50.1	51	Bolivia	61.5
22	Botswana	50.4	52	India	62.4
23	Eritrea	50.6		Iraq	62.4
24	Congo-Brazzaville	50.9	54	Pakistan	63.9
25	Côte d'Ivoire	51.0	55	Russia	64.4
26	Senegal	51.3	56	Turkmenistan	64.6
27	Tanzania	51.4	57	Indonesia	65.1
28	Liberia	51.5	58	South Africa	65.2
29	Nigeria	52.4	59	Libya	65.5
30	Congo	52.9	60	Mongolia	65.8

Lowest male life expectancy
Years, 1995–2000

1	Sierra Leone	36.0	6	Guinea-Bissau	42.4
2	Malawi	40.3	7	Angola	44.9
3	Uganda	40.4	8	Afghanistan	45.0
4	Rwanda	40.8	9	Burkina Faso	45.1
5	Zambia	42.2	10	Gambia, The	45.4

Lowest female life expectancy
Years, 1995–2000

1	Sierra Leone	39.1	6	Guinea-Bissau	45.2
2	Malawi	41.1	7	Afghanistan	46.0
3	Uganda	42.3	8	Burkina Faso	47.0
4	Rwanda	43.4		Guinea	47.0
5	Zambia	43.7	10	Angola	48.1

Death: *the chances*

Highest death rates
Number of deaths per 1,000 population

1	Rwanda	27		Nepal	12
	Sierra Leone	27		Sudan	12
3	Malawi	22	53	Belgium	11
4	Afghanistan	21		Germany	11
	Guinea-Bissau	21		Ghana	11
	Uganda	21		Kenya	11
7	Angola	19		Lesotho	11
	Guinea	19		Moldova	11
	Liberia	19		Norway	11
10	Burkina Faso	18		Poland	11
	Burundi	18		Portugal	11
	Chad	18		Romania	11
	Gambia, The	18		Slovakia	11
	Mali	18		Slovenia	11
	Mozambique	18		Sweden	11
	Niger	18		United Kingdom	11
	Zambia	18		Yemen	11
18	Central African Rep	17	68	Austria	10
	Ethiopia	17		Bangladesh	10
	Somalia	17		Finland	10
21	Congo-Brazzaville	15		Greece	10
	Eritrea	15		Italy	10
	Gabon	15		Luxembourg	10
	Hungary	15		Madagascar	10
	Senegal	15		Myanmar	10
	Togo	15		Papua New Guinea	10
27	Bhutan	14		Serbia, Montenegro	10
	Congo	14		Swaziland	10
	Côte d'Ivoire	14		Uruguay	10
	Laos	14	80	Barbados	9
	Latvia	14		Bolivia	9
	Nigeria	14		France	9
	Russia	14		Georgia	9
	Tanzania	14		India	9
	Ukraine	14		Iraq	9
	Zimbabwe	14		Ireland	9
37	Benin	13		Netherlands	9
	Bulgaria	13		Spain	9
	Cambodia	13		Switzerland	9
	Estonia	13		United States	9
	Haiti	13	91	Argentina	8
	Mauritania	13		Cyprus	8
43	Belarus	12		Indonesia	8
	Botswana	12		Japan	8
	Cameroon	12		Kazakhstan	8
	Croatia	12		New Zealand	8
	Czech Republic	12		Pakistan	8
	Denmark	12		South Africa	8
	Lithuania	12		Turkmenistan	8
	Namibia	12			

Highest infant mortality
Number of deaths per 1,000 live births

1	Niger	191	26	Haiti	94
2	Angola	170		Iraq	94
3	Afghanistan	165	28	Tanzania	93
4	Sierra Leone	164	29	Chad	92
5	Liberia	157	30	Bhutan	90
6	Malawi	137		Côte d'Ivoire	90
7	Mali	134	32	Uganda	88
8	Mozambique	133	33	Gabon	87
9	Guinea-Bissau	132	34	Benin	84
10	Guinea	130	35	Bangladesh	83
11	Congo	128	36	Burkina Faso	82
12	Somalia	125		Nepal	82
13	Mauritania	124	38	Congo-Brazzaville	81
14	Nigeria	114	39	Papua New Guinea	79
15	Ethiopia	113	40	Eritrea	78
16	Zambia	112		Gambia, The	78
17	Cambodia	108		Togo	78
18	Burundi	106		Yemen	78
19	Myanmar	105	44	Senegal	74
	Rwanda	105	45	India	73
21	Central African Rep	103		Sudan	73
22	Laos	102	47	Bolivia	71
23	Madagascar	100	48	Ghana	70
24	Lesotho	96	49	Swaziland	68
25	Pakistan	95	50	Morocco	64

Lowest death rates
No. deaths per 1,000 pop.

1	Kuwait	2
2	Brunei	3
	United Arab Emirates	3
4	Bahrain	4
	Costa Rica	4
	Oman	4
	Qatar	4
	Saudi Arabia	4
9	Bahamas	5
	Dominican Republic	5
	Fiji	5
	Jordan	5
	Malaysia	5
	Mexico	5
	Panama	5
	Singapore	5
	Syria	5
	Venezuela	5

Lowest infant mortality
No. deaths per 1,000 live births

1	Finland	4
	Japan	4
	Singapore	4
	Sweden	4
5	Austria	5
	France	5
	Germany	5
	Hong Kong[a]	5
	Iceland	5
	Netherlands	5
	Norway	5
	Spain	5
	Switzerland	5
13	Australia	6
	Belgium	6
	Canada	6
	Czech Republic	6
	Denmark	6
	Ireland	6
	Italy	6
	Slovenia	6

Note: Both death and, in particular, infant mortality rates can be under-estimated in certain countries where not all deaths are officially recorded.

a Estimate for 1995–2000.

Death and diseases

Cancer[a]
%

1	Netherlands	25.7
2	France	25.3
3	Hong Kong	25.0
4	Switzerland	24.9
5	Canada	24.8
6	Denmark	24.7
7	United Kingdom	24.6
8	Italy	24.5
	New Zealand	24.5
10	Australia	24.2
11	Ireland	23.4
12	Germany	23.3
13	Austria	23.0
	Czech Republic	23.0
15	Japan	22.9
16	United States	22.7
17	Singapore	21.8
	Uruguay	21.8
19	Hungary	21.7
20	Norway	21.6

Heart attack[a]
%

1	Georgia	45.4
2	Armenia	43.8
3	Uzbekistan	42.7
4	Azerbaijan	41.9
5	Lithuania	39.0
	Turkmenistan	39.0
7	Estonia	36.9
8	Austria	36.6
9	Belarus	35.0
10	Latvia	34.7
11	Sweden	34.6
12	United States	34.4
13	Finland	33.4
14	Australia	32.6
	Israel	32.6
16	Argentina	32.5
	Germany	32.5
18	Ireland	32.2
19	Bulgaria	31.8
	Cuba	31.8
	Kazakhstan	31.8

Infectious disease[a]
%

1	Hong Kong	4.7
2	Mexico	4.1
3	Kuwait	3.6
4	Tajikistan	3.4
5	Argentina	3.3
	Turkmenistan	3.3
7	Chile	2.7
8	Singapore	2.6
9	Puerto Rico	2.5
10	China	2.3
11	Kirgizstan	2.2
12	Costa Rica	2.1
	South Korea	2.1
	Uzbekistan	2.1
15	Azerbaijan	2.0
16	Kazakhstan	1.9
17	Mauritius	1.8
	Trinidad & Tobago	1.8
19	Israel	1.6
	Japan	1.6

Motor accident[a]
%

1	South Korea	3.1
2	Latvia	2.2
3	Kuwait	1.9
4	Slovenia	1.8
5	Estonia	1.7
6	Greece	1.6
	Mexico	1.6
	Portugal	1.6
9	Costa Rica	1.5
	Lithuania	1.5
11	Mauritius	1.4
	Poland	1.4
	Puerto Rico	1.4
	Russia	1.4
15	Italy	1.3
	New Zealand	1.3
	Spain	1.3
	Tajikistan	1.3
19	Austria	1.2
	Ukraine	1.2
	United States	1.2

a Data refer to the chances a newborn baby has of eventually dying from one of the causes shown. Statistics are available for only a limited number of countries and many less developed countries are excluded. Latest available.

Tuberculosis[b]
Cases per 100,000 pop., 1995

1	Eritrea	654
2	Botswana	381
3	Philippines	340
4	Zimbabwe	270
5	Lesotho	233
	Swaziland	233
7	South Africa	205
8	Malawi	195
9	Peru	189
10	Papua New Guinea	183
11	Mauritania	165
12	Guinea-Bissau	160
13	Zambia	154
14	Cambodia	142
15	Congo-Brazzaville	135
16	Iraq	131
17	India	129
	Tanzania	129
19	Bolivia	127
20	Uganda	126

Malaria[b]
Cases per 100,000 pop., 1994

1	Malawi	48,116
2	Zambia	42,465
3	Tanzania	25,899
4	Namibia	25,896
5	Kenya	21,956
6	Papua New Guinea	14,307
7	Burundi	13,366
8	Benin	9,830
9	Niger	8,634
10	Guinea	8,081
11	Togo	7,819
12	Angola	5,967
13	Burkina Faso	4,382
14	Zimbabwe	2,834
15	Central African Rep	2,454
16	Bhutan	2,147
17	Botswana	1,994
18	Myanmar	1,527
19	Sri Lanka	1,511
20	Congo-Brazzaville	1,348

AIDS
Cases per 100,000 population[c]

1	Bahamas	904	21	Burundi	147
2	Zambia	543	22	Netherlands Antilles	131
3	Zimbabwe	534	23	Gabon	124
4	Bermuda	531	24	Spain	117
5	Malawi	518	25	Honduras	110
6	Namibia	431	26	Eritrea	106
7	Congo-Brazzaville	383	27	Ghana	105
8	Botswana	360		Martinique	105
9	Barbados	292	29	Thailand	102
10	Tanzania	288	30	Chad	95
11	Swaziland	278	31	Burkina Faso	94
12	Côte d'Ivoire	271	32	Jamaica	88
13	Kenya	269	33	Switzerland	81
14	Uganda	256	34	France	79
15	United States	227	35	Guinea-Bissau	75
16	Central African Rep	210	36	Cameroon	71
17	Trinidad & Tobago	201	37	Italy	70
18	Rwanda	198	38	Brazil	69
19	Togo	190	39	Haiti	68
20	Guadeloupe	170	40	Congo	63

b   Reported cases during specified year.
c   AIDS data refer to the total number of cases reported to the World Health
    Organisation up to November 20 1997. The number of cases diagnosed and
    reported depends on the quality of medical practice and administration and is likely
    to be under-recorded in a number of countries.

Health

Highest health spending
As % of GDP[a]

1	United States	14.2
2	Argentina	10.6
3	Germany	10.4
4	Croatia	10.1
5	Switzerland	10.0
6	France	9.9
7	Canada	9.6
	Czech Republic	9.6
9	Australia	8.9
10	Netherlands	8.8
11	Costa Rica	8.5
	Uruguay	8.5
13	Macedonia, FYR	8.3
14	Portugal	8.1
15	Belgium	8.0
	Norway	8.0
17	Austria	7.9
	Jordan	7.9
	South Africa	7.9
20	Armenia	7.8
	Nicaragua	7.8
22	Finland	7.7
	Italy	7.7
24	Namibia	7.6
	Spain	7.6
26	Azerbaijan	7.5
	Panama	7.5
28	Brazil	7.4
	Colombia	7.4
	New Zealand	7.4

Lowest health spending
As % of GDP[a]

1	Sudan	0.3
2	Cameroon	1.4
	Ghana	1.4
	Nigeria	1.4
5	Indonesia	1.8
6	Sri Lanka	1.9
7	Eritrea	2
8	Bangladesh	2.4
	Philippines	2.4
10	Kenya	2.5
	Malaysia	2.5
	United Arab Emirates	2.5
13	Laos	2.6
	Yemen	2.6
15	Guatemala	2.7
16	Mali	2.9
17	Botswana	3.1
18	Zambia	3.3
19	Côte d'Ivoire	3.4
	Mauritius	3.4
	Morocco	3.4
	Togo	3.4
23	Chad	3.5
	Pakistan	3.5
25	Haiti	3.6
	Sierra Leone	3.6
	Singapore	3.6
28	Egypt	3.7
29	China	3.8
30	Trinidad & Tobago	3.9
	Uganda	3.9

Highest population per doctor
Latest available year

1	Chad	50,000
	Eritrea	50,000
	Gambia, The	50,000
	Malawi	50,000
5	Burkina Faso	33,333
	Mozambique	33,333
	Niger	33,333
8	Angola	25,000
	Ethiopia	25,000
	Ghana	25,000
	Mali	25,000
	Rwanda	25,000
	Somalia	25,000
	Tanzania	25,000
	Uganda	25,000

16	Lesotho	20,000
	Nepal	20,000
18	Benin	16,667
	Burundi	16,667
	Central African Rep	16,667
	Togo	16,667
22	Sierra Leone	14,290
23	Cameroon	14,286
	Senegal	14,286
25	Sudan	10,000
26	Bahrain	9,091
	Mauritania	9,091
	Philippines	9,091
29	Indonesia	8,333
30	Zimbabwe	7,143

Most hospital beds
Beds per 1,000 pop.

1	Switzerland	20.8	31	Slovakia	7.1
2	Japan	16.2	32	Italy	6.5
3	Tajikistan	16.0		Sweden	6.5
4	Norway	13.5	34	Poland	6.3
5	Belarus	12.4	35	Israel	6.0
6	Kazakhstan	12.2	36	Croatia	5.9
	Moldova	12.2	37	Slovenia	5.8
8	Ukraine	12.2	38	Macedonia, FYR	5.5
9	Latvia	11.9	39	Canada	5.4
10	Russia	11.8		Cuba	5.4
11	Mongolia	11.5	41	Denmark	5.0
	Turkmenistan	11.5		Greece	5.0
13	Netherlands	11.3		Ireland	5.0
14	Lithuania	11.1	44	United Kingdom	4.9
15	Bulgaria	10.2	45	Argentina	4.6
16	Finland	10.1	46	Uruguay	4.5
17	Azerbaijan	10.0	47	Portugal	4.3
18	Germany	9.7	48	Libya	4.2
19	Hungary	9.6		United States	4.2
20	Austria	9.4	50	South Korea	4.1
21	France	9.0	51	Papua New Guinea	4.0
22	Australia	8.9		Spain	4.0
23	Uzbekistan	8.7	53	Vietnam	3.8
24	Estonia	8.4	54	Singapore	3.6
25	Georgia	8.2	55	Congo-Brazzaville	3.3
26	Armenia	7.8	56	Chile	3.2
27	Romania	7.7		Gabon	3.2
28	Belgium	7.6		Trinidad & Tobago	3.2
29	Czech Republic	7.4	59	Lebanon	3.1
30	New Zealand	7.3		Mauritius	3.1

Lowest population per doctor
Latest available year

1	Cuba	193	16	Turkmenistan	283
2	Italy	211	17	Hungary	297
3	Israel	218	18	Uzbekistan	299
4	Georgia	229	19	Bulgaria	300
5	Ukraine	233	20	Austria	306
6	Vietnam	247	21	Slovakia	308
7	Spain	250	22	Norway	309
8	Lithuania	251	23	Germany	313
9	Azerbaijan	256	24	Armenia	321
10	Greece	258		Estonia	321
11	Russia	263	26	Kirgizstan	323
12	Belarus	264	27	Uruguay	324
13	Belgium	274	28	Latvia	330
14	Kazakhstan	278	29	Switzerland	332
15	Moldova	281	30	Sweden	334

a Latest available year.

Till death us do part

Highest marriage rates[a]

Number of marriages per 1,000 population

1	Cuba	17.1	31	Canada		7.0
2	Bermuda	14.2		Jordan		7.0
3	Lithuania	12.9	33	Malta		6.9
4	Barbados	11.2		Philippines		6.9
5	Bangladesh	10.9	35	Denmark		6.8
6	Tajikistan	9.6		Poland		6.8
7	Mauritius	9.5		Romania		6.8
8	Bahamas	9.3	38	Chile		6.5
9	Egypt	9.2		Portugal		6.5
	Puerto Rico	9.2	40	Azerbaijan		6.4
	Sri Lanka	9.2		Costa Rica		6.4
12	Moldova	9.0		United Kingdom		6.4
13	United States	8.9	43	Japan		6.3
14	Singapore	8.8		New Zealand		6.3
15	Kazakhstan	8.7	45	Ecuador		6.2
16	Syria	8.6		Réunion		6.2
17	Cyprus	8.4		Uruguay		6.2
18	Thailand	8.3	48	Australia		6.1
19	Turkey	8.0		Israel		6.1
20	Taiwan	7.9		Jamaica		6.1
21	Kuwait	7.8	51	Ukraine		6.0
	Uzbekistan	7.8	52	Bahrain		5.9
23	Albania	7.6		Hong Kong		5.9
	China	7.6		Russia		5.9
25	South Korea	7.5		Tunisia		5.9
26	Iran	7.4	56	Kirgizstan		5.8
27	Belarus	7.3		Netherlands		5.8
28	Mexico	7.2	58	Algeria		5.7
29	Brunei	7.1	58	Switzerland		5.7
	Macedonia, FYR	7.1	60	Trinidad & Tobago		5.6

Lowest marriage rates[a]

Number of marriages per 1,000 population

1	Qatar	2.5		Slovenia		4.2
2	South Africa	3.3	14	Ghana		4.5
3	Dominican Republic	3.6		Iceland		4.5
	Paraguay	3.6		Ireland		4.5
5	Estonia	3.8	17	Argentina		4.6
	Sweden	3.8		Armenia		4.6
7	Latvia	3.9		Finland		4.6
8	United Arab Emirates	4.0		Norway		4.6
9	Martinique	4.1	21	Guadeloupe		4.7
	Peru	4.1		Guatemala		4.7
11	Bulgaria	4.2		Suriname		4.7
	El Salvador	4.2				

a   Latest available year.

Note: Marriage rates refer to registered marriages only and, therefore, reflect the customs surrounding registry and efficiency of administration. The data are based on latest available figures and hence will be affected by the population age structure at the time.

Highest divorce rates[a]

Number of divorces per 1,000 population

1	Cuba	6.0		Guadeloupe	2.0
2	China	4.6	32	Germany	1.9
	Russia	4.6		Iceland	1.9
	United States	4.6	34	Kuwait	1.8
5	Belarus	4.3		Luxembourg	1.8
6	Ukraine	4.0	36	Bahamas	1.7
7	Estonia	3.7		Slovakia	1.7
	Puerto Rico	3.7	38	Azerbaijan	1.6
9	Moldova	3.4		Egypt	1.6
10	Latvia	3.2		Israel	1.6
	Uruguay	3.2	41	Romania	1.5
12	Czech Republic	3.0		Uzbekistan	1.5
	United Kingdom	3.0	43	Barbados	1.4
14	Lithuania	2.8		Japan	1.4
15	Australia	2.7		Singapore	1.4
	Canada	2.7		Turkmenistan	1.4
	Finland	2.7	47	Dominican Republic	1.3
	Kazakhstan	2.7		Réunion	1.3
	New Zealand	2.7	49	Bahrain	1.2
	Norway	2.7		Jordan	1.2
21	Netherlands Antilles	2.6		Kirgizstan	1.2
22	Denmark	2.5		Portugal	1.2
	Suriname	2.5		South Korea	1.2
	Sweden	2.5	54	Brunei	1.1
25	Austria	2.3		Costa Rica	1.1
	Hungary	2.3		United Arab Emirates	1.1
27	Netherlands	2.2	57	Croatia	1.0
	Switzerland	2.2		Hong Kong	1.0
29	Belgium	2.1		Poland	1.0
30	France	2.0		Venezuela	1.0

Lowest divorce rates[a]

Number of divorces per 1,000 population

1	Guatemala	0.2		Brazil	0.6
	Nicaragua	0.2		Macau	0.6
3	Macedonia, FYR	0.3	15	Albania	0.7
4	Italy	0.4		Ecuador	0.7
	Mexico	0.4		Serbia, Montenegro	0.7
6	Chile	0.5		Greece	0.7
	El Salvador	0.5		Mauritius	0.7
	Iran	0.5		Spain	0.7
	Jamaica	0.5	21	Cyprus	0.8
	Libya	0.5		Martinique	0.8
	Turkey	0.5		Slovenia	0.8
12	Bermuda	0.6		Syria	0.8

Households and prices

Biggest households[a]
Population per dwelling

1	Gabon	8.3		Mauritania	5.5
2	Iraq	7.1		Tunisia	5.5
3	Algeria	7.0	29	Benin	5.4
4	Pakistan	6.8		Congo	5.4
	Yemen	6.8		Venezuela	5.4
6	Guinea	6.7	32	Congo-Brazzaville	5.3
	Jordan	6.7		Tanzania	5.3
8	Bahrain	6.6	34	Cambodia	5.2
9	Niger	6.4		Cameroon	5.2
10	Syria	6.3		Guatemala	5.2
11	Burkina Faso	6.2		Iran	5.2
	Liberia	6.2		Myanmar	5.2
13	Afghanistan	5.9		Paraguay	5.2
	Morocco	5.9		Philippines	5.2
15	Brunei	5.8	41	Kenya	5.1
	Côte d'Ivoire	5.8		Nigeria	5.1
	Fiji	5.8	43	Egypt	4.9
	Nepal	5.8		India	4.9
19	Bangladesh	5.7		Malaysia	4.9
	Croatia	5.7		South Africa	4.9
	Togo	5.7		Sri Lanka	4.9
	Ukraine	5.7	48	Mexico	4.6
23	Mali	5.6		Vietnam	4.6
	Qatar	5.6	49	Indonesia	4.5
	Sudan	5.6		Peru	4.5
26	Bosnia	5.5			

Highest cost of living[b]
December 1997, USA=100

1	Japan	154		South Korea	101
2	Hong Kong	122	17	United States	100
	Russia	122	18	Finland	94
4	Norway	121		Netherlands	94
5	Switzerland	117	20	Australia	93
6	France	112		Brazil	93
7	Gabon	108	22	Belgium	92
8	United Kingdom	107		Côte d'Ivoire	92
9	Singapore	106		Germany	92
	Taiwan	106		Ireland	92
11	Sweden	105		Russia	92
12	Austria	104	27	Argentina	91
	Denmark	104	28	Papua New Guinea	89
14	China	101		Spain	89
	Israel	101	30	Luxembourg	86

a Latest available year.
b The cost of living index shown is compiled by The Economist Intelligence Unit for
use by companies in determining expatriate compensation: it is a comparison of the
cost of maintaining a typical international lifestyle in the country rather than a
comparison of the purchasing power of a citizen of the country. The index is based
on typical urban prices an international executive and family will face abroad. The

Smallest households[a]
Population per dwelling

1	Denmark	2.2	**26**	Cyprus	2.9
2	Germany	2.3		Czech Republic	2.9
	Iceland	2.3		Greece	2.9
	Norway	2.3		Luxembourg	2.9
	Sweden	2.3		New Zealand	2.9
6	Finland	2.4		Romania	2.9
	Netherlands	2.4	**32**	Japan	3.0
8	Austria	2.5	**33**	Malta	3.1
	France	2.5		Taiwan	3.1
	Switzerland	2.5	**35**	Albania	3.2
11	Australia	2.6	**36**	Belarus	3.3
	Bermuda	2.6		China	3.3
	Hungary	2.6		Hong Kong	3.3
	Italy	2.6		Poland	3.3
	Latvia	2.6		Puerto Rico	3.3
	Spain	2.6		Serbia, Montenegro	3.3
	United States	2.6		South Korea	3.3
18	Argentina	2.7		Uruguay	3.3
	Belgium	2.7	**44**	Gambia, The	3.4
	Canada	2.7	**45**	Barbados	3.6
	Portugal	2.7		Estonia	3.6
	United Kingdom	2.7		Macau	3.6
23	Bulgaria	2.8		Slovenia	3.6
	Russia	2.8	**49**	Lithuania	3.7
	Slovakia	2.8	**50**	Moldova	3.8

Lowest cost of living[b]
December 1997, USA=100

1	Iran	44		Sri Lanka	62
2	India	45	**17**	Turkey	63
3	Libya	47	**18**	Bangladesh	64
4	Hungary	49		Tunisia	64
5	Zimbabwe	52	**20**	Vietnam	66
6	Pakistan	53	**21**	Malaysia	67
7	Czech Republic	55	**22**	Kuwait	68
8	Algeria	56		Paraguay	68
	Ecuador	56		Venezuela	68
10	Philippines	58	**25**	Mexico	69
	Thailand	58	**26**	Colombia	70
12	Kenya	59		Panama	70
13	Poland	60	**28**	Saudi Arabia	71
	Serbia, Montenegro	60	**29**	Indonesia	72
15	Romania	62		Peru	72

prices are for products of international comparable quality found in a supermarket or department store. Prices found in local markets and bazaars are not used unless the available merchandise is of the specified quality and the shopping area itself is safe for executive and family members. New York City prices are used as the base, so USA = 100.

Consumer goods: *ownership*

TV
Number of people per receiver

1	Bermuda	1.2		Norway	2.5
2	Japan	1.5		Russia	2.5
	Malta	1.5	28	Switzerland	2.6
	United States	1.5	29	Ukraine	2.7
5	Canada	1.7	30	Slovenia	2.9
6	France	1.8	31	Australia	3.0
	Germany	1.8		Portugal	3.0
	Latvia	1.8	33	Luxembourg	3.1
9	Denmark	1.9	34	Bahrain	3.2
10	Croatia	2.0	35	Poland	3.4
	Czech Republic	2.0	36	Iceland	3.4
	Finland	2.0		Netherlands Antilles	3.4
13	Hungary	2.1		Qatar	3.4
	Netherlands	2.1	39	Ireland	3.5
15	Austria	2.2		Oman	3.5
	Italy	2.2	41	Singapore	3.6
	Slovakia	2.2	42	Hong Kong	3.8
	Sweden	2.2		Lebanon	3.8
19	Belgium	2.3		Trinidad & Tobago	3.8
	Estonia	2.3	45	Barbados	3.9
	United Kingdom	2.3		Moldova	3.9
22	Bulgaria	2.4	47	Kuwait	4.2
	Spain	2.4	48	Belarus	4.3
24	Lithuania	2.5	49	Kazakhstan	4.4
	New Zealand	2.5	50	Puerto Rico	4.5

Telephone
Number of people per telephone line

1	Sweden	1.5	23	Cyprus	2.7
2	Bermuda	1.6		New Zealand	2.7
3	Denmark	1.7		South Korea	2.7
4	Switzerland	1.8		Spain	2.7
5	Finland	1.9	27	Portugal	2.8
	France	1.9	28	Martinique	2.9
	Norway	1.9	29	Australia	3.0
8	Canada	2.0		Ireland	3.0
	United States	2.0		Singapore	3.0
10	Germany	2.1	32	Latvia	3.2
	Greece	2.1		Slovenia	3.2
	Hong Kong	2.1	34	Barbados	3.3
	Iceland	2.1		Puerto Rico	3.3
	Japan	2.1	36	Guadeloupe	3.4
	Luxembourg	2.1		Israel	3.4
	Netherlands	2.1	38	Estonia	3.5
	United Kingdom	2.1	39	Croatia	3.6
18	Italy	2.2		Macau	3.6
19	Austria	2.3	40	Lithuania	4.0
	Belgium	2.3	41	United Arab Emirates	4.3
21	Malta	2.5	42	Czech Republic	4.6
22	Bulgaria	2.6	43	Hungary	5.3

Video cassette recorder
% of households owning

1	South Korea	88		Qatar	77
2	Japan	86	12	Hong Kong	75
	Singapore	86	13	Lebanon	72
4	Kuwait	85	14	Bahrain	71
5	Australia	84	15	Denmark	69
6	Canada	82		Ireland	69
7	United States	81		Norway	69
8	United Kingdom	79	18	Bermuda	68
9	Netherlands	77		France	68
	New Zealand	77	20	Saudi Arabia	66

Computer
Computers per 100 people

1	United States	45.0	16	Hong Kong	26.1
2	Australia	36.6	17	Belgium	24.9
3	Canada	36.4	18	Austria	24.6
4	Norway	36.3	19	France	23.4
5	Iceland	35.6	20	Germany	23.1
6	Finland	35.4	21	Japan	22.8
7	Sweden	35.3	22	Israel	21.9
8	Denmark	34.9	23	Italy	15.8
9	New Zealand	32.0	24	Taiwan	14.7
10	Singapore	31.6	25	Spain	12.7
11	Luxemburg	30.0	26	South Korea	12.4
12	Switzerland	29.9	27	Portugal	10.3
13	Netherlands	29.2	28	Hungary	9.0
14	United Kingdom	28.3	29	Czech Republic	8.1
15	Ireland	26.3	30	Greece	7.3

Mobile telephone
Subscribers per 100 people

1	Finland	41.9	16	Austria	14.4
2	Norway	38.3	17	United Kingdom	14.2
3	Sweden	35.8	18	Canada	13.8
4	Hong Kong	32.3	19	Spain	11.0
5	Australia	29.2	20	Netherlands	10.8
6	Denmark	28.2	21	Malaysia	10.2
7	Iceland	24.5	22	Germany	10.1
8	Japan	22.9	23	France	9.9
	Singapore	22.9	24	Belgium	9.7
10	United States	20.6	25	Greece	9.3
11	Italy	20.0	26	Ireland	8.1
12	New Zealand	16.6	27	Hungary	6.7
13	Portugal	15.1	28	Taiwan	6.5
14	South Korea	14.9	29	Czech Republic	5.4
15	Switzerland	14.7	30	Argentina	5.3

Books and newspapers

Book sales

$m

1	United States	26,127
2	Germany	9,775
3	Japan	4,678
4	United Kingdom	3,650
5	France	3,307
6	Spain	2,982
7	South Korea	2,733
8	Brazil	2,678
9	Italy	2,484
10	China	1,868
11	Canada	1,253
12	Australia	1,242
13	Netherlands	1,147
14	Belgium	1,084
15	Switzerland	764
16	Taiwan	674
17	Sweden	643
18	Argentina	639
19	Mexico	630
20	Norway	604
21	Austria	522
22	South Africa	448
23	Finland	442
24	Vietnam	431
25	Denmark	402
26	Russia	359
27	India	346

Per head, $

1	Norway	132
2	Germany	119
3	Luxembourg	113
4	Belgium	105
5	Switzerland	100
6	Finland	84
	United States	84
8	Spain	77
9	Denmark	76
10	Netherlands	71
11	Singapore	70
	Sweden	70
13	New Zealand	68
14	Austria	62
	United Kingdom	62
16	Ireland	56
17	France	55
18	South Korea	53
19	Australia	47
20	Italy	45
21	Canada	37
	Japan	37
23	Taiwan	31
24	Israel	26
25	Portugal	24
26	Greece	23
27	Argentina	15

Daily newspapers

Copies per '000 population, 1994

1	Hong Kong	719
2	Macau	628
3	Norway	607
4	Japan	576
5	Croatia	575
6	Iceland	515
7	Sweden	483
8	Finland	473
9	Austria	472
10	Switzerland	409
11	South Korea	404
12	Kuwait	401
13	Luxembourg	384
14	Denmark	365
15	Singapore	364
16	United Kingdom	351
17	Netherlands	334
18	Belgium	321
19	Germany	317
20	New Zealand	297

	Romania	297
22	Israel	281
23	Netherlands Antilles	269
24	Russia	267
25	Australia	258
26	Slovakia	256
27	Bermuda	254
28	Estonia	242
29	France	237
	Uruguay	237
31	Hungary	228
	Latvia	228
	United States	228
34	Czech Republic	219
35	Venezuela	215
36	North Korea	213
37	Canada	189
38	Belarus	187
39	Slovenia	185
40	Puerto Rico	184

Music and the Internet

Music sales[a]

$m			$ per head	
1	United States	12,298	1 Denmark	58
2	Japan	6,762	Norway	58
3	Germany	3,179	3 Japan	54
4	United Kingdom	2,710	4 Switzerland	53
5	France	2,318	5 Iceland	50
6	Brazil	1,394	6 Austria	47
7	Canada	912	7 United Kingdom	46
8	Australia	815	8 Sweden	44
9	Netherlands	660	9 Belgium	43
10	Italy	637	10 Netherlands	41
11	Spain	585	11 United States	40
12	South Korea	517	12 France	39
13	Belgium	443	Germany	39
14	Taiwan	416	14 Australia	31
15	Sweden	403	15 Finland	28
16	Switzerland	401	New Zealand	28
17	Mexico	399	17 Canada	27
18	Austria	397	18 Hong Kong	26
19	Denmark	307	19 Ireland	23
20	India	298	20 Singapore	20
21	Argentina	285	21 Cyprus	17
22	Indonesia	270	22 Portugal	16

Internet hosts[b]

By country, March 1998			Per 1,000 pop., March 1998	
1	United States	20,623,995	1 Finland	85.4
2	Japan	1,168,956	2 United States	66.4
3	Germany	994,926	3 Norway	62.7
4	United Kingdom	987,774	4 Iceland	55.2
5	Canada	839,141	5 New Zealand	38.4
6	Finland	450,044	6 Sweden	34.6
7	Netherlands	381,172	7 Denmark	30.0
8	France	333,306	8 Bermuda	28.0
9	Sweden	319,065	9 Australia	25.3
10	Norway	286,338	10 Canada	24.5
11	Italy	243,250	11 Netherlands	23.6
12	Taiwan	179,836	12 United Kingdom	16.7
13	New Zealand	169,264	13 Switzerland	15.0
14	Spain	168,913	14 Singapore	14.4
15	Denmark	159,358	15 Austria	12.9
16	South Africa	122,025	16 Germany	12.1
17	South Korea	121,932	17 Ireland	10.3
18	Brazil	117,200	18 Hong Kong	10.2
19	Switzerland	114,816	19 Japan	9.3
20	Austria	109,154	Luxembourg	9.3
21	Russia	94,137	21 Israel	8.8
22	Belgium	87,938	22 Belgium	8.5
23	Poland	77,594	23 Taiwan	8.2

a Includes vinyl, tape and compact disc sales.
b Includes all hosts ending ".com", ".net" and ".org", which exaggerates the numbers.

Nobel prize winners: *1901–97*

Peace

1	United States	16
2	United Kingdom	10
3	France	9
4	Sweden	5
5	Germany	4
6	Belgium	3
7	Norway	3
8	South Africa	3
9	Argentina	2
	Austria	2
	Israel	2
	Russia	2
	Switzerland	2

Economics[a]

1	United States	22
2	United Kingdom	7
3	Norway	2
	Sweden	2
5	France	1
	Germany	1
	Netherlands	1
	Russia	1

Literature

1	France	13
2	United States	12
3	United Kingdom	8
4	Germany	6
	Sweden	6
6	Italy	5
	Spain	5
8	Norway	3
	Poland	3
	Russia	3

Physiology or medicine

1	United States	42
2	United Kingdom	18
3	Germany	14
4	France	6
	Sweden	6
	Switzerland	6
7	Austria	5
	Denmark	5
9	Belgium	3
	Italy	3

Physics

1	United States	40
2	United Kingdom	19
3	Germany	17
4	France	8
5	Netherlands	5
6	Russia	4
	Sweden	4
	Switzerland	4
9	Austria	3
	Italy	3
	Japan	3

Chemistry

1	United States	34
2	United Kingdom	22
3	Germany	14
4	France	6
5	Sweden	5
	Switzerland	5
7	Canada	4
8	Argentina	1
	Austria	1
	Belgium	1
	Czech Republic	1
	Denmark	1
	Finland	1
	Italy	1
	Japan	1
	Netherlands	1
	Norway	1
	Russia	1

a 1969–97
Prizes by country of residence at time awarded. When prizes have been shared in the same field, one credit given to each country.

Olympic medal winners

Summer games, 1896–1996

		Gold	Silver	Bronze
1	United States	833	634	548
2	Soviet Union[a]	485	395	354
3	Germany	360	375	391
4	United Kingdom	177	233	225
5	France	176	181	205
6	Italy	166	136	142
7	Hungary	142	128	155
8	Sweden	134	152	173
9	Finland	99	80	113
10	Japan	93	89	98
11	Australia	87	85	122
12	Romania	63	77	99
13	China	52	63	49
14	Poland	50	67	110
15	Canada	49	77	91
16	Netherlands	49	57	81
17	Switzerland	46	68	60
18	Bulgaria	43	76	63
19	Denmark	39	60	57
20	Belgium	37	50	49

Winter games, 1924–1998

		Gold	Silver	Bronze
1	Germany	96	89	80
2	Soviet Union[a]	87	63	67
3	Norway	83	87	69
4	United States	59	59	41
5	Austria	39	53	53
6	Sweden	39	28	25
7	Finland	38	49	48
8	Switzerland	29	31	32
9	Italy	27	27	23
10	Canada	25	25	29
11	Russia	21	14	7
12	Netherlands	19	23	19
13	France	18	17	26
14	South Korea	9	3	4
15	Japan	8	9	12
16	United Kingdom	7	4	13
17	Poland	1	1	2
18	Czech Republic	1	1	1
19	Bulgaria	1	0	0
20	China	0	10	4

a Includes unified team in 1992.

Drinking and smoking

Beer drinkers
Litres consumed per head

1	Czech Republic	160.0
2	Ireland	142.5
3	Germany	134.5
4	Denmark	117.6
5	Austria	116.0
6	Luxembourg	109.0
7	United Kingdom	102.3
8	Belgium	102.0
9	Australia	95.4
10	New Zealand	93.9
11	Slovakia	90.2
12	Netherlands	83.7
13	United States	83.5
14	Finland	82.1
15	Hungary	79.4
16	Venezuela	75.0
17	Canada	67.5
18	Spain	64.7
19	Portugal	61.9
20	Switzerland	60.2

Wine drinkers
Litres consumed per head

1	Portugal	60.6
2	France	60.0
3	Luxembourg	58.0
4	Italy	55.0
5	Switzerland	43.3
6	Argentina	42.3
7	Greece	34.0
8	Uruguay	32.0
9	Austria	31.5
10	Spain	30.3
11	Hungary	30.0
12	Denmark	28.3
13	Belgium	25.0
14	Romania	23.3
15	Germany	22.8
16	Bulgaria	21.7
17	Australia	18.2
18	Netherlands	17.1
19	Czech Republic	16.9
20	New Zealand	16.6

Pure alcohol
Litres consumed per head

1	Luxembourg	11.8
2	Portugal	11.2
3	France	11.1
4	Czech Republic	10.1
5	Denmark	10.0
6	Austria	9.8
	Germany	9.8
8	Hungary	9.5
9	Spain	9.3
	Switzerland	9.3
11	Slovakia	9.2
12	Ireland	9.1
13	Belgium	9.0
14	Greece	8.7
	Romania	8.7
16	Italy	8.2
17	Netherlands	8.0
18	Bulgaria	7.8
19	United Kingdom	7.6
20	Australia	7.5
	Cyprus	7.5

Smokers
Av. ann. consumption of cigarettes per head per day

1	Greece	7.4
2	Japan	7.3
3	South Korea	6.6
4	Bulgaria	6.4
	Poland	6.4
6	Switzerland	5.8
7	Czech Republic	5.4
	Hungary	5.4
9	Spain	5.0
	United States	5.0
11	Lithuania	4.8
12	Israel	4.7
	Taiwan	4.7
14	Estonia	4.6
15	Germany	4.5
	Ireland	4.5
	Portugal	4.5
	Slovakia	4.5
19	Australia	4.4
	Austria	4.4

Crime and punishment

Serious assault[a]

No. per 100,000 pop., 1995

1	Sweden	616.00
2	Jamaica	595.32
3	Swaziland	565.50
4	Australia	560.62
5	New Zealand	541.24
6	South Africa	524.18
7	Bahrain	501.49
8	Belgium	453.63
9	South Korea	442.99
10	United States	418.33
11	Botswana	416.15
12	Kazakhstan	373.84
13	Zambia	308.65
14	Luxembourg	291.22
15	Israel	285.49
16	Bermuda	214.87
17	Netherlands	180.92
18	Slovakia	177.74
19	Canada	165.39
20	Denmark	165.29

Theft[a]

No. per 100,000 pop., 1995

1	Sweden	7,759.00
2	New Zealand	7,577.92
3	Netherlands	5,799.36
4	Bermuda	5,535.95
5	Canada	4,884.73
6	United States	4,813.95
7	Germany	4,797.46
8	Norway	4,540.75
9	France	4,137.09
10	Switzerland	3,946.65
11	Australia	3,532.33
12	Luxembourg	3,431.46
13	Belgium	3,388.84
14	Denmark	3,365.14
15	South Africa	2,925.86
16	Puerto Rico	2,760.86
17	Finland	2,745.47
18	Austria	2,640.27
19	Ireland	2,468.49
20	Italy	2,357.33

Prisoners[b]

Total prison pop., 1995

1	United States	1,585,000
2	Russia	1,018,123
3	Ukraine	203,988
4	Germany	66,146
5	Poland	61,136
6	United Kingdom	58,662
7	France	53,178
8	Belarus	52,033
9	Turkey	49,895
10	Italy	49,642
11	Romania	46,456
12	Japan[c]	45,057
13	Spain	40,157
14	Canada	33,785
15	Czech Republic	19,832
16	Australia	15,327
17	Lithuania	13,228
18	Hungary	12,455
19	Portugal	12,150
20	Moldova	10,363

Per 100,000 pop., 1995

1	Russia	695
2	United States	600
3	Belarus	505
4	Ukraine	390
5	Latvia	375
6	Lithuania	355
7	Moldova	275
8	Estonia	270
9	Romania	205
10	Czech Republic	190
11	Poland	170
12	Slovakia	145
13	Portugal	125
14	Hungary	120
	New Zealand[d]	120
16	Canada	115
	Luxembourg	115
18	Bulgaria	105
	Spain	105
20	United Kingdom	100

a Crime statistics are based on offences recorded by the police. The number will therefore depend partly on the efficiency of police administration systems, the definition of offences, and the proportion of crimes reported, and therefore may not be strictly comparable.
b Only developed countries and other countries in Europe considered.
c 1993
d 1994

Environment: *trees and disasters*

Top deforesters

Average annual rate, km² 1990–95

1	Brazil	25,544	21	Papua New Guinea	1,332
2	Indonesia	10,844	22	Madagascar	1,300
3	Bolivia	5,814	23	Cameroon	1,292
4	Mexico	5,080	24	Central African Rep	1,282
5	Venezuela	5,034	25	Nigeria	1,214
6	Malaysia	4,002	26	Ghana	1,172
7	Myanmar	3,874	27	Mozambique	1,162
8	Sudan	3,526	28	Mali	1,138
9	Thailand	3,294	29	Honduras	1,022
10	Paraguay	3,266	30	Chad	942
11	Tanzania	3,226	31	Gabon	910
12	Zambia	2,644	32	Argentina	894
13	Philippines	2,624	33	China	866
14	Colombia	2,622	34	Guatemala	824
15	Angola	2,370	35	Guinea	748
16	Peru	2,168	36	Botswana	708
17	Ecuador	1,890	37	Panama	636
18	Cambodia	1,638	38	Ethiopia	624
19	Nicaragua	1,508	39	Benin	596
20	Vietnam	1,352	40	Uganda	592

Top reafforesters

Average annual rate, km² 1990–95

1	United States	5,886	6	Greece	1,408
2	Uzbekistan	2,260	7	Belarus	688
3	Kazakhstan	1,928	8	New Zealand	434
4	Canada	1,764	9	Latvia	250
5	France	1,608	10	Portugal	240

Fastest forest depletion

% average annual decrease in forested area, 1990–95

1	Lebanon	7.8		Panama	2.1
2	Jamaica	7.2	18	Iran	1.7
3	Philippines	3.5	19	Cambodia	1.6
4	Haiti	3.4		Dominican Republic	1.6
5	El Salvador	3.3		Ecuador	1.6
6	Costa Rica	3.0		Malawi	1.6
	Sierra Leone	3.0	23	Trinidad & Tobago	1.5
8	Pakistan	2.9	24	Myanmar	1.4
9	Paraguay	2.6		Togo	1.4
	Thailand	2.6		Vietnam	1.4
11	Jordan	2.5	27	Ghana	1.3
	Nicaragua	2.5	28	Algeria	1.2
13	Malaysia	2.4		Benin	1.2
14	Honduras	2.3		Bolivia	1.2
15	Syria	2.2		Cuba	1.2
16	Guatemala	2.1			

Most forested countries
% of total area covered with forest, 1995

1	Suriname[a]	90.5	13	Slovenia	55.0
2	Guinea-Bissau	82.1	14	Bosnia	52.9
3	Papua New Guinea	81.5	15	Peru	52.8
4	South Korea	76.8	16	North Korea	51.7
5	Gabon	69.4	17	Colombia	51.0
6	Japan	66.6	18	Greece	50.4
7	Finland	65.6	19	Venezuela	49.9
8	Brazil	65.2	20	Central African Rep	48.0
9	Indonesia	60.6	21	Estonia	47.6
10	Sweden	59.2	22	Malaysia	47.1
11	Congo-Brazzaville	57.0	23	Austria	47.0
12	Cambodia	55.4	24	Latvia	46.8

Oil tanker spills

	Country affected	Oil spilled ('000 tonnes)	Name	Flag	Year
1	Trinidad & Tobago	276	Atlantic Express	Greece	1979
2	South Africa	256	Castello de Belvar	Spain	1983
3	France	228	Amoco Cadiz	Liberia	1978
4	Canada	140	Odyssey	Liberia	1988
5	United Kingdom	121	Torrey Canyon	Liberia	1967
6	Oman	120	Sea Star	South Korea	1972
7	Greece	102	Irenes Serenade	Greece	1980
8	Spain	101	Urquiola	Spain	1976
9	United States	99	Hawaiian Patriot	Liberia	1977
10	Turkey	95	Independenta	Romania	1979
11	United Kingdom	85	Braer	Liberia	1993

Industrial disasters, 1988–98[b]

	Location	Origin of accident	Deaths
1988	Islamabad, Pakistan	explosives	100
	Arzamas, Russia	explosives	73
	North Sea, UK	oil explosion	167
	Sverdlosk, Russia	explosives	5
1989	Ionava, Russia	chemical explosion	6
	Acha Ufa, Russia	gas explosion	575
1990	Ufa, Russia	chemical explosion	...
	Bangkok, Thailand	explosion (lorry)	54
	Patna, India	explosion (train)	100
1991	Thailand	explosives	171
	Livorno, Italy	oil explosion	140
	Sterlington, USA	gas explosion	8
1992	Kozlu, Turkey	gas explosion	270
1993	Shenzhen, China	fire (toy factory)	84
	Thailand	fire (toy factory)	189
1996	Dusseldorf, Germany	fire	16
	Lima, Peru	explosives	12
1997	Sichuan, China	explosives	21
	Columbus, USA	chemical fire	25

a 1992   b Not ranked due to difficulties in comparing the effects of each.

Environment: *pollution and waste*

Carbon dioxide emissions
Tonnes per head, 1995

1	Kuwait	31.5	22	Netherlands	8.8
2	United Arab Emirates	27.8		Poland	8.8
3	Singapore	21.3	24	Ukraine	8.5
4	United States	20.8	25	Israel	8.4
5	Norway	16.6	26	South Africa	8.3
6	Australia	16.0		South Korea	8.3
7	Canada	14.7		Venezuela	8.3
8	Saudi Arabia	13.4	29	Libya	7.8
9	Kazakhstan	13.3	30	New Zealand	7.6
	Trinidad & Tobago	13.3	31	Austria	7.4
11	Russia	12.3	32	Greece	7.3
12	North Korea	11.6	33	Italy	7.2
13	Estonia	11.1	34	Slovakia	7.1
14	Czech Republic	10.8	35	Bulgaria	6.7
15	Denmark	10.5	36	Turkmenistan	6.3
16	Belgium	10.2	37	Slovenia	5.9
	Germany	10.2		Spain	5.9
18	Finland	10.0	39	France	5.8
19	United Kingdom	9.3	40	Azerbaijan	5.7
20	Ireland	9.0		Belarus	5.7
	Japan	9.0			

Nitrogen oxide emissions in cities
Micrograms per cubic metre

1	Milan, Italy	248	11	Cape Town, South Africa	72
2	Mexico City, Mexico	130	12	Bucharest, Romania	71
3	Sofia, Bulgaria	122	13	Tokyo, Japan	68
	Beijing, China	122	14	Athens, Greece	64
5	Cordoba, Argentina	97	15	Seoul, South Korea	60
6	Sao Paulo, Brazil	83	16	Amsterdam, Netherlands	58
7	Santiago, Chile	81	17	Paris, France	57
8	Katowice, Poland	79		Caracas, Venezuela	57
	New York, USA	79	19	Copenhagen, Denmark	54
10	London, UK	77	20	Munich, Germany	53

Sulphur dioxide emissions in cities
Micrograms per cubic metre

1	Tehran, Iran	209	11	Sao Paulo, Brazil	43
2	Rio de Janeiro, Brazil	129	12	Budapest, Hungary	39
3	Istanbul, Turkey	120		Sofia, Bulgaria	39
4	Moscow, Russia	109	14	Athens, Greece	34
5	Beijing, China	90	15	Bombay, India	33
6	Katowice, Poland	83		Caracas, Venezuela	33
7	Tianjin, China	82	17	Prague, Czech Republic	32
8	Mexico City, Mexico	74	18	Milan, Italy	31
9	Cairo, Egypt	69		Quito, Ecuador	31
10	Seoul, South Korea	44		Zagreb, Croatia	31

Solid hazardous waste generated
Kg per head

1	Belgium	2,731	11	Poland	90
2	United States	1,059	12	Austria	84
3	Czech Republic	808		Mexico	84
4	Slovenia	507	14	Germany	82
5	Canada	267	15	Hungary	78
6	Luxembourg	214	16	France	69
7	Portugal	139	17	Italy	59
8	Switzerland	117	18	Sweden	57
9	Finland	110	19	Greece	43
10	Netherlands	93	20	Spain	43

Industrial waste generated
Kg per head

1	United States	485.4	11	Austria	16.1
2	Canada	138.0	12	Finland	14.9
3	Hungary	61.6		France	12.3
4	Japan	52.6	14	France	12.3
5	Switzerland	42.6		Greece	10.0
6	Germany	32.5	16	Australia	8.4
7	Luxembourg	31.4	17	Spain	8.3
8	Netherlands	30.3	18	Mexico	6.1
9	Iceland	21.4	19	Poland	4.6
10	Norway	16.6			

Solid municipal waste generated
Kg per head

1	United States	730	11	Austria	430
2	Australia	690	12	Japan	410
3	Canada	660	13	Belgium	400
4	Finland	620		Switzerland	400
5	Iceland	560	15	Turkey	390
6	Norway	510		Hungary	390
7	Netherlands	500	17	Sweden	370
8	Luxembourg	490	18	Germany	360
9	France	470		Slovakia	360
10	Denmark	460		Spain	360

The statistics for all tables (including those on page 94) except carbon dioxide emissions, fresh water resources and water use cover OECD and emerging Eastern European countries only. They normally refer to various years in the late 1980s to early 1990s, though some refer to an earlier period.

Environment: *recycling and water*

Glass recycling
Recovery rates, %, 1994

1	Switzerland	84		Sweden	56
2	Netherlands	77	12	Italy	54
3	Austria	76	13	Finland	50
4	Canada[a]	75	14	France	48
5	Germany	75	15	Australia[a]	36
	Iceland[a]	75	16	Portugal	32
7	Norway	72	17	Ireland	31
8	Belgium	67		Spain	31
	Denmark	67	19	Greece	29
10	Japan[a]	56	20	United Kingdom	28

Paper recycling
Recovery rates, %, 1993

1	Austria[b]	78	11	France	42
	Spain	78	12	Portugal[a]	41
3	Switzerland	54	13	Turkey[a]	39
4	Netherlands[c]	53	14	Denmark[a]	36
5	Japan[a]	51	15	United States	34
6	Australia[c]	50	16	Canada[a]	32
	Sweden	50		Norway	32
8	Italy[c]	47		United Kingdom	32
9	Germany	46	19	Greece	30
10	Finland[a]	45		Iceland[c]	30

Freshwater resources
Cubic metres per head, '000

1	Congo-Brazzaville	345.6	11	Venezuela	38.4
2	Papua New Guinea	182.0	12	Sierra Leone	34.6
3	Gabon	145.8	13	Guinea	33.4
4	Canada	95.1	14	Chile	32.5
5	New Zealand	90.0	15	Brazil	32.2
6	Norway	87.7	16	Russia	29.2
7	Panama	53.9	17	Colombia	28.6
8	Central African Rep	42.2	18	Costa Rica	27.6
9	Bolivia	39.5	19	Ecuador	26.8
10	Nicaragua	38.9	20	Madagascar	24.6

Water use
Cubic metres per head, latest year

1	Turkmenistan	5,487	11	Canada	1,520
2	Uzbekistan	3,542	12	Lithuania	1,180
3	Kirgizstan	2,461	13	Chile	1,165
4	Kazakhstan	2,253	14	Romania	1,148
5	Estonia	2,243	15	Pakistan	1,112
6	Tajikistan	2,123	16	Hong Kong	1,098
7	Azerbaijan	2,081	17	Madagascar	1,062
8	Iraq	2,077	18	Armenia	1,045
9	United States	1,734	19	Iran	1,000
10	Bulgaria	1,641	20	Syria	988

a 1992
b 1990

c 1991

Part II
COUNTRY PROFILES

ALGERIA

Area	2,381,741 sq km	Currency	Algerian dinar (AD)
Capital	Algiers		

People

Population	28.8m	Life expectancy: men		67.5 yrs
Pop. per sq km	12		women	70.3 yrs
Av. ann. growth		Adult literacy		59.4%
in pop. 1990–2000	2.37%	Fertility rate (per woman)		3.8
Pop. under 15	39.2%	Urban population		56%
Pop. over 65	3.6%			per 1,000 pop.
No. of men per 100 women	102.5	Crude birth rate		29.2
Human Development Index	73.7	Crude death rate		6

The economy

GDP	AD2,468bn	GDP per head	$1,520
GDP	$44bn	GDP per head in purchasing	
Av. ann. growth in real		power parity (USA=100)	17
GDP 1990–96	0.6		

Origins of GDP		Components of GDP[a]	
	% of total		% of total
Agriculture	10.3	Private consumption	55.5
Industry, of which:	67.1	Public consumption	15.7
manufacturing	...	Investment	32.0
Services	22.6	Exports	26.7
		Imports	-29.9

Structure of employment[b]

	% of total		% of labour force
Agriculture	26	Unemployed 1992	23.8
Industry	31	Av. ann. rate 1990–92	21.5
Services	43		

Energy

	m TCE		
Total output	170.503	% output exported	70.1
Total consumption	46.141	% consumption imported	2.7
Consumption per head,			
kg coal equivalent	1,642		

Inflation and finance

Consumer price		av. ann. increase 1989–96	
inflation 1996	21.6%	Narrow money (M1)	10.9%
Av. ann. inflation 1990–96	25.0%	Broad money	15.4%

Exchange rates

	end 1997		December 1997
AD per $	58.41	Effective rates	1990 = 100
AD per SDR	78.82	– nominal	...
AD per Ecu	64.25	– real	...

Principal exports[a]

	$bn fob		$bn fob
Energy & products	9.3	Total including others	**10.3**

Main export destinations

	% of total		% of total
Italy	20.2	Spain	8.7
United States	16.8	Germany	7.5
France	13.0	Netherlands	5.7

Principal imports[a]

	$bn cif		$bn cif
Food	3.5		
Hydrocarbon sector	2.0	Total incl. others	**10.2**

Main origins of imports

	% of total		% of total
France	31.9	United States	8.2
Italy	9.5	Germany	5.3
Spain	9.1	Canada	3.7

Balance of payments[b], reserves and debt, $bn

Visible exports fob	12.3	Overall balance	1.0
Visible imports fob	-6.9	Change in reserves	2.0
Trade balance	5.5	Level of reserves	
Invisibles inflows	0.5	end Dec.	6.3
Invisibles outflows	-3.8	No. months of import cover	5.7
Net transfers	0.2	Foreign debt	33.3
Current account balance	2.4	– as % of GDP	75.7
– as % of GDP	5.3	Debt service paid	4.2
Capital balance	-1.0	Debt service ratio	27.7

Family life

No. of households	3.3m	Divorces per 1,000 pop.	...
Av. no. per household	7.0	Cost of living, Dec. 1997	
Marriages per 1,000 pop.	5.7	New York = 100	56

a 1995
b 1991

ARGENTINA

Area	2,766,889 sq km	Currency	Peso (P)
Capital	Buenos Aires		

People

Population	35.2m	Life expectancy: men	69.6 yrs
Pop. per sq km	13	women	76.8 yrs
Av. ann. growth		Adult literacy	96.0%
in pop. 1990–2000	1.3%	Fertility rate (per woman)	2.6
Pop. under 15	28.9%	Urban population	88%
Pop. over 65	9.4%		per 1,000 pop.
No. of men per 100 women	96.3	Crude birth rate	19.9
Human Development Index	88.4	Crude death rate	8

The economy

GDP	P297bn	GDP per head	$8,380
GDP	$295bn	GDP per head in purchasing	
Av. ann. growth in real		power parity (USA=100)	35
GDP 1990–96	4.9%		

Origins of GDP		Components of GDP	
	% of total		% of total
Agriculture	7.2	Private consumption[a]	82.5
Industry, of which:	35.2	Public consumption	…
manufacturing	24.3	Investment	21.5
Services	57.6	Exports	13.8
		Imports	-17.8

Structure of employment

	% of total		% of labour force
Agricultural	2	Unemployed 1996	16.3
Industry	25	Av. ann. rate 1991–96	11.1
Services	73		

Energy

	m TCE		
Total output	95.425	% output exported	26.1
Total consumption	76.962	% consumption imported	11.4
Consumption per head			
kg coal equivalent	2,214		

Inflation and finance

Consumer price		av. ann. increase 1989–96	
inflation 1997	0.5%	Narrow money (M1)	272%
Av. ann. inflation 1990–97	31.4%	Broad money	162%
Money market rate, 1997	6.63%		

Exchange rates

	end 1997		December 1997
P per $	1.00	Effective rates	1990 = 100
P per SDR	1.35	– nominal	…
P per Ecu	1.10	– real	…

Principal exports

	$bn fob		$bn fob
Vegetable products	4.5	Live animals	2.2
Processed foods	3.8	Oils & fats	1.9
Minerals	3.1	Total incl. others	**23.8**

Main export destinations

	% of total		% of total
Brazil	27.8	Netherlands	5.2
United States	8.2	Italy	3.3
Chile	7.4		

Principal imports

	$bn cif		$bn cif
Machinery & industrial		Plastics	1.5
equipment	7.6	Metals	1.5
Chemicals	3.7	Total incl. others	**23.8**
Transport equipment	3.4		

Main origins of imports

	% of total		% of total
Brazil	22.4	Germany	6.0
United States	19.9	France	5.0
Italy	6.3		

Balance of payments, reserves and debt, $bn

Visible exports fob	23.8	Overall balance	3.2
Visible imports fob	-22.2	Change in reserves	3.7
Trade balance	1.6	Level of reserves	
Invisibles inflows	7.9	end Dec.	19.7
Invisibles outflows	-13.6	No. months of import cover	6.6
Net transfers	0.3	Foreign debt	93.8
Current account balance	-3.8	– as % of GDP	31.2
– as % of GDP	-1.3	Debt service paid	14.0
Capital balance	7.0	Debt service ratio	44.2

Family life

No. of households	12.6m	Divorces per 1,000 pop.	...
Av. no. per household	2.7	Cost of living, Dec. 1997	
Marriages per 1,000 pop.	4.6	New York = 100	91

a Including public consumption.

AUSTRALIA

Area	7,682,300 sq km	Currency	Australian dollar (A$)
Capital	Canberra		

People

Population	18.1m	Life expectancy: men	75.4 yrs
Pop. per sq km	2	women	81.2 yrs
Av. ann. growth		Adult literacy	99.0%
in pop. 1990–2000	1.1%	Fertility rate (per woman)	1.9
Pop. under 15	21.5%	Urban population	85%
Pop. over 65	11.7%		per 1,000 pop.
No. of men per 100 women	99.7	Crude birth rate	14.3
Human Development Index	93.1	Crude death rate	7

The economy

GDP	A$500bn	GDP per head	$20,370
GDP	$368bn	GDP per head in purchasing	
Av. ann. growth in real		power parity (USA=100)	73
GDP 1990–96	3.7%		

Origins of GDP[a]

	% of total	Components of GDP[a]	% of total
Agriculture & mining	8.4	Private consumption	60.1
Industry, of which:	23.5	Public consumption	16.5
manufacturing	17.1	Investment	22.7
Services	68.1	Exports	23.3
		Imports	-22.7

Structure of employment[b]

	% of total		% of labour force
Agriculture	5	Unemployed 1996	8.6
Industry	23	Av. ann. rate 1990–96	9.3
Services	72		

Energy

	m TCE		
Total output	261.022	% output exported	57.7
Total consumption	140.766	% consumption imported	20.0
Consumption per head,			
kg coal equivalent	7,879		

Inflation and finance

Consumer price		av. ann. increase 1989–96	
inflation 1997	0.3%	Narrow money (M1)	11.4%
Av. ann. inflation 1990–97	2.8%	Broad money	10.2%
Treasury bill rate, 1997	5.25%		

Exchange rates

	end 1997		December 1997
A$ per $	1.53	Effective rates	1990 = 100
A$ per SDR	2.07	– nominal	105.1
A$ per Ecu	1.68	– real	

Principal exports[a]

	$bn fob		$bn fob
Ores & minerals	14.2	Gold	4.9
Coal & oil	9.4		
Machinery	7.6	Total incl. others	**59.9**

Main export destinations

	% of total		% of total
Japan	21.6	United States	6.1
Asean[c]	15.5	Developing countries	45.7
EU	11.1		

Principal imports[a]

	$bn cif		$bn cif
Machinery	19.3	Energy & products	3.3
Consumer goods	14.2	Chemicals	2.3
Motor vehicles & other transport equipment	9.1	Total incl. others	**60.7**

Main origins of imports

	% of total		% of total
United States	22.6	Asean[c]	9.4
EU15	24.9	Developing countries	29.2
Japan	13.9		

Balance of payments, reserves and aid, $bn

Visible exports fob	60.3	Capital balance	17.6
Visible imports fob	-61.0	Overall balance	2.5
Trade balance	-0.6	Change in reserves	2.5
Invisibles inflows	24.6	Level of reserves	
Invisibles outflows	-39.9	end Dec.	17.4
Net transfers	0.1	No. months of import cover	2.1
Current account balance	-15.9	Aid given	1.12
– as % of GDP	-4.3	– as % of GDP	0.3

Family life

No. of households	6.8m	Divorces per 1,000 pop.	2.7
Av. no. per household	2.6	Cost of living, Dec. 1997	
Marriages per 1,000 pop.	6.1	New York = 100	93

a Year ending June 30, 1997.
b 1994
c Brunei, Indonesia, Malaysia, Philippines, Singapore, Thailand, Vietnam, but excluding Laos and Myanmar which joined Asean in 1997.

AUSTRIA

Area	83,855 sq km	Currency	Schilling (ASch)
Capital	Vienna		

People

Population	8.1m	Life expectancy: men	73.7 yrs
Pop. per sq km	97	women	80.1 yrs
Av. ann. growth		Adult literacy	99.0%
in pop. 1990–2000	0.73%	Fertility rate (per woman)	1.4
Pop. under 15	17.7%	Urban population	56%
Pop. over 65	14.7%		per 1,000 pop.
No. of men per 100 women	96.8	Crude birth rate	10.3
Human Development Index	93.2	Crude death rate	10

The economy

GDP	ASch2,422bn	GDP per head	$27,940
GDP	$227bn	GDP per head in purchasing	
Av. ann. growth in real		power parity (USA=100)	78
GDP 1990–96	1.6%		

Origins of GDP		Components of GDP	
	% of total		% of total
Agriculture	2.1	Private consumption	55.7
Industry, of which:	35.2	Public consumption	18.8
manufacturing	…	Investment	26.7
Services	62.7	Exports	38.8
		Imports	-40.0

Structure of employment

	% of total		% of labour force
Agriculture	6	Unemployed 1996	4.1
Industry	29	Av. ann. rate 1990–96	3.7
Services	65		

Energy

	m TCE		
Total output	8.696	% output exported	27.3
Total consumption	34.458	% consumption imported	84.1
Consumption per head,			
kg coal equivalent	4,283		

Inflation and finance

Consumer price		av. ann. increase 1989–96	
inflation 1997	1.3%	Narrow money (M1)	7.1%
Av. ann. inflation 1990–97	2.8%	Broad money	6.2%
Money market rate, 1997	3.27%		

Exchange rates

	end 1997		December 1997
ASch per $	12.63	Effective rates	1990 = 100
ASch per SDR	17.05	– nominal	102.6
ASch per Ecu	13.89	– real	84.0

Principal exports

	$bn fob		$bn fob
Machinery & transport equipment	29.6	Chemicals	6.8
		Food, drink & tobacco	3.2
Manufactured goods	19.9	Raw materials	2.6
Consumer goods	9.7	Total incl. others	**73.0**

Main export destinations

	% of total		% of total
Germany	37.4	France	4.3
Italy	8.3	Hungary	3.6
Switzerland	5.4	EU15	64.1

Principal imports

	$bn cif		$bn cif
Machinery & transport equipment	29.5	Chemicals	8.0
		Food, drink & tobacco	4.7
Manufactured products	14.1	Fuel & energy	4.1
Consumer goods	13.8	Total incl. others	**77.7**

Main origins of imports

	% of total		% of total
Germany	42.9	United States	4.5
Italy	8.8	Switzerland	3.6
France	4.8	EU15	70.8

Balance of payments, reserves and aid, $bn

Visible exports fob	55.9	Capital balance	4.5
Visible imports fob	-63.7	Overall balance	1.1
Trade balance	-7.8	Change in reserves	3.5
Invisibles inflows	48.4	Level of reserves	
Invisibles outflows	-43.6	end Dec.	26.8
Net transfers	-1.0	No. months of import cover	3.0
Current account balance	-4.0	Aid given	0.56
– as % of GDP	-1.8	– as % of GDP	0.24

Family life

No. of households	3.3m	Divorces per 1,000 pop.	2.3
Av. no. per household	2.5	Cost of living, Dec. 1997	
Marriages per 1,000 pop.	5.3	New York = 100	104

BANGLADESH

Area	143,998 sq km	Currency	Taka (Tk)
Capital	Dhaka		

People

Population	120.1m	Life expectancy: men	58.1 yrs
Pop. per sq km	834	women	58.2 yrs
Av. ann. growth		Adult literacy	37.3%
in pop. 1990–2000	1.57%	Fertility rate (per woman)	3.1
Pop. under 15	41.6%	Urban population	18%
Pop. over 65	3.3%		per 1,000 pop.
No. of men per 100 women	105.4	Crude birth rate	26.8
Human Development Index	36.8	Crude death rate	10

The economy

GDP	Tk1,302bn	GDP per head	$260
GDP	$31bn	GDP per head in purchasing	
Av. ann. growth in real		power parity (USA=100)	4
GDP 1990–96	4.3%		

Origins of GDP[a]		Components of GDP[a]	
	% of total		% of total
Agriculture	29.8	Private consumption	76.5
Industry, of which:	15.2	Public consumption	14.0
manufacturing	9.3	Investment	17.4
Services	55.0	Exports	15.5
		Imports	-23.4

Structure of employment

	% of total		% of labour force
Agriculture	63	Unemployed 1996	2.5
Industry	10	Av. ann. rate 1990–96	…
Services	27		

Energy

	m TCE		
Total output	9.287	% output exported	0.0
Total consumption	11.891	% consumption imported	29.7
Consumption per head,			
kg coal equivalent	101		

Inflation and finance

Consumer price		av. ann. increase 1989–96	
inflation 1997	5.7%	Narrow money (M1)	13.0%
Av. ann. inflation 1990–97	4.6%	Broad money	13.4%
Deposit rate, 1997	8.11%		

Exchange rates

	end 1997		December 1997
Tk per $	45.45	Effective rates	1990 = 100
Tk per SDR	61.32	– nominal	…
Tk per Ecu	49.99	– real	…

BANGLADESH **105**

Principal exports[a]

	$bn fob		$bn fob
Clothing	3.0	Leather	0.2
Fish & fish products	0.3		
Jute goods	0.3	Total incl. others	**3.5**

Main export destinations

	% of total		% of total
United States	32.1	France	6.9
United Kingdom	11.4	Netherlands	4.9
Germany	10.2	Italy	4.8

Principal imports[a]

	$bn cif		$bn cif
Textiles	1.6	Chemicals	0.4
Machinery & transport equipment	1.0	Fuels	0.3
Foods	0.6	Total incl. others	**6.8**

Main origins of imports

	% of total		% of total
India	16.2	Singapore	5.9
China	10.3	South Korea	5.8
Japan	8.6	United States	3.3

Balance of payments, reserves and debt, $bn

Visible exports fob	4.0	Overall balance	-0.6
Visible imports fob	-6.2	Change in reserves	-0.5
Trade balance	-2.3	Level of reserves	
Invisibles inflows	0.7	end Dec.	1.9
Invisibles outflows	-1.3	No. months of import cover	2.9
Net transfers	1.9	Foreign debt	16.1
Current account balance	-1.0	– as % of GDP	51.9
– as % of GDP	-3.1	Debt service paid	0.7
Capital balance	0.4	Debt service ratio	11.7

Family life

No. households	14.8m	Divorces per 1,000 pop.	…
Av. no. per household	5.7	Cost of living, Dec. 1997	
Marriages per 1,000 pop.	10.9	New York = 100	64

a Fiscal year ending June 30 1997.

BELGIUM

Area	30,520 sq km	Currency	Belgian franc (BFr)
Capital	Brussels		

People

Population	10.2m	Life expectancy: men	73.9 yrs
Pop. per sq km	333	women	80.6 yrs
Av. ann. growth		Adult literacy	99.0%
in pop. 1990–2000	0.3%	Fertility rate (per woman)	1.6
Pop. under 15	17.8%	Urban population	97%
Pop. over 65	15.8%		*per 1,000 pop.*
No. of men per 100 women	96.1	Crude birth rate	11.2
Human Development Index	93.2	Crude death rate	11

The economy

GDP	BFr8,305bn	GDP per head	$26,440
GDP	$269bn	GDP per head in purchasing	
Av. ann. growth in real		power parity (USA=100)	81
GDP 1990–96	1.2%		

Origins of GDP		Components of GDP	
	% of total		*% of total*
Agriculture	1.3	Private consumption	63.1
Industry, of which:	30.7	Public consumption	14.5
manufacturing	22.9	Investment	17.6
Services	68.0	Exports	68.5
		Imports	-63.8

Structure of employment[a]

	% of total		*% of labour force*
Agriculture	3	Unemployed 1996	9.6
Industry	31	Av. ann. rate 1990–96	8.4
Services	66		

Energy

	m TCE		
Total output	15.761	% output exported[b]	158.4
Total consumption	69.439	% consumption imported[b]	129.9
Consumption per head,			
kg coal equivalent	6,857		

Inflation and finance

Consumer price		*av. ann. increase 1993–96*	
inflation 1997	1.6%	Narrow money (M1)	1.1%
Av. ann. inflation 1990–97	2.4%	Broad money	5.9%
Money market rate, 1997	3.46%		

Exchange rates

	end 1997		*December 1997*
BFr per $	36.92	Effective rates	*1990 = 100*
BFr per SDR	49.81	– nominal	102.0
BFr per Ecu	40.77	– real	104.3

Principal exports[c]

	$bn fob		$bn fob
Vehicles	25.8	Rubber & plastic goods	13.3
Chemicals	21.8	Precious stones & jewellery	12.4
Machinery & electrical goods	21.5		
Metals & products	16.4	Total incl. others	**169.1**

Main export destinations[c]

	% of total		% of total
Germany	20.6	United Kingdom	9.0
France	17.8	United States	4.4
Netherlands	13.3	EU15	75.1

Principal imports[c]

	$bn cif		$bn cif
Machinery & electrical products	26.4	Mineral products	12.9
		Precious stones & jewellery	12.4
Vehicles	20.1		
Chemicals	16.8	Total incl. others	**157.4**

Main origins of imports[c]

	% of total		% of total
Germany	19.9	United Kingdom	9.2
Netherlands	18.5	United States	6.1
France	15.3	EU15	75.7

Balance of payments[c], reserves and aid, $bn

Visible exports fob	154.1	Capital balance	-13.4
Visible imports fob	-145.6	Overall balance	0.6
Trade balance	8.5	Change in reserves	-1.5
Invisibles inflows	97.5	Level of reserves	
Invisibles outflows	-87.8	end Dec.	22.6
Net transfers	-4.2	No. months of import cover	1.2
Current account balance	14.0	Aid given	0.91
– as % of GDP	5.2	– as % of GDP	0.34

Family life

No. of households	3.7m	Divorces per 1,000 pop.	2.1
Av. no. per household	2.7	Cost of living, Dec. 1997	
Marriages per 1,000 pop.	5.1	New York = 100	92

a 1992
b Energy trade data are distorted by transitory and oil refining activities.
c Including Luxembourg.

BRAZIL

Area	8,511,965 sq km	Currency	Real (R)
Capital	Brasilia		

People

Population	161.1m	Life expectancy: men	63.4 yrs
Pop. per sq km	19	women	71.2 yrs
Av. ann. growth		Adult literacy	82.7%
in pop. 1990–2000	1.34%	Fertility rate (per woman)	2.2
Pop. under 15	31.6%	Urban population	78%
Pop. over 65	4.8%		per 1,000 pop.
No. of men per 100 women	97.9	Crude birth rate	19.6
Human Development Index	78.3	Crude death rate	7

The economy

GDP	R779bn	GDP per head	$4,410
GDP	$710bn	GDP per head in purchasing	
Av. ann. growth in real		power parity (USA=100)	23
GDP 1990–96	2.9%		

Origins of GDP[a]		Components of GDP[a]	
	% of total		% of total
Agriculture	10.7	Private consumption	65.1
Industry, of which:	42.0	Public consumption	15.2
manufacturing	28.3	Investment	21.6
Services	47.3	Exports	11.7
		Imports	-13.6

Structure of employment[a]

	% of total		% of labour force
Agriculture	26	Unemployed 1995	6.1
Industry	20	Av. ann. rate 1990–95	…
Services	54		

Energy

	m TCE		
Total output	93.543	% output exported	3.6
Total consumption	144.969	% consumption imported	45.0
Consumption per head,			
kg coal equivalent	912		

Inflation and finance

		av. ann. increase 1989–96	
Consumer price			
inflation 1997	6.9%	Narrow money (M1)	689%
Av. ann. inflation 1990–97	234.3%	Broad money	691%
Money market rate, 1997	25.00%		

Exchange rates

	end 1997		December 1997
R per $	1.12	Effective rates	1990 = 100
R per SDR	1.51	– Nominal	…
R per Ecu	1.23	– Real	…

Principal exports

	$bn fob		$bn fob
Manufactures	29.7	Coffee	2.1
Iron ore	4.5		
Soyabeans etc.	2.9	Total incl. others	**47.7**

Main export destinations

	% of total		% of total
United States	19.5	Japan	6.4
Argentina	10.8	Germany	4.4

Principal imports

	$bn cif		$bn cif
Machines & electrical		Fuels & lubricants	6.1
materials	15.7	Transport equipment & parts	4.5
Chemical products	8.0	Total incl. others	**53.3**

Main origins of imports

	% of total		% of total
United States	22.2	Argentina	9.0
Germany	12.7	Japan	5.2

Balance of payments[a], reserves and debt, $bn

Visible exports fob	46.5	Overall balance	13.0
Visible imports fob	-49.7	Change in reserves	8.2
Trade balance	-3.2	Level of reserves	
Invisibles inflows	9.6	end Dec.	59.7
Invisibles outflows	-28.2	No. months of import cover	8.3
Net transfers	3.6	Foreign debt	179.0
Current account balance	-18.1	– as % of GDP	25.2
– as % of GDP	-3.1	Debt service paid	25.1
Capital balance	29.7	Debt service ratio	41.1

Family life

No. of households	38.4m	Divorces per 1,000 pop.	0.6
Av. no. per household	4.0	Cost of living, Dec. 1997	
Marriages per 1,000 pop.	5.2	New York = 100	93

a 1995

BULGARIA

Area	110,994 sq km	Currency	Lev (BGL)
Capital	Sofia		

People

Population	8.5m	Life expectancy: men	67.8 yrs
Pop. per sq km	76	women	74.9 yrs
Av. ann. growth		Adult literacy	93.0%
in pop. 1990–2000	-0.49%	Fertility rate (per woman)	1.5
Pop. under 15	18.4%	Urban population	71%
Pop. over 65	14.5%		per 1,000 pop.
No. of men per 100 women	95.4	Crude birth rate	10.3
Human Development Index	78.0	Crude death rate	13

The economy

GDP	BGL1,660bn	GDP per head	$1,190
GDP	$10bn	GDP per head in purchasing	
Av. ann. growth in real		power parity (USA=100)	15
GDP 1990–96	-3.5%		

Origins of GDP		**Components of GDP**	
	% of total		% of total
Agriculture	11.7	Private consumption	77.3
Industry, of which:	32.6	Public consumption	12.4
manufacturing	...	Investment	11.5
Services	55.7	Exports	41.7
		Imports	-43.0

Structure of employment[a]

	% of total		% of labour force
Agriculture	14	Unemployed 1996	12.5
Industry	50	Av. ann. rate 1990–96	11.5
Services	36		

Energy

	m TCE		
Total output	14.449	% output exported	20.0
Total consumption	31.005	% consumption imported	70.8
Consumption per head,			
kg coal equivalent	3,644		

Inflation and finance

av. ann increase 1989–96

Consumer price			
inflation 1997	1,082.6%	Narrow money (M1)	...
Av. ann. inflation 1990–96	72.1%	Broad money	...

Exchange rates

	end 1997		December 1997
BGL per $	1,763.50	Effective rates	1990 = 100
BGL per SDR	2,380.73	– Nominal	...
BGL per Ecu	1,939.85	– Real	...

Principal exports

	$bn fob		$bn fob
Chemicals, plastics & rubber	1.0	Machinery & transport	
Animal & vegetable products	0.9	equipment	0.7
Base metals	0.9	Total incl. others	**4.9**

Main export destinations

	% of total		% of total
Italy	10.9	EU15	36.5
Russia	9.8		

Principal imports

	$bn fob		$bn fob
Mineral products & fuels	1.9	Chemicals	0.6
Machinery & transport equip.	0.9	Total incl. others	**4.7**

Main origins of imports

	% of total		% of total
Russia	28.4	EU15	31.3
Germany	10.9		

Balance of payments, reserves and debt, $bn

Visible exports fob	4.7	Overall balance	-0.7
Visible imports fob	-4.6	Change in reserves	-0.8
Trade balance	0.1	Level of reserves	
Invisibles inflows	1.5	end Dec.	0.9
Invisibles outflows	-1.8	No. months of import cover	1.6
Net transfers	0.1	Foreign debt	9.8
Current account balance	-0.0	– as % of GDP	98
– as % of GDP	-0.2	Debt service paid	1.3
Capital balance	-0.8	Debt service ratio	20.5

Family life

No. of households	3.1m	Divorces per 1,000 pop.	1.3
Av. no. per household	2.8	Cost of living, Dec. 1997	
Marriages per 1,000 pop.	4.2	New York = 100	...

a 1990

CAMEROON

Area	475,442 sq km	Currency	CFA franc (CFAfr)
Capital	Yaoundé		

People

Population	13.6m	Life expectancy: men	54.5 yrs
Pop. per sq km	29	women	57.2 yrs
Av. ann. growth		Adult literacy	62.1%
in pop. 1990–2000	2.76%	Fertility rate (per woman)	5.3
Pop. under 15	44.2%	Urban population	45%
Pop. over 65	3.6%		per 1,000 pop.
No. of men per 100 women	98.7	Crude birth rate	39.3
Human Development Index	46.8	Crude death rate	12

The economy

GDP	CFAfr5,017bn	GDP per head	$610
GDP	$8.4bn	GDP per head in purchasing	
Av. ann. growth in real		power parity (USA=100)	6
GDP 1990–96	-1.0%		

Origins of GDP[a]

	% of total
Agriculture	33.5
Industry, of which:	21.1
manufacturing	10.2
Services	45.4

Components of GDP[a]

	% of total
Private consumption	67.8
Public consumption	8.3
Investment	17.9
Exports	23.2
Imports	-17.2

Structure of employment[b]

	% of total		% of labour force
Agriculture	70	Unemployed 1996	…
Industry	9	Av. ann. rate 1990–96	…
Services	21		

Energy

	m TCE		
Total output	7.584	% output exported	71.7
Total consumption	1.910	% consumption imported	5.9
Consumption per head,			
kg coal equivalent	145		

Inflation and finance

			av. ann. change 1989–96
Consumer price			
inflation 1996	4.7%	Narrow money (M1)	-3.6%
Av. ann. inflation 1990–96	6.7%	Broad money	-2.7%

Exchange rates

	end 1997		December 1997
CFAfr per $	598.8	Effective rates	1990 = 100
CFAfr per SDR	807.9	– nominal	79.6
CFAfr per Ecu	658.7	– real	

Principal exports[a]

	$m fob		$m fob
Crude oil	457	Cocoa	95
Timber	239	Coffee	93
		Total incl. others	**1,761**

Main export destinations

	% of total		% of total
Italy	17.7	Spain	16.5
France	15.8	Netherlands	6.7

Principal imports[c]

	$m fob		$m fob
Capital goods	190	Fuel	7
Food	89	Total incl. others	**1,241**

Main origins of imports

	% of total		% of total
France	36.7	Belgium/Luxembourg	7.1
Italy	7.5	United States	6.5

Balance of payments[d], reserves and debt, $bn

Visible exports fob	1.7	Overall balance	0.0
Visible imports fob	-1.1	Change in reserves	0.00
Trade balance	0.6	Level of reserves	
Invisibles inflows	0.3	end Dec.	0.01
Invisibles outflows	-0.9	No. months of import cover	0.1
Net transfers	0.1	Foreign debt	9.5
Current account balance	0.1	– as % of GDP	113.1
– as % of GDP	1.0	Debt service paid	0.5
Capital balance	0.1	Debt service ratio	23.6

Family life

No. of households	1.4m	Divorces per 1,000 pop.	...
Av. no. per household	5.2	Cost of living, Dec. 1997	
Marriages per 1,000 pop.	...	New York = 100	74

a Fiscal year ending June 30 1996.
b 1990
c Fiscal year ending June 30 1995.
d 1995

CANADA

Area[a]	9,970,610 sq km	Currency	Canadian dollar (C$)
Capital	Ottawa		

People

Population	29.7m	Life expectancy: men		76.1 yrs
Pop. per sq km	3		women	81.8 yrs
Av. ann. growth		Adult literacy		99.0%
in pop. 1990–2000	0.99%	Fertility rate (per woman)		1.6
Pop. under 15	20.4%	Urban population		77%
Pop. over 65	12.0%			per 1,000 pop.
No. of men per 100 women	98.3	Crude birth rate		11.9
Human Development Index	96.0	Crude death rate		7

The economy

GDP	C$820bn	GDP per head	$19,200
GDP	$570bn	GDP per head in purchasing	
Av. ann. growth in real		power parity (USA=100)	78
GDP 1990–96	1.9%		

Origins of GDP

	% of total
Agriculture	2.6
Industry, of which:	30.5
manufacturing & mining	21.3
Services	66.9

Components of GDP

	% of total
Private consumption	58.3
Public consumption	20.6
Investment	17.3
Exports	39.1
Imports	-35.3

Structure of employment

	% of total		% of labour force
Agriculture	4	Unemployed 1996	9.7
Industry	23	Av. ann. rate 1990–96	10.1
Services	73		

Energy

	m TCE		
Total output	496.012	% output exported	48.4
Total consumption	320.860	% consumption imported	18.5
Consumption per head,			
kg coal equivalent	10,913		

Inflation and finance

Consumer price		av. ann. increase 1989–96	
inflation 1997	1.6%	Narrow money (M1)	7.0%
Av. ann. inflation 1990–97	2.4%	Broad money	8.2%
Money market rate, 1997	4.34%		

Exchange rates

	end 1997		December 1997
C$ per $	1.43	Effective rates	1990 = 100
C$ per SDR	1.93	– nominal	82.6
C$ per Ecu	1.57	– real	78.3

Principal exports

	$bn fob		$bn fob
Motor vehicles & other		Forest products	25.4
transport equipment	46.6	Energy products	18.8
Machinery & industrial		Agric. products &	
equipment	45.7	foodstuffs	17.9
Industrial supplies	38.3	Total incl. others	**205.8**

Main export destinations

	% of total		% of total
United States	79.1	United Kingdom	1.7
Japan	4.5		

Principal imports

	$bn fob		$bn fob
Machinery & industrial		Consumer goods	19.0
equipment	56.3	Agric. products & foodstuffs	10.4
Motor vehicles & other		Energy products	7.1
transport equipment	37.8		
Industrial supplies	34.2	Total incl. others	**175.7**

Main origins of imports

	% of total		% of total
United States	75.9	United Kingdom	2.3
Japan	3.0		

Balance of payments, reserves and aid, $bn

Visible exports fob	205.8	Capital balance	0.4
Visible imports fob	-175.7	Overall balance	5.5
Trade balance	30.1	Change in reserves	5.2
Invisibles inflows	47.6	Level of reserves	
Invisibles outflows	-75.2	end Dec.	21.6
Net transfers	0.3	No. months of import cover	1.0
Current account balance	2.8	Aid given	1.80
– as % of GDP	0.5	– as % of GDP	0.32

Family life

No. of households	10.8m	Divorces per 1,000 pop.	2.7
Av. no. per household	2.7	Cost of living, Dec. 1997	
Marriages per 1,000 pop.	7.0	New York = 100	81

a Including freshwater.

CHILE

Area	756,945 sq km	Currency	Chilean peso (peso)
Capital	Santiago		

People

Population	14.4m	Life expectancy: men		72.3 yrs
Pop. per sq km	19	women		78.3 yrs
Av. ann. growth		Adult literacy		75.5%
in pop. 1990–2000	1.5%	Fertility rate (per woman)		2.4
Pop. under 15	29.4%	Urban population		84%
Pop. over 65	6.6%		per 1,000 pop.	
No. of men per 100 women	98.0	Crude birth rate		19.9
Human Development Index	89.1	Crude death rate		6

The economy

GDP	28,536bn pesos	GDP per head	$4,860
GDP	$70bn	GDP per head in purchasing	
Av. ann. growth in real		power parity (USA=100)	42
GDP 1990–96	7.2%		

Origins of GDP		Components of GDP	
	% of total		% of total
Agriculture	7.1	Private consumption	69.6
Industry, of which:	35.9	Public consumption	8.1
manufacturing	17.8	Investment	31.7
Services	57.0	Exports	38.8
		Imports	-48.3

Structure of employment[a]

	% of total		% of labour force
Agriculture	16	Unemployed 1996	5.4
Industry	26	Av. ann. rate 1990–96	5.1
Services	58		

Energy

	m TCE		
Total output	6.840	% output exported	2.4
Total consumption	21.956	% consumption imported	70.5
Consumption per head,			
kg coal equivalent	1,545		

Inflation and finance

			av. ann. increase 1989–96
Consumer price			
inflation 1997	6.1%	Narrow money (M1)	23.1%
Av. ann. inflation 1990–97	12.0%	Broad money	23.2%
Deposit rate, 1997	12.02%		

Exchange rates

	end 1997		December 1997
			1990 = 100
Peso per $	439.8	Effective rates	
Peso per SDR	593.4	– nominal	166.8
Peso per Ecu	483.8	– real	136.3

Principal exports

	$bn fob		$bn fob
Copper	6.0	Fish meal	0.6
Cellulose	1.0	Total incl. others	**15.4**

Main export destinations

	% of total		% of total
United States	16.6	South Korea	5.6
Japan	16.2	Germany	4.8
Brazil	6.1	Argentina	4.6
United Kingdom	5.8		

Principal imports

	$bn cif		$bn cif
Intermediate goods	9.9	Consumer goods	3.2
Capital goods	4.7	Total incl. others	**17.8**

Main origins of imports

	% of total		% of total
United States	23.7	Mexico	5.3
Argentina	9.4	Germany	4.2
Brazil	6.1	France	3.4
Japan	5.5		

Balance of payments, reserves and debt, $bn

Visible exports fob	15.4	Overall balance	2.5
Visible imports fob	-16.5	Change in reserves	0.7
Trade balance	-1.1	Level of reserves	
Invisibles inflows	4.1	end Dec.	15.5
Invisibles outflows	-6.3	No. months of import cover	8.2
Net transfers	0.5	Foreign debt	27.9
Current account balance	-2.9	– as % of GDP	39.1
– as % of GDP	-4.2	Debt service paid	6.3
Capital balance	6.3	Debt service ratio	32.3

Family life

No. of households	3.3m	Divorces per 1,000 pop.	0.5
Av. no. per household	4.2	Cost of living, Dec. 1997	
Marriages per 1,000 pop.	6.5	New York = 100	78

a 1995

CHINA

Area	9,560,900 sq km	Currency	Yuan
Capital	Beijing		

People

Population	1,232.1m	Life expectancy: men	68.2 yrs
Pop. per sq km	128	women	71.7 yrs
Av. ann. growth		Adult literacy	80.9%
in pop. 1990–2000	1.00%	Fertility rate (per woman)	1.8
Pop. under 15	26.3%	Urban population	30%
Pop. over 65	6.1%		per 1,000 pop.
No. of men per 100 women	106.2	Crude birth rate	16.2
Human Development Index	62.6	Crude death rate	7

The economy

GDP	Yuan6,976bn	GDP per head	$750
GDP	$906bn	GDP per head in purchasing	
Av. ann. growth in real		power parity (USA=100)	12
GDP 1990–96	12.3%		

Origins of GDP		Components of GDP	
	% of total		% of total
Agriculture	19.9	Private consumption	46.7
Industry, of which:	48.6	Public consumption	10.9
manufacturing	…	Investment	34.6
Services	31.5	Exports	22.4
		Imports	-22.4

Structure of employment

	% of total		% of labour force
Agriculture	48	Unemployed 1996	3.0
Industry	21	Av. ann. rate 1990–96	2.6
Services	31		

Energy

	m TCE		
Total output	1,237.323	% output exported	4.9
Total consumption	1,170.693	% consumption imported	3.8
Consumption per head,			
kg coal equivalent	976		

Inflation and finance

Consumer price		av. ann. increase 1989–96	
inflation 1997	2.8%	Narrow money (M1)	24.0%
Av. ann. inflation 1991–97	10.9%	Broad money	29.5%
Deposit rate, 1997	5.67%		

Exchange rates

	end 1997		December 1997
Yuan per $	8.28	Effective rates	1990 = 100
Yuan per SDR	11.17	– nominal	…
Yuan per Ecu	9.12	– real	…

Principal exports

	$bn fob		$bn fob
Textiles & clothing	37.1	Food & tobacco	11.6
Machinery & electrical		Chemicals	8.9
equipment	35.3	Total incl. others	**151.2**

Main export destinations

	% of total		% of total
Hong Kong	21.8	South Korea	5.0
Japan	20.4	Germany	3.9
United States	17.7	Singapore	2.5

Principal imports

	$bn cif		$bn cif
Machinery & electrical	54.8	Iron & steel	7.2
equipment		Fuels	6.9
Chemicals	18.1		
Textiles	12.0	Total incl. others	**138.9**

Main origins of imports

	% of total		% of total
Japan	21.0	Hong Kong	5.6
Taiwan	11.7	Germany	5.3
United States	11.6	Russia	3.7
South Korea	9.0	Singapore	2.6

Balance of payments, reserves and debt, $bn

Visible exports fob	151.1	Overall balance	31.7
Visible imports fob	-131.5	Change in reserves	31.4
Trade balance	19.5	Level of reserves	
Invisibles inflows	27.9	end Dec.	111.7
Invisibles outflows	-42.3	No. months of import cover	7.7
Net transfers	2.1	Foreign debt	128.8
Current account balance	7.2	- as % of GDP	14.2
- as % of GDP	0.8	Debt service paid	15.7
Capital balance	40.0	Debt service ratio	8.7

Family life

No. of households	357m	Divorces per 1,000 pop.	4.6
Av. no. per household	3.3	Cost of living, Dec. 1997	
Marriages per 1,000 pop.	7.6	New York = 100	101

COLOMBIA

Area	1,141,748 sq km	Currency	Colombian peso (peso)
Capital	Bogota		

People

Population	36.4m	Life expectancy: men		68.2 yrs
Pop. per sq km	32		women	73.7 yrs
Av. ann. growth		Adult literacy		91.1%
in pop. 1990–2000	1.77%	Fertility rate (per woman)		2.7
Pop. under 15	34.3%	Urban population		73%
Pop. over 65	4.4%			per 1,000 pop.
No. of men per 100 women	98.5	Crude birth rate		23.4
Human Development Index	84.8	Crude death rate		6

The economy

GDP	88,829bn pesos	GDP per head	$2,140
GDP	$80bn	GDP per head in purchasing	
Av. ann. growth in real		power parity (USA=100)	25
GDP 1990–96	4.5%		

Origins of GDP		Components of GDP	
	% of total		% of total
Agriculture	20.6	Private consumption	67.8
Industry, of which:	29.1	Public consumption	16.0
manufacturing	19.2	Investment	19.2
Services	50.3	Exports	14.9
		Imports	-18.0

Structure of employment[a]

	% of total		% of labour force
Agriculture	1	Unemployed 1996	11.2
Industry	30	Av. ann. rate 1992–96	9.6
Services	69		

Energy

	m TCE		
Total output	76.510	% output exported	58.3
Total consumption	32.106	% consumption imported	7.1
Consumption per head,			
kg coal equivalent	896		

Inflation and finance

Consumer price		av. ann. increase 1991–96	
inflation 1997	18.5%	Narrow money (M1)	29.4%
Av. ann. inflation 1990–97	24.0%	Broad money	30.4%
Money market rate, 1997	23.8%		

Exchange rates

	end 1997		December 1997
			1990 = 100
Peso per $	1,294	Effective rates	
Peso per SDR	1,745	– nominal	77.6
Peso per Ecu	1,423	– real	155.7

Principal exports

	$bn fob		$bn fob
Petroleum & products	2.9	Gold	0.3
Coffee	1.6		
Coal	0.8	Total incl. others	**10.7**

Main export destinations

	% of total		% of total
United States	39.9	EU15	21.4
Japan	27.9	Andean Group[b]	17.4

Principal imports

	$bn fob		$bn fob
Industrial supplies	6.5	Consumer goods	2.6
Capital goods	4.6	Total	**13.7**

Main origins of imports

	% of total		% of total
United States	40.9	Andean Group[b]	13.1
EU15	17.4	Japan	5.2

Balance of payments, reserves and debt, $bn

Visible exports fob	10.7	Overall balance	1.6
Visible imports fob	-12.8	Change in reserves	1.5
Trade balance	-2.1	Level of reserves	
Invisibles inflows	4.8	end Dec.	9.7
Invisibles outflows	-8.0	No. months of import cover	5.6
Net transfers	0.5	Foreign debt	28.9
Current account balance	-4.8	– as % of GDP	36.1
– as % of GDP	-5.9	Debt service paid	5.4
Capital balance	6.8	Debt service ratio	34.6

Family life

No. of households	8.5m	Divorces per 1,000 pop.	...
Av. no. per household	4.1	Cost of living, Dec. 1997	
Marriages per 1,000 pop.	2.4	New York = 100	70

a   Main cities.
b   Bolivia, Colombia, Ecuador, Peru, Venezuela.

CÔTE D'IVOIRE

Area	322,463 sq km	Currency	CFA franc (CFAfr)
Capital	Abidjan/Yamoussoukro		

People

Population	14.0m	Life expectancy: men	50.0 yrs
Pop. per sq km	43	women	52.2 yrs
Av. ann. growth		Adult literacy	39.4%
in pop. 1990–2000	2.6%	Fertility rate (per woman)	5.1
Pop. under 15	44.8%	Urban population	44%
Pop. over 65	2.8%		per 1,000 pop.
No. of men per 100 women	104.0	Crude birth rate	37.2
Human Development Index	36.8	Crude death rate	14

The economy

GDP	CFAfr5,440bn	GDP per head	$660
GDP	$9.4bn	GDP per head in purchasing	
Av. ann. growth in real		power parity (USA=100)	6
GDP 1990–96	2.4%		

Origins of GDP[a]		Components of GDP	
	% of total		% of total
Agriculture	30.7	Private consumption	60.0
Industry, of which:	19.4	Public consumption	11.6
manufacturing	13.4	Investment	16.1
Services	49.9	Exports	47.2
		Imports	-35.0

Structure of employment[b]

	% of total		% of labour force
Agriculture	60	Unemployed 1996	…
Industry	10	Av. ann. rate 1990–96	…
Services	30		

Energy

	m TCE		
Total output	0.647	% output exported	61.8
Total consumption	3.346	% consumption imported	145.2
Consumption per head,			
kg coal equivalent	244		

Inflation and finance

Consumer price			av. ann. change 1989–96
inflation 1996	2.5%	Narrow money (M1)	6.6%
Av. ann. inflation 1990–96	6.8%	Broad money	5.8%

Exchange rates

	end 1997		December 1997
CFAfr per $	598.8	Effective rates	1990 = 100
CFAfr per SDR	807.9	– nominal	82.8
CFAfr per Ecu	658.7	– real	72.2

Principal exports

	$m fob		$m fob
Cocoa beans & products	1,571	Coffee & products	297
Petroleum products	657		
Timber & products	316	Total incl. others	**4,996**

Main export destinations[c]

	% of total		% of total
France	18	Netherlands	8
Germany	8	Italy	8

Principal imports[c]

	$m cif		$m cif
Indusrial imports	877	Fuel	467
Transport equipment	499		
Food & drinks	498	Total incl. others	**3,038**

Main origins of imports[c]

	% of total		% of total
France	32	Ghana	4
Nigeria	20	Germany	4
United States	6		

Balance of payments, reserves and debt, $bn

Visible exports fob	4.4	Overall balance	-0.4
Visible imports fob	-2.5	Change in reserves	0.1
Trade balance	1.9	Level of reserves	
Invisibles inflows	0.8	end Dec.	0.6
Invisibles outflows	-2.5	No. months of import cover	1.5
Net transfers	-0.4	Foreign debt	19.7
Current account balance	-0.2	– as % of GDP	209.6
– as % of GDP	-2.2	Debt service paid	1.3
Capital balance	-0.1	Debt service ratio	26.2

Family life

No. of households	2.4m	Divorces per 1,000 pop.	...
Av. no. per household	5.8	Cost of living, Dec. 1997	
Marriages per 1,000 pop.	...	New York = 100	92

a 1994
b 1990
c 1995

CZECH REPUBLIC

Area	78,864 sq km	Currency	Koruna (Kc)
Capital	Prague		

People

Population	10.3m	Life expectancy: men	69.8 yrs
Pop. per sq km	130	women	76.0 yrs
Av. ann. growth		Adult literacy	99.0%
in pop. 1990–2000	-0.11	Fertility rate (per woman)	1.4
Pop. under 15	18.9%	Urban population	65%
Pop. over 65	12.6%		*per 1,000 pop.*
No. of men per 100 women	95.6	Crude birth rate	10.7
Human Development Index	88.2	Crude death rate	12

The economy

GDP	Kcs1,414bn	GDP per head	$4,770
GDP	$49bn	GDP per head in purchasing	
Av. ann. growth in real		power parity (USA=100)	40
GDP 1990–96	-1.0%		

Origins of GDP		Components of GDP	
	% of total		*% of total*
Agriculture	5.0	Private consumption	57.9
Industry, of which:	40.6	Public consumption	19.2
manufacturing	...	Investment	30.9
Services	54.4	Exports	56.9
		Imports	-65.0

Structure of employment

	% of total		*% of labour force*
Agriculture	6	Unemployed 1996	3.9
Industry	42	Av. ann. rate 1993–96	3.7
Services	58		

Energy

	m TCE		
Total output	41.234	% output exported	27.8
Total consumption	50.895	% consumption imported	46.2
Consumption per head,			
kg coal equivalent	4,959		

Inflation and finance

Consumer price		*av. ann. increase 1994–96*	
inflation 1997	8.4%	Narrow money (M1)	18.9%
Av. ann. inflation 1991–97	16.8%	Broad money	18.3%
Refinancing rate, 1997	23.00%		

Exchange rates

	end 1997		*December 1997*
Kc per $	34.64	Effective rates	*1990 = 100*
Kc per SDR	46.73	– nominal	...
Kc per Ecu	38.10	– real	...

Principal exports

	$bn fob		$bn fob
Machinery & industrial		Raw materials	1.0
equipment	7.1	Fuels	1.0
Market goods	6.2	Total incl. others	**21.7**

Main export destinations

	% of total		% of total
Slovakia	13.9	EU15	60.9

Principal imports

	$bn fob		$bn fob
Machinery & transport		Fuel	2.4
equipment	10.5		
Market goods	5.3	Total incl. others	**27.6**

Main origins of imports

	% of total		% of total
Slovakia	11.8	EU15	61.1

Balance of payments, reserves and debt, $bn

Visible exports fob	21.7	Overall balance	-0.8
Visible imports fob	-27.6	Change in reserves	-1.5
Trade balance	-5.9	Level of reserves	
Invisibles inflows	9.4	end Dec.	13.1
Invisibles outflows	-8.2	No. months of import cover	4.4
Net transfers	0.4	Foreign debt	20.1
Current account balance	-4.3	– as % of GDP	41.0
– as % of GDP	-8.8	Debt service paid	2.6
Capital balance	4.3	Debt service ratio	8.3

Family life

No. of households	3.4m	Divorces per 1,000 pop.	3.0
Av. no. per household	2.9	Cost of living, Dec. 1997	
Marriages per 1,000 pop.	5.3	New York = 100	55

DENMARK

Area	43,075 sq km	Currency	Danish krone (DKr)
Capital	Copenhagen		

People

Population	5.2m	Life expectancy: men	73.0 yrs
Pop. per sq km	122	women	78.3 yrs
Av. ann. growth		Adult literacy	99.0%
in pop. 1990–2000	0.26	Fertility rate (per woman)	1.8
Pop. under 15	17.5%	Urban population	85%
Pop. over 65	15.1%		per 1,000 pop.
No. of men per 100 women	98.1	Crude birth rate	13.0
Human Development Index	92.7	Crude death rate	12

The economy

GDP	DKr1,066bn	GDP per head	$32,250
GDP	$169bn	GDP per head in purchasing	
Av. ann. growth in real		power parity (USA=100)	81
GDP 1990–96	2.2%		

Origins of GDP		Components of GDP	
	% of total		% of total
Agriculture	4.1	Private consumption	53.7
Industry, of which:	28.6	Public consumption	25.2
manufacturing	19.6	Investment	16.8
Services	67.3	Exports	34.6
		Imports	-30.2

Structure of employment

	% of total		% of labour force
Agriculture	4	Unemployed 1996	6.9
Industry	27	Av. ann. rate 1994–96	7.3
Services	69		

Energy

	m TCE		
Total output	20.402	% output exported	76.8
Total consumption	25.175	% consumption imported	100.2
Consumption per head,			
kg coal equivalent	4,820		

Inflation and finance

Consumer price		av. ann. increase 1989–96	
inflation 1997	2.2%	Narrow money (M1)	4.7%
Av. ann. inflation 1990–97	2.1%	Broad money	4.1%
Money market rate, 1997	3.71%		

Exchange rates

	end 1997		December 1997
DKr per $	6.83	Effective rates	1990 = 100
DKr per SDR	9.21	– nominal	104.3
DKr per Ecu	7.51	– real	105.6

Principal exports

	$bn fob		$bn fob
Manufactured goods	37.4	Ships	0.9
Agric. products	6.4		
Energy & products	2.3	Total incl. others	**49.0**

Main export destinations

	% of total		% of total
Germany	22.5	Norway	6.5
Sweden	11.2	France	5.2
United Kingdom	8.9	Netherlands	4.5

Principal imports

	$bn cif		$bn cif
Intermediate goods	20.8	Transport equipment	3.0
Consumer goods	12.3		
Capital goods	5.5	Total incl. others	**44.1**

Main origins of imports

	% of total		% of total
Germany	22.8	Netherlands	7.4
Sweden	12.2	France	5.4
United Kingdom	7.6	Norway	5.1

Balance of payments, reserves and aid, $bn

Visible exports fob	50.7	Capital balance	2.1
Visible imports fob	-43.2	Overall balance	3.6
Trade balance	7.5	Change in reserves	3.1
Invisibles inflows	54.1	Level of reserves	
Invisibles outflows	57.2	end Dec.	14.9
Net transfers	-1.6	No. months of import cover	1.8
Current account balance	2.9	Aid given	1.77
– as % of GDP	1.7	– as % of GDP	1.04

Family life

No. of households	2.3m	Divorces per 1,000 pop.	2.5
Av. no. per household	2.2	Cost of living, Dec. 1997	
Marriages per 1,000 pop.	6.8	New York = 100	104

EGYPT

Area	1,000,250 sq km	Currency	Egyptian pound (£E)
Capital	Cairo		

People

Population	63.3m	Life expectancy: men	64.7 yrs
Pop. per sq km	63	women	67.3 yrs
Av. ann. growth		Adult literacy	50.5%
in pop. 1990–2000	1.91%	Fertility rate (per woman)	3.4
Pop. under 15	38.0%	Urban population	45%
Pop. over 65	4.2%		*per 1,000 pop.*
No. of men per 100 women	103.1	Crude birth rate	26.1
Human Development Index	61.4	Crude death rate	7

The economy

GDP	£E228bn	GDP per head	$1,080
GDP	$64bn	GDP per head in purchasing	
Av. ann. growth in real		power parity (USA=100)	10
GDP 1990–96	3.7%		

Origins of GDP[a]		Components of GDP[a]	
	% of total		*% of total*
Agriculture	16.6	Private consumption	71.2
Industry, of which:	33.8	Public consumption	11.2
manufacturing	...	Investment	21.9
Services	49.6	Exports	27.7
		Imports	-32.0

Structure of employment[b]

	% of total		*% of labour force*
Agriculture	34	Unemployed 1995	11.3
Industry	22	Av. ann. rate 1990–95	10.1
Services	44		

Energy

	m TCE		
Total output	86.314	% output exported	42.4
Total consumption	45.994	% consumption imported	3.0
Consumption per head,			
kg coal equivalent	741		

Inflation and finance

		av. ann. increase 1989–96	
Consumer price			
inflation 1997	4.6%	Narrow money (M1)	10.1%
Av. ann. inflation 1990–97	12.1%	Broad money	16.1%
Deposit rate, 1997	9.8%		

Exchange rates

	end 1997		*December 1997*
£E per $	3.39	Effective rates	*1990 = 100*
£E per SDR	4.57	– nominal	...
£E per Ecu	3.73	– real	...

Principal exports[a]

	$m fob		$m fob
Petroleum & products	2,226	Other agric. products	230
Cotton yarn & textiles	574	Raw cotton	91
Industrial goods	371	Total incl. others	**4,593**

Main export destinations

	% of total		% of total
Italy	20.1	Germany	5.0
United States	12.4	France	4.0
United Kingdom	7.7	Turkey	3.7

Principal imports[a]

	$m cif		$m cif
Machinery & transport		Chemicals & rubber	2,021
equipment	3,313	Base metals & manufactures	1,452
Agric. products &		Wood, paper & textiles	1,374
foodstuffs	2,887	Total incl. others	**13,826**

Main origins of imports

	% of total		% of total
United States	17.7	France	8.0
Germany	9.6	Japan	4.5
Italy	8.1	United Kingdom	3.8

Balance of payments, reserves and debt, $bn

Visible exports fob	4.8	Overall balance	-1.7
Visible imports fob	-13.2	Change in reserves	1.2
Trade balance	-8.4	Level of reserves	
Invisibles inflows	11.2	end Dec.	18.3
Invisibles outflows	-6.6	No. months of import cover	11.1
Net transfers	3.7	Foreign debt	31.4
Current account balance	-0.2	– as % of GDP	49.1
– as % of GDP	-0.3	Debt service paid	2.3
Capital balance	-1.5	Debt service ratio	11.6

Family life

No. of households	9.7m	Divorces per 1,000 pop.	1.6
Av. no. per household	4.9	Cost of living, Dec. 1997	
Marriages per 1,000 pop.	9.2	New York = 100	85

a Year ending June 30, 1996.
b 1995

FINLAND

Area	338,145 sq km	Currency	Markka (Fmk)
Capital	Helsinki		

People

Population	5.1m	Life expectancy: men	73.0 yrs
Pop. per sq km	15	women	80.1 yrs
Av. ann. growth		Adult literacy	99.0%
in pop. 1990–2000	0.38%	Fertility rate (per woman)	1.8
Pop. under 15	19.0%	Urban population	63%
Pop. over 65	14.1%		per 1,000 pop.
No. of men per 100 women	95.1	Crude birth rate	12.0
Human Development Index	94.0	Crude death rate	10

The economy

GDP	Fmk569bn	GDP per head	$23,230
GDP	$119bn	GDP per head in purchasing	
Av. ann. growth in real		power parity (USA=100)	66
GDP 1990–96	0.3%		

Origins of GDP		Components of GDP	
	% of total		% of total
Agriculture	5.0	Private consumption	50.9
Industry, of which:	33.1	Public consumption	20.8
manufacturing	25.1	Investment	20.8
Services	61.9	Exports	35.2
		Imports	-27.8

Structure of employment

	% of total		% of labour force
Agriculture	7	Unemployed 1996	16.1
Industry	27	Av. ann. rate 1990–96	13.3
Services	66		

Energy

	m TCE		
Total output	11.630	% output exported[a]	48.5
Total consumption	36.787	% consumption imported[a]	74.2
Consumption per head,			
kg coal equivalent	7,203		

Inflation and finance

Consumer price		av. ann. increase 1992–96	
inflation 1997	1.2%	Narrow money (M1)	9.4%
Av. ann. inflation 1990–97	2.3%	Broad money	1.0%
Money market rate, 1997	3.23%		

Exchange rates

	end 1997		December 1997
Fmk per $	5.42	Effective rates	1990 = 100
Fmk per SDR	7.31	– nominal	80.9
Fmk per Ecu	5.96	– real	63.9

Principal exports

	$bn fob		$bn fob
Metals & engineering		Chemicals	3.9
equipment	16.3	Wood & products	2.7
Paper & products	9.4	Total incl. others	**40.3**

Main export destinations

	% of total		% of total
Germany	12.1	United States	7.9
Sweden	10.7	Russia	6.1
United Kingdom	10.2	EU15	54.5

Principal imports

	$bn cif		$bn cif
Raw materials	15.4	Energy & products	2.7
Consumer goods	6.5		
Capital goods	4.6	Total incl. others	**30.7**

Main origins of imports

	% of total		% of total
Germany	15.1	Russia	7.3
Sweden	11.9	United States	7.3
United Kingdom	8.8	EU15	60.3

Balance of payments, reserves and aid, $bn

Visible exports fob	40.5	Capital balance	-8.0
Visible imports fob	-29.5	Overall balance	-3.0
Trade balance	11.1	Change in reserves	-3.2
Invisibles inflows	10.1	Level of reserves	
Invisibles outflows	-15.3	end Dec.	7.5
Net transfers	-1.1	No. months of import cover	2.0
Current account balance	4.8	Aid given	0.41
– as % of GDP	4.0	– as % of GDP	0.34

Family life

No. of households	2.1m	Divorces per 1,000 pop.	2.7
Av. no. per household	2.4	Cost of living, Dec. 1997	
Marriages per 1,000 pop.	4.6	New York = 100	94

a Energy trade data are distorted by transitory and oil refinery activities.

FRANCE

Area	543,965 sq km	Currency	Franc (FFr)
Capital	Paris		

People

Population	58.3m	Life expectancy: men	74.6 yrs
Pop. per sq km	106	women	82.9 yrs
Av. ann. growth		Adult literacy	99.0%
in pop. 1990–2000	0.41%	Fertility rate (per woman)	1.6
Pop. under 15	19.4%	Urban population	73%
Pop. over 65	15.2%		per 1,000 pop.
No. of men per 100 women	95.0	Crude birth rate	11.6
Human Development Index	94.6	Crude death rate	9

The economy

GDP	FFr7,870bn	GDP per head	$26,290
GDP	$1,534bn	GDP per head in purchasing	
Av. ann. growth in real		power parity (USA=100)	78
GDP, 1990–96	1.1%		

Origins of GDP		Components of GDP	
	% of total		% of total
Agriculture	2.5	Private consumption	60.7
Industry, of which:	23.5	Public consumption	19.6
manufacturing	…	Investment	17.1
Services	74.0	Exports	24.0
		Imports	-21.4

Structure of employment[a]

	% of total		% of labour force
Agriculture	5	Unemployed 1996	12.4
Industry	27	Av. ann. rate 1990–96	10.9
Services	68		

Energy

	m TCE		
Total output	160.032	% output exported	16.9
Total consumption	308.633	% consumption imported	62.8
Consumption per head,			
kg coal equivalent	5,309		

Inflation and finance

Consumer price		av. ann. increase 1989–96	
inflation 1997	1.2%	Narrow money (M1)	2.1%
Av. ann. inflation 1990–97	2.2%	Broad money	4.2%
Money market rate, 1997	3.24%		

Exchange rates

	end 1997		December 1997
FFr per $	5.99	Effective rates	1990 = 100
FFr per SDR	8.08	– nominal	105.5
FFr per Ecu	6.61	– real	91.6

Principal exports

	$bn fob		$bn fob
Capital equipment	79.7	Motor vehicles & other	
Non-durable consumer		transport equipment	38.5
goods	44.5	Steel & other metals	24.0
Chemicals	43.8		
Agric. products & foodstuffs	42.6	Total incl. others	**290.9**

Main export destinations

	% of total		% of total
Germany	17.1	Spain	7.8
United Kingdom	9.3	United States	6.1
Italy	9.2	Netherlands	4.5
Belgium/Luxembourg	8.4	EU15	62.9

Principal imports

	$bn cif		$bn cif
Capital equipment	69.0	Agric. products	
Chemicals	43.4	& foodstuffs	31.8
Non-durable consumer		Steel & other metals	23.4
goods	43.1	Energy products	22.2
Motor vehicles & other			
transport equipment	32.5	Total incl. others	**275.6**

Main origins of imports

	% of total		% of total
Germany	17.4	United States	7.9
Italy	10.1	Spain	7.0
Belgium/Luxembourg	8.4	Netherlands	5.2
United Kingdom	8.4	EU15	63.0

Balance of payments, reserves and aid, $bn

Visible exports fob	281.8	Capital balance	-21.1
Visible imports fob	-266.9	Overall balance	0.2
Trade balance	14.9	Change in reserves	-1.5
Invisibles inflows	131.1	Level of reserves	
Invisibles outflows	-117.5	end Dec.	57.0
Net transfers	-7.9	No. months of import cover	1.8
Current account balance	20.6	Aid given[b]	7.5
– as % of GDP	1.3	– as % of GDP	0.48

Family life

No. of households	22.8m	Divorces per 1,000 pop.	2.0
Av. no. per household	2.5	Cost of living, Dec. 1997	
Marriages per 1,000 pop.	4.4	New York = 100	112

a 1994
b Including aid to French overseas territories.

GERMANY

Area	357,868 sq km	Currency	Deutschemark (DM)
Capital	Berlin		

People

Population	81.9m	Life expectancy: men		73.4 yrs
Pop. per sq km	230		women	79.9 yrs
Av. ann. growth		Adult literacy		99.0%
in pop. 1990–2000	0.41%	Fertility rate (per woman)		1.3
Pop. under 15	16.0%	Urban population		87%
Pop. over 65	15.2%			per 1,000 pop.
No. of men per 100 women	95.9	Crude birth rate		9.3
Human Development Index	92.4	Crude death rate		11

The economy

GDP	DM3,540bn	GDP per head	$28,860
GDP	$2,365bn	GDP per head in purchasing	
Av. ann. growth in real		power parity (USA=100)	77
GDP 1990–96[a]	2.8%		

Origins of GNP

	% of total
Agriculture	1.0
Industry, of which:	32.3
manufacturing	…
Services	66.7

Components of GNP

	% of total
Private consumption	57.6
Public consumption	19.7
Investment	21.3
Exports	24.2
Imports	-22.9

Structure of employment

	% of total		% of labour force
Agriculture	3	Unemployed 1996	8.8
Industry	35	Av. ann. rate 1991–96	9.9
Services	62		

Energy

	m TCE		
Total output	199.956	% output exported	14.4
Total consumption	461.018	% consumption imported	66.3
Consumption per head,			
kg coal equivalent	5,650		

Inflation and finance

Consumer price		av. ann. increase 1989–96	
inflation 1997	1.8%	Narrow money (M1)	10.1%
Av. ann. inflation 1990–97	2.5%	Broad money	7.9%
Money market rate, 1997	3.2%		

Exchange rates

	end 1997		December 1997
DM per $	1.79	Effective rates	1990 = 100
DM per SDR	2.42	– nominal	103.2
DM per Ecu	1.97	– real	111.9

Principal exports

	$bn fob		*$bn fob*
Machinery	162.2	Textiles & clothing	21.0
Road vehicles	84.4	Iron & steel	15.3
Chemicals	67.5		
Food, drink & tobacco	24.4	Total incl. others	**519.4**

Main export destinations

	% of total		*% of total*
France	10.9	Italy	7.4
United Kingdom	8.0	Netherlands	7.4
United States	7.8	EU15	56.7

Principal imports

	$bn cif		*$bn cif*
Machinery	99.2	Food, drink & tobacco	40.1
Road vehicles	45.4	Chemicals	39.5
Textiles & clothing	40.5	Total incl. others	**448.2**

Main origins of imports

	% of total		*% of total*
France	10.6	United States	7.3
Netherlands	8.6	United Kingdom	6.8
Italy	8.2	EU15	55.1

Balance of payments, reserves and aid, $bn

Visible exports fob	519.4	Capital balance	14.2
Visible imports fob	-448.2	Overall balance	-1.2
Trade balance	71.2	Change in reserves	-3.5
Invisibles inflows	161.4	Level of reserves	
Invisibles outflows	-209.3	end Dec.	118.3
Net transfers	-36.4	No. months of import cover	2.1
Current account balance	-13.1	Aid given	7.6
– as % of GDP	-0.6	– as % of GDP	0.33

Family life

No. of households	35.1m	Divorces per 1,000 pop.	1.9
Av. no. per household	2.3	Cost of living, Dec. 1997	
Marriages per 1,000 pop.	5.3	New York = 100	92

GREECE

Area	131,957 sq km	Currency	Drachma (Dr)
Capital	Athens		

People

Population	10.5m	Life expectancy: men	75.5 yrs
Pop. per sq km	79	women	80.6 yrs
Av. ann. growth		Adult literacy	96.7%
in pop. 1990–2000	0.36%	Fertility rate (per woman)	1.4
Pop. under 15	16.8%	Urban population	65%
Pop. over 65	15.9%		per 1,000 pop.
No. of men per 100 women	96.9	Crude birth rate	10.0
Human Development Index	92.3	Crude death rate	10

The economy

GDP	Dr29,861bn	GDP per head	$11,440
GDP	$120bn	GDP per head in purchasing	
Av. ann. growth in real		power parity (USA=100)	46
GDP 1990–96	1.6%		

Origins of GDP		Components of GDP	
	% of total		% of total
Agriculture	11.2	Private consumption	74.0
Industry, of which:	25.3	Public consumption	14.3
manufacturing	...	Investment	21.3
Services	63.5	Exports	15.9
		Imports	-26.4

Structure of employment[a]

	% of total		% of labour force
Agriculture	20	Unemployed 1995	10.0
Industry	23	Av. ann. rate 1990–95	8.8
Services	57		

Energy

	m TCE		
Total output	11.917	% output exported[b]	40.8
Total consumption	34.382	% consumption imported[b]	91.9
Consumption per head,			
kg coal equivalent	3,289		

Inflation and finance

Consumer price		av. ann. increase 1989–96	
inflation 1997	5.5%	Narrow money (M1)	17.3%
Av. ann. inflation 1990–97	12.8%	Broad money	13.7%
Deposit rate, 1997	10.11%		

Exchange rates

	end 1997		December 1997
Dr per $	282.6	Effective rates	1990 = 100
Dr per SDR	381.3	– nominal	65.5
Dr per Ecu	310.9	– real	111.2

Principal exports

	$bn fob		$bn fob
Manufactured products	3.1	Minerals	0.2
Food & beverages	1.3		
Petroleum products	0.5		
Raw materials & industrial supplies	0.3	Total incl. others	**10.9**

Main export destinations

	% of total		% of total
Germany	27.7	France	6.6
United States	17.7	United Kingdom	6.6
Italy	8.9	EU15	56.5

Principal imports

	$bn cif		$bn cif
Manufactured consumer goods	8.9	Petroleum	1.2
		Chemicals & products	1.1
Capital goods	5.7	Iron & steel	0.8
Foodstuffs	3.2	Total incl. others	**25.5**

Main origins of imports

	% of total		% of total
Germany	17.9	France	8.2
Italy	15.7	United Kingdom	6.9
United States	9.0	EU15	64.5

Balance of payments, reserves and debt, $bn

Visible exports fob	5.9	Overall balance	4.2
Visible imports fob	-21.4	Change in reserves	2.7
Trade balance	-15.5	Level of reserves	
Invisibles inflows	10.5	end Dec.	18.8
Invisibles outflows	-7.6	No. months of import cover	7.8
Net transfers	8.0	Aid given	0.18
Current account balance	-4.6	– as % of GDP	0.16
– as % of GDP	-3.8		
Capital balance	8.7		

Family life

No. of households	3.7m	Divorces per 1,000 pop.	0.7
Av. no. per household	2.9	Cost of living, Dec. 1997	
Marriages per 1,000 pop.	6.2	New York = 100	97

a 1995
b Energy trade figures are distorted by transitory and oil refining activities.

HONG KONG

Area	1,075 sq km	Currency	Hong Kong dollar (HK$)
Capital	Victoria		

People

Population	6.2m	Life expectancy: men	76.1 yrs
Pop. per sq km	5,924	women	81.8 yrs
Av. ann. growth		Adult literacy	92.3%
in pop. 1990–2000	1.11%	Fertility rate (per woman)	1.3
Pop. under 15	19.6%	Urban population	95%
Pop. over 65	9.8%		per 1,000 pop.
No. of men per 100 women	107.6	Crude birth rate	10.6
Human Development Index	91.4	Crude death rate[c]	6.2

The economy

GDP	HK$1,192bn	GDP per head	$24,760
GDP	$153bn	GDP per head in purchasing	
Av. ann. growth in real		power parity (USA=100)	90
GDP 1990–96	5.9%		

Origins of GDP		Components of GDP	
	% of total		% of total
Agriculture	0.1	Private consumption	60.5
Industry, of which:	15.4	Public consumption	8.9
manufacturing	7.2	Investment	32.3
Services	84.5	Exports	141.3
		Imports	-143.0

Structure of employment

	% of total		% of labour force
Agriculture	0	Unemployed 1996	2.8
Industry	26	Av. ann. rate 1990–96	2.1
Services	74		

Energy

	m TCE		
Total output	nil	% output exported	nil
Total consumption	12.645	% consumption imported	245.3
Consumption per head,			
kg coal equivalent	2,065		

Inflation and finance

Consumer price		av. ann. increase 1992–96	
inflation 1997	5.7%	Narrow money (M1)	11.8%
Av. ann. inflation 1990–97	8.2%	Broad money	11.5%
Treasury bill rate, 1997	4.5%		

Exchange rates

	end 1997		December 1997
HK$ per $	7.75	Effective rates	1990 = 100
HK$ per SDR	10.46	– nominal	…
HK$ per Ecu	8.53	– real	…

Principal exports[a]

	$bn fob		$bn fob
Clothing	9.0	Watches, clocks &	
Electrical machinery		photographic equipment	1.5
& apparatus	3.9		
Textiles	1.8	Total incl. others	**27.4**

Main export destinations[b]

	% of total		% of total
China	34.3	Germany	4.2
United States	21.2	United Kingdom	3.3
Japan	6.5	Singapore	2.7

Principal imports

	$bn cif		$bn cif
Consumer goods	74.0	Agric. products & foodstuffs	8.4
Raw materials & semi-		Fuels	4.2
manufactured products	70.0		
Capital goods	41.9	Total incl. others	**198.9**

Main origins of imports

	% of total		% of total
China	37.1	United States	7.9
Japan	13.6	Singapore	5.3
Taiwan	8.0	South Korea	4.8

Balance of payments, reserves and debt, $bn

Visible exports fob	180.6	Overall balance	...
Visible imports cif	-198.9	Change in reserves	8.4
Trade balance	-18.3	Level of reserves	
Invisibles inflows	37.3	end Dec.	63.8
Invisibles outflows	-21.5	No. months of import cover	3.2
Net transfers	...	Foreign debt	18.1
Current account balance	-2.6	– as % of GDP	13.4
– as % of GDP	-1.7	Debt service paid	3.1
Capital balance	...	Debt service ratio	1.1

Family life

No. of households	1.8m	Divorces per 1,000 pop.	1.0
Av. no. per household	3.3	Cost of living, Dec. 1997	
Marriages per 1,000 pop.	5.9	New York = 100	122

a Domestic.
b Including re-exports.
c Estimate.
Note: Hong Kong became part of China from July 1 1997.

HUNGARY

Area	93,030 sq km	Currency	Forint (Ft)
Capital	Budapest		

People

Population	10.0m	Life expectancy: men	64.5 yrs
Pop. per sq km	108	women	73.8 yrs
Av. ann. growth		Adult literacy	99.0%
in pop. 1990–2000	-0.55%	Fertility rate (per woman)	1.4
Pop. under 15	18.0%	Urban population	65%
Pop. over 65	14.0%		per 1,000 pop.
No. of men per 100 women	91.6	Crude birth rate	10.2
Human Development Index	85.7	Crude death rate	15

The economy

GDP	Ft5,562bn	GDP per head	$4,410
GDP	$44bn	GDP per head in purchasing	
Av. ann. growth in real		power parity (USA=100)	25
GDP 1990–96	-0.4%		

Origins of GDP[a]		Components of GDP[a]	
	% of total		% of total
Agriculture	7.2	Private consumption	65.9
Industry, of which:	31.8	Public consumption	11.9
manufacturing	...	Investment	27.3
Services	61.0	Exports	38.5
		Imports	-43.6

Structure of employment[b]

	% of total		% of labour force
Agriculture	13	Unemployed 1996	9.9
Industry	35	Av. ann. rate 1992–96	10.5
Services	52		

Energy

	m TCE		
Total output	18.307	% output exported	13.0
Total consumption	33.707	% consumption imported	60.4
Consumption per head,			
kg coal equivalent	3,335		

Inflation and finance

Consumer price		av. ann. increase 1989–95	
inflation 1997	18.3%	Narrow money (M1)	19.2%
Av. ann. inflation 1990–97	24.6%	Broad money	21.4%

Exchange rates

	end 1997		December 1997
Ft per $	203.5	Effective rates	1990 = 100
Ft per SDR	274.6	– nominal	42.3
Ft per Ecu	223.9	– real	

Principal exports

	$bn fob		$bn fob
Machinery & transport		Food & beverages	2.0
equipment	4.8	Raw materials	0.6
Other manufactures	5.3	Total incl. others	**13.1**

Main export destinations

	% of total		% of total
Germany	29.0	CIS	8.7
Austria	10.6	Italy	8.0

Principal imports

	$bn cif		$bn cif
Machinery & transport		Fuels	1.9
equipment	5.9	Food & food products	0.7
Other manufactures	7.1	Total incl. others	**16.2**

Main origins of imports

	% of total		% of total
Germany	23.6	Austria	9.5
CIS	14.8	Italy	8.1

Balance of payments, reserves and debt, $bn

Visible exports fob	14.2	Overall balance	-1.2
Visible imports fob	-16.8	Change in reserves	-2.3
Trade balance	-2.7	Level of reserves	
Invisibles inflows	6.2	end Dec.	9.8
Invisibles outflows	-6.2	No. months of import cover	5.1
Net transfers	0.9	Foreign debt	27.0
Current account balance	-1.7	– as % of GDP	61.4
– as % of GDP	-3.8	Debt service paid	8.4
Capital balance	-1.4	Debt service ratio	41.0

Family life

No. of households	3.9m	Divorces per 1,000 pop.	2.3
Av. no. per household	2.6	Cost of living, Dec. 1997	
Marriages per 1,000 pop.	5.3	New York = 100	49

a 1995
b 1992

INDIA

Area	3,287,263 sq km	Currency	Indian rupee (Rs)
Capital	New Delhi		

People

Population	944.6m	Life expectancy: men	62.1 yrs
Pop. per sq km	287	women	62.7 yrs
Av. ann. growth		Adult literacy	51.2%
in pop. 1990–2000	1.69%	Fertility rate (per woman)	3.1
Pop. under 15	35.0%	Urban population	27%
Pop. over 65	4.6%		*per 1,000 pop.*
No. of men per 100 women	106.8	Crude birth rate	25.2
Human Development Index	44.6	Crude death rate	9

The economy

GDP	Rs12,770bn	GDP per head	$380
GDP	$358bn	GDP per head in purchasing	
Av. ann. growth in real		power parity (USA=100)	6
GDP 1990–96	5.8%		

Origins of GDP[a]		**Components of GDP**[a]	
	% of total		*% of total*
Agriculture	28.8	Private consumption	62.0
Industry, of which:	29.2	Public consumption	9.9
manufacturing	...	Investment	26.0
Services	41.2	Exports	8.9
		Imports	-6.8

Structure of employment[b]

	% of total		*% of labour force*
Agriculture	64	Unemployed 1996	...
Industry	16	Av. ann. rate 1990–96	...
Services	20		

Energy

	m TCE		
Total output	310.950	% output exported	nil
Total consumption	358.722	% consumption imported	20.6
Consumption per head,			
kg coal equivalent	386		

Inflation and finance

Consumer price		*av. ann. increase 1989–96*	
inflation 1996	9.0%	Narrow money (M1)	12.4%
Av. ann. inflation 1990–97	9.2%	Broad money	16.2%
Money market rate, 1997	5.29%		

Exchange rates

	end 1997		*December 1997*
Rs per $	39.28	Effective rates	*1990 = 100*
Rs per SDR	53.00	– nominal	...
Rs per Ecu	43.21	– real	...

Principal exports[a]

	$bn fob		$bn fob
Gems & jewellery	5.3	Textiles	3.7
Engineering goods	4.1		
Garments	3.8	Total incl. others	**30.7**

Main export destinations[a]

	% of total		% of total
United States	17.4	United Kingdom	6.3
Japan	7.0	Germany	6.2

Principal imports[a]

	$bn cif		$bn cif
Capital goods	8.2	Gems	1.9
Crude oil & products	7.2	Total incl. others	**34.8**

Main origins of imports[a]

	% of total		% of total
United States	10.5	Japan	6.7
Germany	8.6	United Kingdom	5.2

Balance of payments, reserves and debt, $bn

Visible exports fob	33.7	Overall balance	4.0
Visible imports fob	-43.1	Change in reserves	2.0
Trade balance	-9.5	Level of reserves	
Invisibles inflows	9.1	end Dec.	24.9
Invisibles outflows	-15.4	No. months of import cover	5.1
Net transfers	10.4	Foreign debt	89.8
Current account balance	-5.3	– as % of GDP	25.1
– as % of GDP	-1.5	Debt service paid	12.7
Capital balance	10.9	Debt service ratio	24.1

Family life

No. of households	185m	Divorces per 1,000 pop.	…
Av. no. per household	4.9	Cost of living, Dec. 1997	
Marriages per 1,000 pop.	…	New York = 100	45

a Year ending March 31, 1996.
b 1990

INDONESIA

Area	1,919,445 sq km	Currency	Rupiah (Rp)
Capital	Jakarta		

People

Population	200.5m	Life expectancy: men	63.3 yrs
Pop. per sq km	105	women	67.0 yrs
Av. ann. growth		Adult literacy	83.2%
in pop. 1990–2000	1.51%	Fertility rate (per woman)	2.6
Pop. under 15	32.9%	Urban population	35%
Pop. over 65	4.3%		*per 1,000 pop.*
No. of men per 100 women	99.5	Crude birth rate	23.1
Human Development Index	66.8	Crude death rate	8

The economy

GDP	Rp532,631bn	GDP per head	$1,080
GDP	$213bn	GDP per head in purchasing	
Av. ann. growth in real		power parity (USA=100)	12
GDP 1990–96	7.7%		

Origins of GDP		Components of GDP	
	% of total		*% of total*
Agriculture	16.3	Private consumption	61.7
Industry, of which:	41.6	Public consumption	7.7
manufacturing	24.6	Investment	33.6
Services	42.1	Exports	26.6
		Imports	-29.7

Structure of employment

	% of total		*% of total*
Agriculture	44	Unemployed 1996	4.0
Industry	18	Av. ann. rate 1990–96	…
Services	38		

Energy

	m TCE		
Total output	266.739	% output exported	50.9
Total consumption	109.650	% consumption imported	21.4
Consumption per head,			
kg coal equivalent	555		

Inflation and finance

Consumer price		*av. ann. increase 1993–96*	
inflation 1997	6.6%	Narrow money (M1)	17.1%
Av. ann. inflation 1990–97	8.4%	Broad money	23.6%
Money market rate, 1997	27.82%		

Exchange rates

	end 1997		*December 1997*
Rp per $	4,650	Effective rates	*1990 = 100*
Rp per SDR	6,274	– nominal	…
Rp per Ecu	5,115	– real	…

Principal exports

	$bn fob		$bn fob
Petroleum & products	7.2	Plywood	3.6
Textiles & clothing	6.6	Rubber & products	2.2
Natural gas	4.5	Total incl. others	**49.8**

Main export destinations

	% of total		% of total
Japan	25.9	South Korea	6.6
United States	13.6	China	4.1
Singapore	7.8	Netherlands	3.3

Principal imports

	$bn cif		$bn cif
Machinery & transport		Food, drink & tobacco	4.2
equipment	17.5	Fuels	3.7
Other manufactures	6.6	Raw materials	3.5
Chemicals	6.0	Total incl. others	**42.9**

Main origins of imports

	% of total		% of total
Japan	19.8	Singapore	6.7
United States	11.7	Australia	5.9
Germany	7.0	South Korea	5.6

Balance of payments[a], reserves and debt, $bn

Visible exports fob	45.5	Overall balance	1.6
Visible imports fob	-39.8	Change in reserves	4.5
Trade balance	5.7	Level of reserves	
Invisibles inflows	7.0	end Dec.	19.4
Invisibles outflows	-20.6	No. months of import cover	3.5
Net transfers	0.8	Foreign debt	129.0
Current account balance	-7.0	– as % of GDP	60.6
– as % of GDP	-3.7	Debt service paid	21.5
Capital balance	10.4	Debt service ratio	36.8

Family life

No. of households	43.1m	Divorces per 1,000 pop.	0.8
Av. no. per household	4.5	Cost of living, Dec. 1997	
Marriages per 1,000 pop.	7.4	New York = 100	72

a 1995

IRAN

Area	1,648,000 sq km	Currency	Rial (IR)
Capital	Tehran		

People

Population	70.0m	Life expectancy: men	68.5 yrs
Pop. per sq km	42	women	70.0 yrs
Av. ann. growth		Adult literacy	68.6%
in pop. 1990–2000	2.55%	Fertility rate (per woman)	4.8
Pop. under 15	44.4%	Urban population	59%
Pop. over 65	3.8%		per 1,000 pop.
No. of men per 100 women	103.5	Crude birth rate	34.0
Human Development Index	78.0	Crude death rate	6

The economy

GDP	IR232,742bn	GDP per head	$1,302
GDP	$82bn	GDP per head in purchasing	
Av. ann. growth in real		power parity (USA=100)	17
GDP 1990–96	4.2%		

Origins of GDP[a]		Components of GDP[a]	
	% of total		% of total
Agriculture	25.2	Private consumption	53.0
Industry, of which:	34.4	Public consumption	12.7
manufacturing	...	Investment	26.7
Services	40.4	Exports	19.9
		Imports	-12.5

Structure of employment[b]

	% of total		% of labour force
Agriculture	39	Unemployed 1996	...
Industry	23	Av. ann. rate 1990–96	...
Services	38		

Energy

	m TCE		
Total output	323.134	% output exported	59.5
Total consumption	130.049	% consumption imported	5.5
Consumption per head,			
kg coal equivalent	1,902		

Inflation and finance

Consumer price		av. ann. increase 1989–96	
inflation 1997	17.2%	Narrow money (M1)	26.2%
Av. ann. inflation 1990–97	24.3%	Broad money	27.0%

Exchange rates

	end 1997		December 1997
IR per $	1,754	Effective rates	1990 = 100
IR per SDR	2,367	– nominal	...
IR per Ecu	1,929	– real	...

Principal exports[a]

	$bn fob		$bn fob
Oil & gas	15.1	Fruit	0.5
Carpets	0.9	Total incl. others	**18.4**

Main export destinations

	% of total		% of total
Japan	13.5	France	5.3
Italy	8.1	Spain	4.0
South Korea	6.8	Netherlands	3.1
South Africa	6.1	Germany	3.0

Principal imports[c]

	$bn cif		$bn cif
Raw materials & intermediate goods	12.6	Consumer goods	2.2
Capital goods	5.1	Total incl. others	**20.0**

Main origins of imports

	% of total		% of total
Germany	14.9	France	5.1
United Arab Emirates	8.3	United Kingdom	4.8
Japan	6.0	Italy	4.7
Argentina	5.8	Netherlands	2.6

Balance of payments[d], reserves and debt, $bn

Visible exports fob	22.4	Overall balance	2.4
Visible imports fob	-15.0	Change in reserves	...
Trade balance	7.4	Level of reserves	
Invisibles inflows	1.3	end Dec.	...
Invisibles outflows	-4.0	No. months of import cover	...
Net transfers	0.5	Foreign debt	21.2
Current account balance	5.2	– as % of GDP[e]	25.9
– as % of GDP	3.9	Debt service paid[f]	3.4
Capital balance	-5.5	Debt service ratio[f]	29.3

Family life

No. of households	10.8m	Divorces per 1,000 pop.	0.5
Av. no. per household	5.2	Cost of living, Dec. 1997	
Marriages per 1,000 pop.	7.4	New York = 100	47

a Iranian year ending March 20, 1996.
b 1990
c Iranian year ending March 20, 1994.
d Iranian year ending March 20, 1997.
e 1992
f 1995

IRAQ

Area	438,317 sq km	Currency	Iraqi dinar (ID)
Capital	Baghdad		

People

Population	20.6m	Life expectancy: men	60.9 yrs
Pop. per sq km	47	women	63.9 yrs
Av. ann. growth		Adult literacy	56.8%
in pop. 1990–2000	2.46%	Fertility rate (per woman)	5.3
Pop. under 15	42.8%	Urban population	75%
Pop. over 65	3.0%		per 1,000 pop.
No. of men per 100 women	103.6	Crude birth rate	36.4
Human Development Index	53.1	Crude death rate	9

The economy

GDP	ID73bn	GDP per head	$1,095
GDP	$23bn	GDP per head in purchasing	
Av. ann. growth in real		power parity (USA=100)	4
GDP 1985–95	-9.3%		

Origins of GDP[a]		Components of GDP[a]	
	% of total		% of total
Agriculture	5.1	Private consumption	56.1
Industry, of which:	72.9	Public consumption	32.9
manufacturing	11.6	Investment	8.1
Services	22.0	Exports	26.7
		Imports	-23.8

Structure of employment

	% of total		% of labour force
Agriculture	…	Unemployed 1996	…
Industry	…	Av. ann. rate 1990–96	…
Services	…		

Energy

	m TCE		
Total output	58.207	% output exported	10.0
Total consumption	36.782	% consumption imported	nil
Consumption per head,			
kg coal equivalent	1,830		

Inflation and finance

			av. ann. increase 1989–96
Consumer price			
inflation 1996	57%	Narrow money (M1)	…
Av. ann. inflation 1990–96	56.0%	Broad money	…

Exchange rates

	end 1997		December 1997
ID per $	0.31	Effective rates	1990 = 100
ID per SDR	0.42	– nominal	208.3
ID per Ecu	0.34	– real	…

Principal exports[ab]

	$bn fob		$bn fob
Crude oil	14.5	Total incl. others	**14.6**

Main export destinations[bc]

	% of total		% of total
Jordan	83.9	EU15	7.6
Greece	5.1		

Principal imports[ab]

	$bn cif		$bn cif
Civilian goods	5.0		
Military goods	2.7	Total incl. others	**7.7**

Main origins of imports[bc]

	% of total		% of total
Jordan	48.7	Switzerland	7.6
Hungary	14.6	Germany	2.1

Balance of payments[b], reserves and debt, $bn

Visible exports fob	1.5	Overall balance	...
Visible imports fob	-1.8	Change in reserves	...
Trade balance	-0.3	Level of reserves	
Invisibles inflows	...	end Dec.	...
Invisibles outflows	...	No. months of import cover	...
Net transfers	...	Foreign debt[c]	107.2
Current account balance	-0.3	– as % of GDP[c]	638.1
– as % of GDP	...	Debt service	...
Capital balance	...	Debt service ratio	18.0

Family life

No. of households	2.1m	Divorces per 1,000 pop.	...
Av. no. per household	7.1	Cost of living, Dec. 1997	
Marriages per 1,000 pop.	...	New York = 100	...

a   1989
b   Trade, balance of payments and debt data for Iraq are estimates based on limited
    and inconsistent information.
c   1995

IRELAND

Area	70,282 sq km	Currency	Punt (I£)
Capital	Dublin		

People

Population	3.6m	Life expectancy: men	74.0 yrs
Pop. per sq km	51	women	79.4 yrs
Av. ann. growth		Adult literacy	99.0%
in pop. 1990–2000	0.2%	Fertility rate (per woman)	1.8
Pop. under 15	24.1%	Urban population	58%
Pop. over 65	11.3%		*per 1,000 pop.*
No. of men per 100 women	99.7	Crude birth rate	13.0
Human Development Index	92.9	Crude death rate	9

The economy

GDP	I£42bn	GDP per head	$17,450
GDP	$62bn	GDP per head in purchasing	
Av. ann. growth in real		power parity (USA=100)	60
GDP 1990–96	6.1%		

Origins of GDP		Components of GDP	
	% of total		*% of total*
Agriculture	8	Private consumption	55.4
Industry, of which:	38	Public consumption	14.8
manufacturing	…	Investment	18.8
Services	54	Exports	80.3
		Imports	-69.3

Structure of employment

	% of total		*% of labour force*
Agriculture	11	Unemployed 1996	11.9
Industry	27	Av. ann. rate 1990–96	13.9
Services	62		

Energy

	m TCE		
Total output	5.316	% output exported	24.4
Total consumption	15.072	% consumption imported	78.6
Consumption per head,			
kg coal equivalent	4,250		

Inflation and finance

Consumer price		*av. ann. increase 1989–96*	
inflation 1997	1.4%	Narrow money (M1)	10.0%
Av. ann. inflation 1990–97	2.4%	Broad money	12.4%
Treasury bill rate, 1997	6.05%		

Exchange rates

	end 1997		*December 1997*
I£ per $	0.69	Effective rates	*1990 = 100*
I£ per SDR	0.94	– nominal	96.6
I£ per Ecu	0.76	– real	…

Principal exports

	$bn fob		$bn fob
Machinery & transport		Agric. products &	
equipment	16.7	foodstuffs	6.6
Chemicals	10.7	Total incl. others	**48.6**

Main export destinations

	% of total		% of total
United Kingdom	24.8	Netherlands	6.8
Germany	12.8	Italy	3.6
United States	9.4	EU15	68.6
France	8.3		

Principal imports

	$bn cif		$bn cif
Machinery & transport		Manufactured goods	3.9
equipment	15.1		
Chemicals	4.4	Total incl. others	**36.1**

Main origins of imports

	% of total		% of total
United Kingdom	34.8	France	3.9
United States	15.5	Netherlands	2.9
Germany	6.9	EU15	56.8
Japan	5.4		

Balance of payments, reserves and aid, $bn

Visible exports fob	48.5	Capital balance	-2.1
Visible imports fob	-33.3	Overall balance	-0.1
Trade balance	15.2	Change in reserves	-0.4
Invisibles inflows	11.1	Level of reserves	
Invisibles outflows	-27.1	end Dec.	8.3
Net transfers	2.2	No. months of import cover	1.7
Current account balance	1.4	Aid given	0.18
– as % of GDP	2.3	– as % of GDP	0.31

Family life

No. of households	0.9m	Divorces per 1,000 pop.	…
Av. no. per household	4.1	Cost of living, Dec. 1997	
Marriages per 1,000 pop.	4.5	New York = 100	92

ISRAEL

Area	20,770 sq km	Currency	New Shekel (NIS)
Capital	Jerusalem		

People

Population	5.7m	Life expectancy: men		75.7 yrs
Pop. per sq km	269		women	79.5 yrs
Av. ann. growth		Adult literacy		95.0%
in pop. 1990–2000	2.66%	Fertility rate (per woman)		2.8
Pop. under 15	29.3%	Urban population		91%
Pop. over 65	9.5%			*per 1,000 pop.*
No. of men per 100 women	98.7	Crude birth rate		20.3
Human Development Index	91.3	Crude death rate		6

The economy

GDP	NIS304bn	GDP per head	$15,940
GDP	$90bn	GDP per head in purchasing	
Av. ann. growth in real		power parity (USA=100)	66
GDP 1990–96	6.4%		

Origins of NDP[a]		Components of GDP	
	% of total		*% of total*
Agriculture	2.4	Private consumption	61.8
Industry, of which:	30.4	Public consumption	29.9
manufacturing	21.5	Investment	24.0
Services	67.2	Exports	30.8
		Imports	-46.6

Structure of employment

	% of total		*% of labour force*
Agriculture	3	Unemployed 1996	6.7
Industry	28	Av. ann. rate 1995–96	6.8
Services	69		

Energy

	m TCE		
Total output	0.04	% output exported[b]	10,422.5
Total consumption	18.369	% consumption imported[b]	135.7
Consumption per head,			
kg coal equivalent	3,325		

Inflation and finance

Consumer price		*av. ann. increase 1989–95*	
inflation 1997	9.0%	Narrow money (M1)	23.9%
Av. ann. inflation 1990–97	12.7%	Broad money	21.8%
Treasury bill rate, 1997	13.9%		

Exchange rates

	end 1997		*December 1997*
NIS per $	3.54	Effective rates	*1990 = 100*
NIS per SDR	4.77	– nominal	...
NIS per Ecu	3.89	– real	...

Principal exports

	$bn fob		$bn fob
Metals, machinery & electronics	5.6	Chemicals	2.5
Diamonds	4.1	Total incl. others	**20.6**

Main export destinations

	% of total		% of total
United States	30.8	Belgium/Luxembourg	5.4
Japan	6.9	Germany	5.1
United Kingdom	6.7		

Principal imports

	$bn cif		$bn cif
Diamonds	4.8	Fuel	2.8
Metals, machinery & electronics	3.6	Total incl. others	**31.7**

Main origins of imports

	% of total		% of total
United States	19.9	United Kingdom	8.8
Belgium/Luxembourg	12.2	Italy	7.8
Germany	9.4		

Balance of payments, reserves and debt[c], $bn

Visible exports fob	20.4	Overall balance	3.4
Visible imports fob	-28.4	Change in reserves	3.3
Trade balance	-8.0	Level of reserves	
Invisibles inflows	9.8	end Dec.	11.4
Invisibles outflows	-15.1	No. months of import cover	3.2
Net transfers	6.2	Foreign debt	28.9
Current account balance	-7.1	– as % of GDP	33.4
– as % of GDP	-7.8	Debt service	5.2
Capital balance	8.2	Debt service ratio	8.1

Family life

No. of households	1.4m	Divorces per 1,000 pop.	1.6
Av. no. per household	3.9	Cost of living, Dec. 1997	
Marriages per 1,000 pop.	6.1	New York = 100	101

a   1993
b   Energy trade data are distorted by transitory and oil refining activities.
c   1995

ITALY

Area	301,245 sq km	Currency	Lira (L)
Capital	Rome		

People

Population	57.2m	Life expectancy: men	75.1 yrs
Pop. per sq km	190	women	81.4 yrs
Av. ann. growth		Adult literacy	98.1%
in pop. 1990–2000	0.03%	Fertility rate (per woman)	1.2
Pop. under 15	14.9%	Urban population	67%
Pop. over 65	16.1%		*per 1,000 pop.*
No. of men per 100 women	94.6	Crude birth rate	9.1
Human Development Index	92.1	Crude death rate	10

The economy

GDP	L1,873,500bn	GDP per head	$19,930
GDP	$1,141bn	GDP per head in purchasing	
Av. ann. growth in real		power parity (USA=100)	72
GDP 1990–96	1.0%		

Origins of GDP		**Components of GDP**	
	% of total		*% of total*
Agriculture	3.4	Private consumption	62.2
Industry, of which:	33.2	Public consumption	16.6
manufacturing	...	Investment	17.1
Services	63.4	Exports	24.1
		Imports	-20.0

Structure of employment[a]

	% of total		*% of labour force*
Agriculture	7	Unemployed 1996	12.1
Industry	41	Av. ann. rate 1993–96	11.5
Services	52		

Energy

	m TCE		
Total output	42.928	% output exported	53.3
Total consumption	235.644	% consumption imported	92.6
Consumption per head,			
kg coal equivalent	4,118		

Inflation and finance

Consumer price		*av. ann. increase 1989–96*	
inflation 1997	2.0%	Narrow money (M1)	5.3%
Av. ann. inflation 1990–97	4.7%	Broad money	5.8%
Money market rate, 1997	6.88%		

Exchange rates

	end 1997		*December 1997*
L per $	1,759	Effective rates	*1990 = 100*
L per SDR	2,374	– nominal	75.9
L per Ecu	1,935	– real	80.7

Principal exports

	$bn fob		$bn fob
Industrial & agricultural		Electrical equipment	23.1
machinery	45.6	Chemicals	20.5
Textiles & clothing	28.4	Motor vehicles	18.4
Metal & metal products	24.9	Total incl. others	**233.8**

Main export destinations

	% of total		% of total
Germany	17.4	United Kingdom	6.5
France	12.5	Spain	4.9
United States	7.3	Switzerland	3.7

Principal imports

	$bn cif		$bn cif
Chemicals	29.3	Industrial & agricultural	
Metals & metal products	22.9	machinery	15.5
Electrical equipment	20.2		
Motor vehicles	20.0	Total incl. others	**193.0**

Main origins of imports

	% of total		% of total
Germany	18.5	Netherlands	6.0
France	13.5	United States	4.9
United Kingdom	6.6		

Balance of payments, reserves and aid, $bn

Visible exports fob	250.8	Capital balance	-7.8
Visible imports fob	-190.0	Overall balance	11.9
Trade balance	60.8	Change in reserves	9.9
Invisibles inflows	110.1	Level of reserves	
Invisibles outflows	-122.6	end Dec.	70.6
Net transfers	-7.3	No. months of import cover	2.7
Current account balance	41.0	Aid given	2.42
– as % of GDP	3.6	– as % of GDP	0.2

Family life

No. of households	22.3m	Divorces per 1,000 pop.	0.4
Av. no. per household	2.6	Cost of living, Dec. 1997	
Marriages per 1,000 pop.	4.9	New York = 100	81

a 1995

JAPAN

Area	377,727 sq km	Currency	Yen (¥)
Capital	Tokyo		

People

Population	125.4m	Life expectancy: men		76.9 yrs
Pop. per sq km	332		women	82.9 yrs
Av. ann. growth		Adult literacy		99.0%
in pop. 1990–2000	0.24%	Fertility rate (per woman)		1.5
Pop. under 15	16.2%	Urban population		78%
Pop. over 65	14.2%			per 1,000 pop.
No. of men per 100 women	96.5	Crude birth rate		10.3
Human Development Index	94.0	Crude death rate		8

The economy

GDP	¥500,356bn	GDP per head	$41,080
GDP	$5,149bn	GDP per head in purchasing	
Av. ann. growth in real		power parity (USA=100)	85
GDP 1990–96	1.4%		

Origins of NDP		**Components of GDP**	
	% of total		*% of total*
Agriculture	1.9	Private consumption	59.8
Industry, of which:	38.0	Public consumption	9.8
manufacturing	24.7	Investment	29.8
Services	60.1	Exports	9.9
		Imports	-9.4

Structure of employment

	% of total		*% of labour force*
Agriculture	5	Unemployed 1996	3.4
Industry	33	Av. ann. rate 1990–96	2.6
Services	62		

Energy

	m TCE		
Total output	132.624	% output exported[a]	10.3
Total consumption	638.454	% consumption imported[a]	87.7
Consumption per head,			
kg coal equivalent	5,105		

Inflation and finance

Consumer price		*av. ann. increase 1989–96*	
inflation 1997	1.7%	Narrow money (M1)	6.7%
Av. ann. inflation 1990–97	1.5%	Broad money	4.0%
Money market rate, 1997	0.48%		

Exchange rates

	end 1997		*December 1997*
¥ per $	129.9	Effective rates	*1990 = 100*
¥ per SDR	175.3	– nominal	119.1
¥ per Ecu	142.9	– real	104.4

Principal exports

	$bn fob		$bn fob
Motor vehicles	50.7	Iron & steel products	15.2
Office machinery	29.3		
Chemicals	28.8		
Scientific & optical equipment	17.4	Total incl. others	**410.9**

Main export destinations

	% of total		% of total
United States	27.2	Hong Kong	6.2
South Korea	7.1	China	5.3
Taiwan	6.3	Singapore	5.1

Principal imports

	$bn cif		$bn cif
Mineral fuels	60.6	Chemicals	23.3
Agric. products & foodstuffs	50.8	Wood	9.6
Textiles	25.6	Total incl. others	**349.1**

Main origins of imports

	% of total		% of total
United States	22.7	Indonesia	4.4
China	11.6	Taiwan	4.3
South Korea	4.6	Australia	4.1

Balance of payments, reserves and aid, $bn

Visible exports fob	400.3	Capital balance	-31.4
Visible imports fob	-316.7	Overall balance	35.1
Trade balance	83.6	Change in reserves	33.0
Invisibles inflows	292.8	Level of reserves	
Invisibles outflows	-301.5	end Dec.	225.6
Net transfers	-9.0	No. months of import cover	4.4
Current account balance	65.9	Aid given	9.44
– as % of GDP	1.3	– as % of GDP	0.2

Family life

No. of households	40.5m	Divorces per 1,000 pop.	1.4
Av. no. per household	3.0	Cost of living, Dec. 1997	
Marriages per 1,000 pop.	6.3	New York = 100	154

a   Energy trade data are distorted by transitory and oil refining activities.

KENYA

Area	582,646 sq km	Currency	Kenyan shilling (KSh)
Capital	Nairobi		

People

Population	27.8m	Life expectancy: men	52.3 yrs
Pop. per sq km	48	women	55.7 yrs
Av. ann. growth		Adult literacy	77.0%
in pop. 1990–2000	2.57%	Fertility rate (per woman)	4.9%
Pop. under 15	46.0%	Urban population	28%
Pop. over 65	2.9%		per 1,000 pop.
No. of men per 100 women	100.4	Crude birth rate	36.9
Human Development Index	46.3	Crude death rate	11

The economy

GDP	KSh518bn	GDP per head	$320
GDP	$8.7bn	GDP per head in purchasing	4
Av. ann. growth in real		power parity (USA=100)	
GDP 1990–96	1.9%		

Origins of GDP		Components of GDP	
	% of total		% of total
Agriculture	30.3	Private consumption	66.6
Industry, of which:	...	Public consumption	16.5
manufacturing	10.4	Investment	21.1
Other	59.3	Exports	33.5
		Imports	-37.7

Structure of employment[a]

	% of total		% of labour force
Agriculture	80	Unemployed 1996	...
Industry	7	Av. ann. rate 1990–96	...
Services	13		

Energy

	m TCE		
Total output	0.739	% output exported[b]	72.4
Total consumption	3.785	% consumption imported[b]	94.1
Consumption per head,			
kg coal equivalent	139		

Inflation and finance

Consumer price		av. ann. increase 1989–96	
inflation 1997	12.0%	Narrow money (M1)	19.4%
Av. ann. inflation 1990–97	19.5%	Broad money	23.9%
Treasury bill rate, 1997	22.87%		

Exchange rates

	end 1997		December 1997
KSh per $	62.68	Effective rates	1990 = 100
KSh per SDR	84.57	– nominal	...
KSh per Ecu	68.95	– real	...

Principal exports

	$m fob		$m fob
Tea	397	Petroleum products	123
Coffee	288		
Horticultural products	239	Total incl. others	**2,080**

Main export destinations

	% of total		% of total
Uganda	16.1	United Kingdom	10.4
Tanzania	12.8	Germany	7.5

Principal imports

	$m cif		$m cif
Industrial machinery	463	Iron & steel	169
Petroleum & products	463		
Motor vehicles & chassis	277	Total incl. others	**2,937**

Main origins of imports

	% of total		% of total
United Kingdom	13.2	South Africa	7.6
United Arab Emirates	8.2	Germany	7.4

Balance of payments, reserves and debt, $bn

Visible exports fob	2.1	Overall balance	0.3
Visible imports fob	-2.6	Change in reserves	0.4
Trade balance	-0.5	Level of reserves	
Invisibles inflows	1.0	end Dec.	0.8
Invisibles outflows	-1.1	No. months of import cover	2.5
Net transfers	0.5	Foreign debt	6.9
Current account balance	-0.2	– as % of GDP	79.3
– as % of GDP	-1.9	Debt service paid	0.8
Capital balance	0.6	Debt service ratio	27.5

Family life

No. of households	3.0m	Divorces per 1,000 pop.	...
Av. no. per household	5.1	Cost of living, Dec. 1997	
Marriages per 1,000 pop.	...	New York = 100	58

a 1990
b Energy trade data are distorted by transitory and oil refining activities.

MALAYSIA

Area	332,665 sq km	Currency	Malaysian dollar/ringgit
Capital	Kuala Lumpur		(M$)

People

Population	20.6m	Life expectancy: men	69.9yrs
Pop. per sq km	62	women	74.3 yrs
Av. ann. growth		Adult literacy	83.0%
in pop. 1990–2000	2.21%	Fertility rate (per woman)	3.2
Pop. under 15	38.0%	Urban population	54%
Pop. over 65	3.9%		*per 1,000 pop.*
No. of men per 100 women	101.9	Crude birth rate	25.2
Human Development Index	83.2	Crude death rate	5

The economy

GDP	M$250bn	GDP per head	$4,360
GDP	$90bn	GDP per head in purchasing	
Av. ann. growth in real		power parity (USA=100)	38
GDP 1990–96	8.7%		

Origins of GDP		Components of GDP	
	% of total		*% of total*
Agriculture	12.8	Private consumption	46.4
Industry, of which:	46.2	Public consumption	10.4
manufacturing	34.3	Investment	43.0
Services	41.0	Net exports	0.2

Structure of employment

	% of total		*% of labour force*
Agriculture	19	Unemployed 1996	2.6
Industry	32	Av. ann. rate 1990–96	3.5
Services	49		

Energy

	m TCE		
Total output	89.147	% output exported	56.2
Total consumption	49.391	% consumption imported	29.9
Consumption per head,			
kg coal equivalent	2,452		

Inflation and finance

Consumer price		*av. ann. increase 1989–96*	
inflation 1997	2.7%	Narrow money (M1)	19.7%
Av. ann. inflation 1990–97	3.8%	Broad money	19.4%
Deposit rate, 1996	7.08%		

Exchange rates

	end 1997		*December 1997*
M$ per $	3.89	Effective rates	*1990 = 100*
M$ per SDR	5.25	– nominal	86.9
M$ per Ecu	4.28	– real	82.5

Principal exports

	$bn fob		$bn fob
Electronics & electrical		Textiles, clothing & footwear	2.6
machinery	38.8	Chemicals & products	2.5
Palm oil	4.1	Timber	2.4
Petroleum & LNG	3.9	Total incl. others	**78.2**

Main export destinations

	% of total		% of total
Singapore	20.5	Hong Kong	5.9
United States	18.2	Taiwan	4.1
Japan	13.4	Thailand	4.1

Principal imports

	$bn cif		$bn cif
Manufacturing supplies	30.2	Metal products	2.3
Machinery & transport		Consumer durables	2.2
equipment	11.8	Total incl. others	**78.4**

Main origins of imports

	% of total		% of total
Japan	24.5	South Korea	5.2
United States	15.5	Taiwan	5.0
Singapore	13.3	Germany	4.3

Balance of payments[a], reserves and debt, $bn

Visible exports fob	72.1	Overall balance	-1.8
Visible imports fob	72.2	Change in reserves	3.2
Trade balance	-0.1	Level of reserves	
Invisibles inflows	13.9	end Dec.	27.9
Invisibles outflows	-21.3	No. months of import cover	3.4
Net transfers	0.1	Foreign debt	39.8
Current account balance	-7.4	as % of GDP	44.2
– as % of GDP	-9.4	Debt service paid	7.7
Capital balance	7.3	Debt service ratio	8.2

Family life

No. households	4.0m	Divorces per 1,000 pop.	...
Av. no. per household	4.9	Cost of living, Dec. 1997	
Marriages per 1,000 pop.	3.2	New York = 100	67

a 1995

MEXICO

Area	1,972,545 sq km	Currency	Mexican peso (PS)
Capital	Mexico City		

People

Population	92.7m	Life expectancy: men	69.5 yrs
Pop. per sq km	47	women	75.5 yrs
Av. ann. growth		Adult literacy	72.0%
in pop. 1990–2000	1.73%	Fertility rate (per woman)	2.8
Pop. under 15	35.5%	Urban population	75%
Pop. over 65	4.3%		*per 1,000 pop.*
No. of men per 100 women	98.2	Crude birth rate	24.6
Human Development Index	85.3	Crude death rate	5

The economy

GDP	2,544bn New pesos	GDP per head	$3,690
GDP	$342bn	GDP per head in purchasing	28
Av. ann. growth in real		power parity (USA=100)	
GDP 1990–96	1.8%		

Origins of GDP		Components of GDP	
	% of total		*% of total*
Agriculture	5.4	Private consumption	66.6
Industry, of which:	26.3	Public consumption	10.9
manufacturing	19.6	Investment	20.8
Services	68.3	Exports	18.8
		Imports	-17.5

Structure of employment

	% of total		*% of labour force*
Agriculture	22	Unemployed 1996	3.7
Industry	18	Av. ann. rate 1995–96	4.2
Services	60		

Energy

	m TCE		
Total output	282.781	% output exported	37.3
Total consumption	186.739	% consumption imported	6.5
Consumption per head,			
kg coal equivalent	2,049		

Inflation and finance

Consumer price		*av. ann. increase 1989–96*	
inflation 1997	20.6%	Narrow money (M1)	32.9%
Av. ann. inflation 1990–97	21.0%	Broad money	41.8%
Money market rate, 1997	21.91%		

Exchange rates

	end 1997		*December 1997*
PS per $	8.14	Effective rates	*1990 = 100*
PS per SDR	10.98	– nominal	…
PS per Ecu	8.95	– real	…

Principal exports

	$bn fob		$bn fob
Manufactured products	43.4	Agricultural products	3.6
Crude oil & products	11.7	Total incl. others	**96.0**

Main export destinations

	% of total		% of total
United States	83.9	Japan	1.4
Canada	2.3	Spain	1.0

Principal imports

	$bn cif		$bn cif
Intermediate goods	71.9	Consumer goods	6.7
Capital goods	10.9	Total	**89.5**

Main origins of imports

	% of total		% of total
United States	75.5	Germany	3.5
Japan	4.6	France	1.1

Balance of payments, reserves and debt, $bn

Visible exports fob	96.0	Overall balance	2.6
Visible imports fob	-89.5	Change in reserves	2.5
Trade balance	6.5	Level of reserves	
Invisibles inflows	14.9	end Dec.	19.5
Invisibles outflows	-27.9	No. months of import cover	2.0
Net transfers	4.5	Foreign debt	157.1
Current account balance	-1.9	– as % of GDP	45.9
– as % of GDP	-0.6	Debt service paid	40.8
Capital balance	4.1	Debt service ratio	35.4

Family life

No. of households	19.0m	Divorces per 1,000 pop.	0.4
Av. no. per household	4.6	Cost of living, Dec. 1997	
Marriages per 1,000 pop.	7.2	New York = 100	69

MOROCCO

Area	446,550 sq km	Currency	Dirham (Dh)
Capital	Rabat		

People

Population	27.0m	Life expectancy: men	64.8 yrs
Pop. per sq km	61	women	68.5 yrs
Av. ann. growth		Adult literacy	42.1%
in pop. 1990–2000	1.87%	Fertility rate (per woman)	3.1
Pop. under 15	36.3%	Urban population	48%
Pop. over 65	4.2%		*per 1,000 pop.*
No. of men per 100 women	100.2	Crude birth rate	25.3
Human Development Index	56.6	Crude death rate	7

The economy

GDP	Dh321bn	GDP per head	$1,290
GDP	$35bn	GDP per head in purchasing	
Av. ann. growth in real		power parity (USA=100)	12
GDP 1990–96	2.1%		

Origins of GDP		Components of GDP	
	% of total		*% of total*
Agriculture	20.4	Private consumption	77.7
Industry, of which:	30.5	Public consumption	17.6
manufacturing	16.9	Investment	25.7
Services	49.1	Exports	21.4
		Imports	-40.8

Structure of employment[a]

	% of total		*% of labour force*
Agriculture	4	Unemployed 1992	16.0
Industry	36	Av. ann. rate 1990–92	16.1
Services	60		

Energy

	m TCE		
Total output	0.764	% output exported	nil
Total consumption	11.552	% consumption imported	105.0
Consumption per head,			
kg coal equivalent	436		

Inflation and finance

Consumer price		*av. ann. increase 1989–96*	
inflation 1997	1.0%	Narrow money (M1)	11.6%
Av. ann. inflation 1990–97	5.1%	Broad money	11.3%
Money market rate, 1997	8.00%		

Exchange rates

	end 1997		*December 1997*
Dh per $	9.71	Effective rates	*1990 = 100*
Dh per SDR	13.11	– nominal	122.3
Dh per Ecu	10.68	– real	116.1

Principal exports

	$bn fob		$bn fob
Agricultural products & foodstuffs	1.5	Mineral ores	0.7
		Capital goods	0.2
Semi-finished goods	1.2		
Consumer goods	1.1	Total incl. others	**4.7**

Main export destinations

	% of total		% of total
France	33.0	United Kingdom	6.2
Germany	8.2	Italy	5.9
Spain	8.2		

Principal imports

	$bn cif		$bn cif
Semi-manufactured goods	1.9	Energy & fuels	1.3
Capital goods	1.8	Consumer goods	1.1
Agric. products & foodstuffs	1.3	Total incl. others	**8.2**

Main origins of imports

	% of total		% of total
France	26.2	Italy	7.6
Spain	9.2	United States	5.2
Germany	7.6		

Balance of payments, reserves and debt, $bn

Visible exports fob	6.9	Overall balance	0.2
Visible imports fob	-9.0	Change in reserves	0.2
Trade balance	-2.1	Level of reserves	
Invisibles inflows	2.5	end Dec.	4.1
Invisibles outflows	-3.2	No. months of import cover	3.9
Net transfers	2.4	Foreign debt	21.8
Current account balance	-0.6	– as % of GDP	62.3
– as % of GDP	-1.8	Debt service paid	3.2
Capital balance	0.3	Debt service ratio	27.7

Family life

No. of households	3.4m	Divorces per 1,000 pop.	...
Av. no. per household	5.9	Cost of living, Dec. 1997	
Marriages per 1,000 pop.	...	New York = 100	74

a Urban areas, 1992.

NETHERLANDS

Area[a]	41,526 sq km	Currency	Guilder (Fl)
Capital	Amsterdam		

People

Population	15.6m	Life expectancy: men	75.0 yrs
Pop. per sq km	381	women	80.6 yrs
Av. ann. growth		Adult literacy	99.0%
in pop. 1990–2000	0.6%	Fertility rate (per woman)	1.6
Pop. under 15	18.3%	Urban population	89%
Pop. over 65	13.2%		per 1,000 pop.
No. of men per 100 women	98.2	Crude birth rate	11.9
Human Development Index	94.0	Crude death rate	9

The economy

GDP	Fl662bn	GDP per head	$25,850
GDP	$403bn	GDP per head in purchasing	
Av. ann. growth in real		power parity (USA=100)	75
GDP 1990–96	2.2%		

Origins of GDP		Components of GDP	
	% of total		% of total
Agriculture	3.3	Private consumption	60.2
Industry, of which:	28.2	Public consumption	14.0
manufacturing	...	Investment	20.4
Services	68.5	Exports	53.6
		Imports	-48.1

Structure of employment

	% of total		% of labour force
Agriculture	4	Unemployed 1996	6.6
Industry	22	Av. ann. rate 1990–96	6.7
Services	74		

Energy

	m TCE		
Total output	102.559	% output exported[b]	111.5
Total consumption	114.885	% consumption imported[b]	118.5
Consumption per head,			
kg coal equivalent	7,421		

Inflation and finance

Consumer price		av. ann. increase 1989–96	
inflation 1997	2.2%	Narrow money (M1)	7.2%
Av. ann. inflation 1990–97	2.5%	Broad money	5.5%
Money market rate, 1997	3.07%		

Exchange rates

	end 1997		December 1997
Fl per $	2.02	Effective rates	1990 = 100
Fl per SDR	2.72	– nominal	101.4
Fl per Ecu	2.23	– real	90.8

Principal exports

	$bn fob		$bn fob
Machinery & transport equipment	45.5	Fuels	13.1
		Raw materials, oils & fats	9.4
Food, drink & tobacco	28.1		
Chemicals & plastics	27.6	Total incl. others	**177.0**

Main export destinations

	% of total		% of total
Germany	28.7	United Kingdom	9.6
Belgium/Luxembourg	13.2	Italy	5.9
France	11.1		

Principal imports

	$bn cif		$bn cif
Machinery & transport equipment	49.5	Fuels	12.7
		Textiles & clothing	8.2
Chemicals & plastics	17.2		
Food, drink & tobacco	16.2	Total incl. others	**160.6**

Main origins of imports

	% of total		% of total
Germany	22.4	United States	8.1
Belgium/Luxembourg	11.2	France	7.4
United Kingdom	10.0		

Balance of payments, reserves and aid, $bn

Visible exports fob	175.8	Capital balance	-10.3
Visible imports fob	-154.1	Overall balance	-5.7
Trade balance	21.8	Change in reserves	-7.6
Invisibles inflows	85.3	Level of reserves	
Invisibles outflows	-75.2	end Dec.	39.6
Net transfers	-6.7	No. months of import cover	2.1
Current account balance	25.3	Aid given	3.25
– as % of GDP	6.3	– as % of GDP	0.81

Family life

No. of households	6.4m	Divorces per 1,000 pop.	2.2
Av. no. per household	2.4	Cost of living, Dec. 1997	
Marriages per 1,000 pop.	5.8	New York = 100	94

a Includes water.
b Energy trade data are distorted due to transitory and oil refining activities.

NEW ZEALAND

Area	270,534 sq km	Currency	New Zealand dollar (NZ$)
Capital	Wellington		

People

Population	3.6m	Life expectancy: men	74.7 yrs
Pop. per sq km	13	women	79.7 yrs
Av. ann. growth		Adult literacy	99.0%
in pop. 1990–2000	1.13%	Fertility rate (per woman)	2.0
Pop. under 15	23.2%	Urban population	86%
Pop. over 65	11.4%		per 1,000 pop.
No. of men per 100 women	97.9	Crude birth rate	15.4
Human Development Index	93.7	Crude death rate	8

The economy

GDP	NZ$96bn	GDP per head	$15,850
GDP	$57bn	GDP per head in purchasing	
Av. ann. growth in real		power parity (USA=100)	60
GDP 1990–96	3.3%		

Origins of GDP

	% of total
Agriculture	8.0
Industry, of which:	25.0
manufacturing	18.5
Services	67.0

Components of GDP

	% of total
Private consumption	64.3
Public consumption	15.0
Investment	22.1
Exports	32.8
Imports	-34.1

Structure of employment

	% of total		% of labour force
Agriculture	9	Unemployed 1996	6.1
Industry	25	Av. ann. rate 1990–96	8.4
Services	66		

Energy

	m TCE		
Total output	17.264	% output exported	12.3
Total consumption	20.794	% consumption imported	31.5
Consumption per head,			
kg coal equivalent	5,839		

Inflation and finance

			av. ann. increase 1989–96
Consumer price			
inflation 1997	1.2%	Narrow money (M1)	11.0%
Av. ann. inflation 1990–97	2.5%	Broad money	20.4%
Treasury bill rate, 1997	7.53%		

Exchange rates

	end 1997		December 1997
NZ$ per $	1.72	Effective rates	1990 = 100
NZ$ per SDR	2.32	– nominal	109.2
NZ$ per Ecu	1.89	– real	102.6

Principal exports

	$bn fob		$bn fob
Dairy produce	2.6	Fruit & vegetables	0.7
Meat	1.8	Wool	0.7
Forest products	1.7	Total incl. others	**14.4**

Main export destinations

	% of total		% of total
Australia	20.3	United States	9.1
Japan	15.3	United Kingdom	6.4

Principal imports

	$bn cif		$bn cif
Machinery	2.2	Mineral fuels	0.9
Vehicles & aircraft	2.0		
Electrical machinery	1.5	Total incl. others	**14.8**

Main origins of imports

	% of total		% of total
Australia	23.5	Japan	13.5
United States	15.9	United Kingdom	5.1

Balance of payments, reserves and aid, $bn

Visible exports fob	14.2	Capital balance	0.4
Visible imports fob	-13.7	Overall balance	1.6
Trade balance	0.5	Change in reserves	1.5
Invisibles inflows	5.0	Level of reserves	
Invisibles outflows	-10.0	end Dec.	6.0
Net transfers	0.6	No. months of import cover	3.0
Current account balance	-3.9	Aid given	0.12
– as % of GDP	-6.9	– as % of GDP	0.21

Family life

No. of households	1.2m	Divorces per 1,000 pop.	2.7
Av. no. per household	2.9	Cost of living, Dec. 1997	
Marriages per 1,000 pop.	6.3	New York = 100	85

NIGERIA

Area	923,768 sq km	Currency	Naira (N)
Capital	Abuja		

People

Population	115.0m	Life expectancy: men	50.8 yrs
Pop. per sq km	125	women	54.0 yrs
Av. ann. growth		Adult literacy	55.6%
in pop. 1990–2000	2.92%	Fertility rate (per woman)	6.0
Pop. under 15	45.5%	Urban population	39%
Pop. over 65	2.8%		per 1,000 pop.
No. of men per 100 women	98.4	Crude birth rate	42.3
Human Development Index	39.3	Crude death rate	14

The economy

GDP	N2,157bn	GDP per head	$240
GDP	$28bn	GDP per head in purchasing	
Av. ann. growth in real		power parity (USA=100)	3
GDP 1990–96	2.6%		

Origins of GDP		Components of GDP	
	% of total		% of total
Agriculture	37.3	Private consumption	75.7
Industry, of which:	19.6	Public consumption	11.9
manufacturing	6.5	Investment	5.8
Services	43.1	Exports	13.0
		Imports	-6.4

Structure of employment[a]

	% of total		% of labour force
Agriculture	43	Unemployed 1996	...
Industry	7	Av. ann. rate 1990–96	...
Services	50		

Energy

	m TCE		
Total output	138.317	% output exported	86.8
Total consumption	15.857	% consumption imported	20.2
Consumption per head,			
kg coal equivalent	142		

Inflation and finance

Consumer price		av. ann. increase 1989–96	
inflation 1996	29.3%	Narrow money (M1)	35.3%
Av. ann. inflation 1990–97	38.0%	Broad money	33.0%

Exchange rates

	end 1997		December 1997
N per $	21.89	Effective rates	1990 = 100
N per SDR	29.53	– nominal	30.6
N per Ecu	24.08	– real	

Principal exports

	$bn fob		$bn fob
Petroleum	15.8		
Cocoa beans & products	0.1	Total incl. others	**16.0**

Main export destinations

	% of total		% of total
United States	37.8	India	4.5
Spain	10.2	Germany	4.3
France	8.5		

Principal imports

	$bn cif		$bn cif
Manufactured goods	1.9	Agric products &	
Machinery & transport		foodstuffs	0.9
equipment	1.6		
Chemicals	1.6	Total incl. others	**6.5**

Main origins of imports

	% of total		% of total
United States	13.6	France	8.4
United Kingdom	11.4	Netherlands	5.1
Germany	10.9		

Balance of payments, reserves and debt, $bn

Visible exports fob	14.1	Overall balance	-0.7
Visible imports fob	-5.6	Change in reserves	2.6
Trade balance	8.5	Level of reserves	
Invisibles inflows	0.7	end Dec.	4.3
Invisibles outflows	-7.0	No. months of import cover	4.1
Net transfers	0.8	Foreign debt	31.4
Current account balance	3.1	– as % of GDP	112.1
– as % of GDP	11.2	Debt service paid	2.5
Capital balance	-3.7	Debt service ratio	16.0

Family life

No. households	21.9m	Divorces per 1,000 pop.	…
Av. no. per household	5.1	Cost of living, Dec. 1997	
Marriages per 1,000 pop.	…	New York = 100	78

a 1990

NORWAY

Area	323,878 sq km	Currency	Norwegian krone (Nkr)
Capital	Oslo		

People

Population	4.3m	Life expectancy: men	74.8 yrs
Pop. per sq km	13	women	80.6 yrs
Av. ann. growth		Adult literacy	99.0%
in pop. 1990–2000	0.39%	Fertility rate (per woman)	1.9
Pop. under 15	19.4%	Urban population	73%
Pop. over 65	15.9%		*per 1,000 pop.*
No. of men per 100 women	98.5	Crude birth rate	13.4
Human Development Index	94.3	Crude death rate	11

The economy

GDP	Nkr1,018bn	GDP per head	$34,780
GDP	$151bn	GDP per head in purchasing	
Av. ann. growth in real		power parity (USA=100)	85
GDP 1990–96	3.9%		

Origins of GDP		Components of GDP	
	% of total		*% of total*
Agriculture	2.2	Private consumption	47.6
Industry, of which:	30.0	Public consumption	20.5
manufacturing	...	Investment	22.8
Services	67.8	Exports	40.6
		Imports	-31.4

Structure of employment

	% of total		*% of labour force*
Agriculture	5	Unemployed 1996	4.9
Industry	23	Av. ann. rate 1990–96	5.4
Services	72		

Energy

	m TCE		
Total output	258.250	% output exported	88.5
Total consumption	30.891	% consumption imported	24.2
Consumption per head,			
kg coal equivalent	7,131		

Inflation and finance

Consumer price		*av. ann. increase 1989–96*	
inflation 1996	2.6%	Narrow money (M1)	9.7%
Av. ann. inflation 1990–97	2.5%	Broad money	5.0%
Deposit rate, 1997	3.64%		

Exchange rates

	end 1997		*December 1997*
Nkr per $	7.32	Effective rates	*1990 = 100*
Nkr per SDR	9.87	– nominal	98.7
Nkr per Ecu	8.05	– real	109.5

Principal exports

	$bn fob		$bn fob
Oil, gas & products	24.3	Metal products	4.8
Machinery & transport equipment	5.6	Total incl. others	**49.8**

Main export destinations

	% of total		% of total
United Kingdom	19.6	Sweden	9.1
Netherlands	11.4	France	8.7
Germany	11.1		

Principal imports

	$bn cif		$bn cif
Machinery & transport equipment	12.9	Chemicals	3.4
Metal products	3.5	Total incl. others	**36.9**

Main origins of imports

	% of total		% of total
Sweden	16.5	Denmark	7.5
Germany	13.1	United States	6.7
United Kingdom	9.9	Japan	4.6

Balance of payments, reserves and aid, $bn

Visible exports fob	50.0	Capital balance	1.1
Visible imports fob	-36.0	Overall balance	6.7
Trade balance	13.9	Change in reserves	4.0
Invisibles inflows	18.6	Level of reserves	
Invisibles outflows	-19.8	end Dec.	27.0
Net transfers	-1.5	No. months of import cover	5.8
Current account balance	11.2	Aid given	1.31
– as % of GDP	7.4	– as % of GDP	0.85

Family life

No. households	1.8m	Divorces per 1,000 pop.	2.7
Av. no. per household	2.3	Cost of living, Dec. 1997	
Marriages per 1,000 pop.	4.6	New York = 100	121

PAKISTAN

Area	803,940 sq km	Currency	Pakistan rupee (PRs)
Capital	Islamabad		

People

Population	140.0m	Life expectancy: men	62.9 yrs
Pop. per sq km	176	women	65.1 yrs
Av. ann. growth		Adult literacy	37.1%
in pop. 1990–2000	2.7%	Fertility rate (per woman)	5.0
Pop. under 15	42.7%	Urban population	35%
Pop. over 65	3.1%		per 1,000 pop.
No. of men per 100 women	106.9	Crude birth rate	36.1
Human Development Index	44.5	Crude death rate	8

The economy

GDP	PRs2,175bn	GDP per head	$480
GDP	$64bn	GDP per head in purchasing	
Av. ann. growth in real		power parity (USA=100)	6
GDP 1990–96	4.6%		

Origins of GDP[a]		Components of GDP[a]	
	% of total		% of total
Agriculture	24.8	Private consumption	62.1
Industry, of which:	26.4	Public consumption	26.8
manufacturing	18.1	Investment	18.6
Services	48.8	Exports	15.9
		Imports	-23.4

Structure of employment[a]

	% of total[b]		% of labour force
Agriculture	44	Unemployed 1995	5.4
Industry	18	Av. ann. rate 1990–95	5.0
Services	38		

Energy

	m TCE		
Total output	28.997	% output exported	1.5
Total consumption	46.314	% consumption imported	41.4
Consumption per head,			
kg coal equivalent	340		

Inflation and finance

Consumer price		av. ann. increase 1989–96	
inflation 1997	11.4%	Narrow money (M1)	13.6%
Av. ann. inflation 1990–97	10.8%	Broad money	16.9%
Money market rate, 1997	12.10%		

Exchange rates

	end 1997		December 1997
PRs per $	44.05	Effective rates	1990 = 100
PRs per SDR	59.43	– nominal	…
PRs per Ecu	48.46	– real	…

Principal exports[a]

	$bn fob		$bn fob
Cotton yarn	1.7	Raw cotton	0.2
Cotton fabrics	1.2		
Rice	0.5	Total incl. others	**9.3**

Main export destinations

	% of total		% of total
United States	16.7	Germany	7.1
Hong Kong	9.8	Japan	6.5

Principal imports[a]

	$bn cif		$bn cif
Machinery and transport equipment	3.7	Petroleum & products	2.0
Chemicals	2.2	Total incl. others	**12.1**

Main origins of imports

	% of total		% of total
Japan	10.2	Kuwait	7.4
United States	8.8	Germany	5.0

Balance of payments[c], reserves and debt, $bn

Visible exports fob	8.3	Overall balance	-1.2
Visible imports fob	-11.2	Change in reserves	-1.2
Trade balance	-2.9	Level of reserves	
Invisibles inflows	2.0	end Dec.	1.3
Invisibles outflows	-5.0	No. months of import cover	0.9
Net transfers	2.5	Foreign debt	29.9
Current account balance	-3.3	– as % of GDP	46.7
– as % of GDP	-5.6	Debt service paid	3.3
Capital balance	2.4	Debt service ratio	27.4

Family life

No. households	19.4m	Divorces per 1,000 pop.	…
Av. no. per household	6.8	Cost of living, Dec. 1997	
Marriages per 1,000 pop.	…	New York = 100	53

a Fiscal year ending June 30, 1996.
b Employed labour force.
c 1995

PERU

Area	1,285,216 sq km	Currency	Nuevo Sol (New Sol)
Capital	Lima		

People

Population	23.9m	Life expectancy: men	65.9 yrs
Pop. per sq km	19	women	70.9 yrs
Av. ann. growth		Adult literacy[a]	88.3%
in pop. 1990–2000	1.74%	Fertility rate (per woman)	3.0
Pop. under 15	35.9%	Urban population	72%
Pop. over 65	4.4%		per 1,000 pop.
No. of men per 100 women	98.5	Crude birth rate	24.9
Human Development Index	71.7	Crude death rate	7

The economy

GDP	New Soles 149bn	GDP per head	$2,420
GDP	$59bn	GDP per head in purchasing	
Av. ann. growth in real		power parity (USA=100)	16
GDP 1990–96	1.3%		

Origins of GDP		Components of GDP	
	% of total		% of total
Agriculture	12.9	Private consumption	72.9
Industry, of which:	37.1	Public consumption	8.3
manufacturing	23.3	Investment	23.3
Services	50.0	Exports	11.9
		Imports	-16.4

Structure of employment[b]

	% of total		% of labour force
Agriculture	36	Unemployed 1996[c]	7.0
Industry	18	Av. ann. rate 1991–96	...
Services	46		

Energy

	m TCE		
Total output	11.138	% output exported	16.1
Total consumption	12.919	% consumption imported	46.4
Consumption per head,			
kg coal equivalent	549		

Inflation and finance

Consumer price			av. ann. increase 1989–96
inflation 1997	8.6%	Narrow money (M1)	233%
Av. ann. inflation 1990–97	153%	Broad money	268%
Deposit rate, 1997	15.0%		

Exchange rates

	end 1997		December 1997
New Soles per $	2.73	Effective rates	1990 = 100
New Soles per SDR	3.68	– nominal	...
New Soles per Ecu	3.00	– real	...

Principal exports

	$bn fob		$bn fob
Copper	1.1	Gold	0.6
Fish & fish products	1.1	Textiles	0.5
Agricultural products	0.6	Total incl. others	**5.9**

Main export destinations

	% of total		% of total
United States	19.9	China	7.2
Japan	7.3	Germany	5.2
United Kingdom	7.3	Brazil	4.1

Principal imports

	$bn fob		$bn fob
Industrial supplies	3.2	Consumer goods	1.8
Capital goods	2.4	Total incl. others	**7.9**

Main origins of imports

	% of total		% of total
United States	30.7	Chile	5.7
Colombia	7.3	Spain	5.7

Balance of payments, reserves and debt, $bn

Visible exports fob	5.9	Overall balance	0.4
Visible imports fob	-7.9	Change in reserves	2.3
Trade balance	-2.0	Level of reserves	
Invisibles inflows	2.0	end Dec.	11.0
Invisibles outflows	-4.2	No. months of import cover	10.9
Net transfers	0.6	Foreign debt	29.2
Current account balance	-3.6	– as % of GDP	49.5
– as % of GDP	-6.1	Debt service paid	2.9
Capital balance	3.1	Debt service ratio	35.4

Family life

No. of households	5.1m	Divorces per 1,000 pop.	...
Av. no. per household	4.5	Cost of living, Dec. 1997	
Marriages per 1,000 pop.	4.1	New York = 100	72

a Excluding indigenous jungle population.
b 1990
c Urban areas.

PHILIPPINES

Area	300,000 sq km	Currency	Philippine peso (P)
Capital	Manila		

People

Population	69.3m	Life expectancy: men	66.6 yrs
Pop. per sq km	231	women	70.2 yrs
Av. ann. growth		Adult literacy	94.4%
in pop. 1990–2000	2.11%	Fertility rate (per woman)	3.6
Pop. under 15	38.5%	Urban population	54%
Pop. over 65	3.4%		per 1,000 pop.
No. of men per 100 women	101.4	Crude birth rate	28.4
Human Development Index	67.2	Crude death rate	6

The economy

GDP	P2,197bn	GDP per head	$1,160
GDP	$83bn	GDP per head in purchasing	
Av. ann. growth in real		power parity (USA=100)	13
GDP 1990–96	2.9%		

Origins of GDP		Components of GDP	
	% of total		% of total
Agriculture	21.4	Private consumption	72.8
Industry, of which:	31.8	Public consumption	11.4
manufacturing	22.6	Investment	24.9
Services	46.8	Exports	43.6
		Imports	-54.3

Structure of employment

	% of total		% of labour force
Agriculture	42	Unemployed 1996	7.4
Industry	17	Av. ann. rate 1990–96	8.4
Services	41		

Energy

	m TCE		
Total output	9.191	% output exported	4.3
Total consumption	29.359	% consumption imported	94.1
Consumption per head,			
kg coal equivalent	433		

Inflation and finance

Consumer price		av. ann. increase 1989–96	
inflation 1997	5.1%	Narrow money (M1)	18.2%
Av. ann. inflation 1990–97	9.9%	Broad money	22.7%
Treasury bill rate, 1997	12.89%		

Exchange rates

	end 1997		December 1997
P per $	39.98	Effective rates	1990 = 100
P per SDR	53.93	– nominal	86.4
P per Ecu	43.98	– real	109.0

Principal exports

	$bn fob		$bn fob
Electrical & electronic equipment	10.0	Coconut products	0.7
Clothing	2.4		
Machinery & transport equipment	1.3	Total incl. others	**20.5**

Main export destinations

	% of total		% of total
United States	33.9	Netherlands	5.4
Japan	17.9	United Kingdom	4.6
Singapore	6.0	Hong Kong	4.2

Principal imports

	$bn cif		$bn cif
Electrical equipment parts	5.1	Semi-processed manufactures	3.9
Telecom & electrical machinery	4.2	Total incl. others	**31.8**

Main origins of imports

	% of total		% of total
Japan	21.8	South Korea	5.2
United States	19.7	Saudi Arabia	5.1
Singapore	5.3	Taiwan	5.0

Balance of payments[a], reserves and debt, $bn

Visible exports fob	17.4	Overall balance	1.2
Visible imports fob	-26.4	Change in reserves	4.0
Trade balance	-8.9	Level of reserves	
Invisibles inflows	15.4	end Dec.	11.7
Invisibles outflows	-9.3	No. months of import cover	3.2
Net transfers	0.9	Foreign debt	41.2
Current account balance	-2.0	– as % of GDP	49.6
– as % of GDP	-2.8	Debt service paid	5.8
Capital balance	5.3	Debt service ratio	13.7

Family life

No. of households	12.8m	Divorces per 1,000 pop.	...
Av. no. per household	5.2	Cost of living, Dec. 1997	
Marriages per 1,000 pop.	6.9	New York = 100	58

a 1995

POLAND

Area	312,683 sq km	Currency	Zloty (Zl)
Capital	Warsaw		

People

Population	38.6m	Life expectancy: men	66.7 yrs
Pop. per sq km	119	women	75.7 yrs
Av. ann. growth		Adult literacy	99.0%
in pop. 1990–2000	0.16%	Fertility rate (per woman)	1.7
Pop. under 15	24.9%	Urban population	65%
Pop. over 65	11.0%		per 1,000 pop.
No. of men per 100 women	94.8	Crude birth rate	11.9
Human Development Index	83.4	Crude death rate	11

The economy

GDP	Zl363bn	GDP per head	$3,230
GDP	$125bn	GDP per head in purchasing	
Av. ann. growth in real		power parity (USA=100)	22
GDP 1990–96	3.2%		

Origins of GDP		Components of GDP	
	% of total		% of total
Agriculture	6.0	Private consumption	64.2
Industry, of which:	32.4	Public consumption	18.4
manufacturing	…	Investment	19.0
Services	61.6	Net exports	-2.8

Structure of employment

	% of total		% of labour force
Agriculture	22	Unemployed 1996	12.3
Industry	32	Av. ann. rate 1993–96	13.5
Services	46		

Energy

	m TCE		
Total output	135.480	% output exported	23.2
Total consumption	136.660	% consumption imported	24.4
Consumption per head,			
kg coal equivalent	3,544		

Inflation and finance

Consumer price		av. ann. increase 1989–96	
inflation 1997	15.9%	Narrow money (M1)	76.2%
Av. ann. inflation 1990–97	64.7%	Broad money	81.1%
Money market rate, 1996	20.6%		

Exchange rates

	end 1997		December 1997
Zl per $	3.52	Effective rates	1990 = 100
Zl per SDR	4.75	– nominal	35.8
Zl per Ecu	3.87	– real	

Principal exports

	$bn fob		$bn fob
Manufactured goods	6.3	Chemicals	1.9
Machinery & equipment	5.7	Oil & gas	1.7
Agric. products & foodstuffs	2.5	Total incl. others	**24.4**

Main export destinations

	% of total		% of total
Germany	34.5	United States	4.8
Russia	6.8	Netherlands	4.1
France	5.9	United Kingdom	3.9
Italy	5.6		

Principal imports

	$bn fob		$bn fob
Machinery & equipment	12.3	Oil & gas	3.4
Manufactured goods	7.5	Agric. products & foodstuffs	3.1
Chemicals	5.1	Total incl. others	**37.1**

Main origins of imports

	% of total		% of total
Germany	26.5	Netherlands	4.8
Italy	10.4	France	4.4
Russia	7.3	United States	2.3
United Kingdom	6.3		

Balance of payments, reserves and debt, $bn

Visible exports fob	27.6	Overall balance	3.6
Visible imports fob	-34.8	Change in reserves	3.1
Trade balance	-7.3	Level of reserves	
Invisibles inflows	11.4	end Dec.	18.0
Invisibles outflows	-9.0	No. months of import cover	4.9
Net transfers	1.7	Foreign debt	40.9
Current account balance	-3.3	– as % of GDP	32.7
– as % of GDP	-2.6	Debt service paid	2.6
Capital balance	6.6	Debt service ratio	6.4

Family life

No. of households	11.6m	Divorces per 1,000 pop.	1.0
Av. no. per household	3.3	Cost of living, Dec. 1997	
Marriages per 1,000 pop.	6.8	New York = 100	60

PORTUGAL

Area	88,940 sq km	Currency	Escudo (Esc)
Capital	Lisbon		

People

Population	9.8m	Life expectancy: men	71.8 yrs
Pop. per sq km	106	women	78.9 yrs
Av. ann. growth		Adult literacy	89.6%
in pop. 1990–2000	-0.09%	Fertility rate (per woman)	1.5
Pop. under 15	17.8%	Urban population	36%
Pop. over 65	14.8%		*per 1,000 pop.*
No. of men per 100 women	92.9	Crude birth rate	11.2
Human Development Index	89.0	Crude death rate	11

The economy

GDP	Esc16,524bn	GDP per head	$10,290
GDP	$101bn	GDP per head in purchasing	
Av. ann. growth in real		power parity (USA=100)	49
GDP 1990–96	1.4%		

Origins of GDP		**Components of GDP**	
	% of total		*% of total*
Agriculture	4.1	Private consumption	65.5
Industry, of which:	36.1	Public consumption	19.1
manufacturing	...	Investment	25.6
Services	59.8	Exports	26.7
		Imports	-36.9

Structure of employment

	% of total		*% of labour force*
Agriculture	12	Unemployed 1996	7.2
Industry	31	Av. ann. rate 1990–96	5.6
Services	57		

Energy

	m TCE		
Total output	1.092	% output exported[a]	462.9
Total consumption	23.043	% consumption imported[a]	126.7
Consumption per head,			
kg coal equivalent	2,348		

Inflation and finance

Consumer price		*av. ann. increase 1989–96*	
inflation 1997	2.2%	Narrow money (M1)	11.6%
Av. ann. inflation 1990–97	7.1%	Broad money	13.1%
Money market rate, 1997	5.78%		

Exchange rates

	end 1997		*December 1997*
Esc per $	183.3	Effective rates	*1990 = 100*
Esc per SDR	247.4	– nominal	93.0
Esc per Ecu	201.6	– real	

Principal exports

	$bn fob		$bn fob
Machinery	3.8	Clothing	3.5
Vehicles & transport		Shoes	1.8
equipment	3.7	Total incl. others	**23.2**

Main export destinations

	% of total		% of total
Germany	21.2	United Kingdom	10.8
Spain	14.2	Netherlands	4.9
France	14.1	EU15	80.0

Principal imports

	$bn cif		$bn cif
Machinery	7.2	Chemicals	2.8
Vehicles & transport equipment	5.2		
Agric. products & foodstuffs	3.2	Total incl. others	**34.1**

Main origins of imports

	% of total		% of total
Spain	22.4	Italy	8.3
Germany	15.5	United Kingdom	6.7
France	11.1	EU15	75.6

Balance of payments, reserves and debt, $bn

Visible exports fob	25.5	Overall balance	0.4
Visible imports fob	-34.9	Change in reserves	-0.2
Trade balance	-9.3	Level of reserves	
Invisibles inflows	12.5	end Dec.	21.9
Invisibles outflows	-11.4	No. months of import cover	5.7
Net transfers	6.8	Aid given	0.22
Current account balance	-1.5	– as % of GDP	0.21
– as % of GDP	-1.5		
Capital balance	4.8		

Family life

No. of households	3.2m	Divorces per 1,000 pop.	1.2
Av. no. per household	2.7	Cost of living, Dec. 1997	
Marriages per 1,000 pop.	6.5	New York = 100	76

a Energy trade data are distorted by transitory and oil refining activities.

ROMANIA

˙Area	237,500 sq km	Currency	Leu (L)
Capital	Bucharest		

People

Population	22.7m	Life expectancy: men	66.0 yrs
Pop. per sq km	95	women	73.2 yrs
Av. ann. growth		Adult literacy	96.9%
in pop. 1990–2000	-0.31%	Fertility rate (per woman)	1.4
Pop. under 15	20.5%	Urban population	55%
Pop. over 65	11.8%		*per 1,000 pop.*
No. of men per 100 women	96.8	Crude birth rate	11.0
Human Development Index	74.8	Crude death rate	11

The economy

GDP	L109,515bn	GDP per head	$1,600
GDP	$36bn	GDP per head in purchasing	
Av. ann. growth in real		power parity (USA=100)	17
GDP 1990–96	nil		

Origins of GDP		**Components of GDP**	
	% of total		*% of total*
Agriculture	19.1	Private consumption	69.4
Industry, of which:	42.2	Public consumption	10.8
manufacturing	...	Investment	25.4
Services	38.7	Exports	27.4
		Imports	-33.0

Structure of employment

	% of total		*% of labour force*
Agriculture	38	Unemployed 1996	6.3
Industry	32	Av. ann. rate 1991–96	8.1
Services	30		

Energy

	m TCE		
Total output	43.328	% output exported	15.5
Total consumption	60.583	% consumption imported	46.3
Consumption per head,			
kg coal equivalent	2,666		

Inflation and finance

Consumer price		*av. ann. increase 1989–96*	
inflation 1997	154.8%	Narrow money (M1)	64.6%
Av. ann. inflation 1990–97	108.0%	Broad money	71.9%
Treasury bill rate, 1997	85.7%		

Exchange rates

	end 1997		*December 1997*
L per $	8,023	Effective rates	1990 = 100
L per SDR	10,825	– nominal	...
L per Ecu	8,825	– real	...

Principal exports

	$bn fob		$bn fob
Textiles & footwear	2.2	Mineral products	0.7
Basic metals & products	1.3		
Chemicals	0.9	Total incl. others	**8.1**

Main export destinations

	% of total		% of total
Germany	17.9	Turkey	5.0
Italy	16.6	Netherlands	4.2
France	5.5	China	3.0

Principal imports

	$bn cif		$bn cif
Machinery & equipment	2.9	Food products	0.9
Fuels & minerals	2.7		
Chemicals	1.4	Total incl. others	**11.4**

Main origins of imports

	% of total		% of total
Germany	17.1	France	5.0
Italy	15.6	Egypt	3.8
Russia	12.6	United States	3.8

Balance of payments, reserves and debt, $bn

Visible exports fob	8.1	Overall balance	-0.6
Visible imports fob	-10.6	Change in reserves	0.5
Trade balance	-2.5	Level of reserves	
Invisibles inflows	1.6	end Dec.	3.1
Invisibles outflows	-2.3	No. months of import cover	2.9
Net transfers	0.6	Foreign debt	8.3
Current account balance	-2.6	– as % of GDP	23.1
– as % of GDP	-7.1	Debt service paid	1.2
Capital balance	1.6	Debt service ratio	12.6

Family life

No. of households	7.7m	Divorces per 1,000 pop.	1.5
Av. no. per household	2.9	Cost of living, Dec. 1997	
Marriages per 1,000 pop.	6.8	New York = 100	62

RUSSIA

Area	17,075,400 sq km	Currency	Rouble (Rb)
Capital	Moscow		

People

Population	148.1m	Life expectancy: men	58.0 yrs
Pop. per sq km	9	women	71.5 yrs
Av. ann. growth		Adult literacy	98.7%
in pop. 1990–2000	-0.15%	Fertility rate (per woman)	1.4
Pop. under 15	21.1%	Urban population	76%
Pop. over 65	12.0%		per 1,000 pop.
No. of men per 100 women	88.0	Crude birth rate	9.6
Human Development Index	79.2	Crude death rate	14

The economy

GDP	Rb2,256trn	GDP per head	$2,410
GDP	$356bn	GDP per head in purchasing	
Av. ann. growth in real		power parity (USA=100)	15
GDP 1990–96	-9.0%		

Origins of GDP

	% of total
Agriculture	6.4
Industry, of which:	37.9
manufacturing	...
Services	55.7

Components of GDP

	% of total
Private consumption	49.1
Public consumption	20.1
Investment	23.2
Exports	22.1
Imports	-26.8

Structure of employment[a]

	% of total		% of labour force
Agriculture	16	Unemployed 1996	9.3
Industry	34	Av. ann. rate 1992–96	7.1
Services	50		

Energy

	m TCE		
Total output	1,512.045	% output exported	33.1
Total consumption	1,004.650	% consumption imported	4.3
Consumption per head,			
kg coal equivalent	6,767		

Inflation and finance

		av. ann. increase 1994–96	
Consumer price			
inflation 1997	14.6%	Narrow money (M1)	102%
Av. ann. inflation 1991–97	244.9%	Broad money	108%
Interbank rate, 1997	26.0%		

Exchange rates

	end 1997		December 1997
Rb per $	5.96	Effective rates	1990 = 100
Rb per SDR	8.04	– nominal	...
Rb per Ecu	6.56	– real	...

Principal exports[a]

	$ bn		$ bn
Fuels & raw materials	31.3	Chemicals & rubber	7.4
Metals	14.8		
Machinery & equipment	7.7	Total incl. others	**77.4**

Main export destinations

	% of total		% of total
Ukraine	9.0	China	6.0
Germany	8.0	CIS	20.5
United States	6.0		

Principal imports[a]

	$ bn		$ bn
Machinery & equipment	15.3	Metals	3.4
Food products	12.9		
Chemicals & rubber	4.9	Total incl. others	**46.4**

Main origins of imports

	% of total		% of total
Ukraine	14.0	United States	6.0
Germany	11.0	CIS	29.9
Kazakhstan	7.0		

Balance of payments, reserves and debt, $bn

Visible exports fob	90.5	Overall balance	-22.1
Visible imports fob	-67.4	Change in reserves	-1.8
Trade balance	23.1	Level of reserves	
Invisibles inflows	17.2	end Dec.	16.3
Invisibles outflows	-28.9	No. months of import cover	2.0
Net transfers	0.2	Foreign debt	124.8
Current account balance	11.6	– as % of GDP	35.1
– as % of GDP	3.3	Debt service paid	7.0
Capital balance	-26.7	Debt service ratio	6.6

Family life

No. of households	52.3m	Divorces per 1,000 pop.	4.6
Av. no. per household	2.8	Cost of living, Dec. 1997	
Marriages per 1,000 pop.	5.9	New York = 100	92

a 1995

SAUDI ARABIA

Area	2,200,000 sq km	Currency	Riyal (SR)
Capital	Riyadh		

People

Population	18.8m	Life expectancy: men	69.9 yrs
Pop. per sq km	9	women	73.4 yrs
Av. ann. growth		Adult literacy	61.8%
in pop. 1990–2000	3.00%	Fertility rate (per woman)	5.9
Pop. under 15	41.6%	Urban population	80%
Pop. over 65	2.7%		*per 1,000 pop.*
No. of men per 100 women	125.1	Crude birth rate	34.3
Human Development Index	77.4	Crude death rate	4

The economy

GDP	SR511bn	GDP per head	$7,240
GDP	$136bn	GDP per head in purchasing	
Av. ann. growth in real		power parity (USA=100)	36
GDP 1990–96	1.7%		

Origins of GDP		**Components of GDP**[a]	
	% of total		*% of total*
Agriculture	6.3	Private consumption	42.2
Industry, of which:	53.4	Public consumption	26.1
manufacturing	9.4	Investment	19.5
Services	40.3	Exports	42.1
		Imports	-30.0

Structure of employment[b]

	% of total		*% of labour force*
Agriculture	5	Unemployed 1996	...
Industry	26	Av. ann. rate 1990–96	...
Services	69		

Energy

	m TCE		
Total output	660.695	% output exported	75.9
Total consumption	113.658	% consumption imported	0.0
Consumption per head,			
kg coal equivalent	6,226		

Inflation and finance

Consumer price		*av. ann. increase 1989–96*	
inflation 1996	1.2%	Narrow money (M1)	4.5%
Av. ann. inflation 1990–97	18%	Broad money	4.8%
Deposit rate, 1997	5.79%		

Exchange rates

	end 1997		*December 1997*
SR per $	3.75	Effective rates	*1990 = 100*
SR per SDR	5.05	– nominal	112.5
SR per Ecu	4.13	– real	

Principal exports

	$bn fob		$bn fob
Crude oil & refined		Petrochemicals	2.7
petroleum	50.2	Total incl. others	**56.7**

Main export destinations

	% of total		% of total
Japan	16.9	Singapore	7.9
United States	15.0	France	4.5
South Korea	10.6	Netherlands	3.2

Principal imports

	$bn cif		$bn cif
Machinery	5.8	Textiles & clothing	2.3
Transport equipment	4.2	Chemical products	2.2
Agric. products & foodstuffs	1.2	Total incl. others	**27.8**

Main origins of imports

	% of total		% of total
United States	22.0	Germany	7.7
United Kingdom	11.9	Italy	5.6
Japan	9.1	South Korea	3.3

Balance of payments, reserves and debt[a], $bn

Visible exports fob	56.7	Overall balance	-1.8
Visible imports fob	-25.4	Change in reserves	-1.9
Trade balance	31.3	Level of reserves	
Invisibles inflows	9.1	end Dec.	8.5
Invisibles outflows	-24.4	No. months of import cover	2.0
Net transfers	-15.8	Foreign debt	20.0
Current account balance	0.2	– as % of GDP	16.0
– as % of GDP	0.2	Debt service	2.4
Capital balance	-2.0	Debt service ratio	4.5

Family life

No. of households	...	Divorces per 1,000 pop.	...
Av. no. per household	...	Cost of living, Dec. 1997	
Marriages per 1,000 pop.	...	New York = 100	71

a   1995
b   % of workers, 1994.

SINGAPORE

Area	639 sq km	Currency	Singapore dollar (S$)
Capital	Singapore		

People

Population	3.4m	Life expectancy: men	75.1 yrs
Pop. per sq km	5,476	women	79.5 yrs
Av. ann. growth		Adult literacy	91.0%
in pop. 1990–2000	1.73%	Fertility rate (per woman)	1.8
Pop. under 15	22.5%	Urban population	100%
Pop. over 65	6.3%		per 1,000 pop.
No. of men per 100 women	101.6	Crude birth rate	15.7
Human Development Index	90.0	Crude death rate	5

The economy

GDP	S$133bn	GDP per head	$27,480
GDP	$93bn	GDP per head in purchasing	
Av. ann. growth in real		power parity (USA=100)	88
GDP 1990–96	8.7%		

Origins of GDP		Components of GDP	
	% of total		% of total
Agriculture	0.2	Private consumption	40.7
Industry, of which:	35.5	Public consumption	8.9
manufacturing	26.0	Investment	35.1
Services	64.3	Exports less imports	15.4

Structure of employment

	% of total		% of labour force
Agriculture	0	Unemployed 1996	3.0
Industry	30	Av. ann. rate 1990–96	2.5
Services	70		

Energy

	m TCE		
Total output	...	% output exported	...
Total consumption	28.652	% consumption imported[a]	366.8
Consumption per head,			
kg coal equivalent	8,612		

Inflation and finance

Consumer price		av. ann. increase 1989–96	
inflation 1997	2.0%	Narrow money (M1)	10.7%
Av. ann. inflation 1990–97	2.4%	Broad money	13.0%
Money market rate, 1997	4.35%		

Exchange rates

	end 1997		December 1997
S$ per $	1.68	Effective rates	1990 = 100
S$ per SDR	2.26	– nominal	109.8
S$ per Ecu	1.85	– real	124.5

Principal exports

	$bn fob		$bn fob
Machinery & equipment	82.5	Agric. products & foodstuffs	2.3
Mineral fuels	11.9	Crude materials	1.7
Manufactured products	7.1		
Chemicals	7.0	Total incl. others	**125.0**

Main export destinations

	% of total		% of total
United States	18.4	Thailand	5.7
Malaysia	18.0	Germany	3.1
Hong Kong	8.9	United Kingdom	2.8
Japan	8.2		

Principal imports

	$bn cif		$bn cif
Machinery & equipment	76.0	Agric. products & foodstuffs	3.7
Manufactured products	12.9	Crude minerals	1.5
Mineral fuels	12.3		
Chemicals	7.8	Total incl. others	**131.3**

Main origins of imports

	% of total		% of total
Japan	18.2	Taiwan	4.1
United States	16.3	Saudi Arabia	3.8
Malaysia	15.0	Germany	3.6
Thailand	5.5		

Balance of payments, reserves and debt[b], $bn

Visible exports fob	126.0	Overall balance	7.4
Visible imports fob	-123.7	Change in reserves	8.2
Trade balance	2.3	Level of reserves	
Invisibles inflows	42.1	end Dec.	76.8
Invisibles outflows	-29.1	No. months of import cover	6.0
Net transfers	-1.0	Foreign debt	5.5
Current account balance	14.3	– as % of GDP	10.0
– as % of GDP	15.4	Debt service	0.6
Capital balance	0.4	Debt service ratio	0.6

Family life

No. of households	0.8m	Divorces per 1,000 pop.	1.4
Av. no. per household	4.0	Cost of living, Dec. 1997	
Marriages per 1,000 pop.	8.8	New York = 100	106

a Energy trade data are distorted by transitory and oil refining activities.
b 1995

SLOVAKIA

Area	49,035 sq km	Currency	Koruna (Kc)
Capital	Bratislava		

People

Population	5.3m	Life expectancy: men	67.0 yrs
Pop. per sq km	109	women	75.8 yrs
Av. ann. growth		Adult literacy	99.0%
in pop. 1990–2000	0.22%	Fertility rate (per woman)	1.5
Pop. under 15	24.7%	Urban population	59%
Pop. over 65	10.7%		per 1,000 pop.
No. of men per 100 women	94.9	Crude birth rate	11.7
Human Development Index	87.3	Crude death rate	11

The economy

GDP	Kc581bn	GDP per head	$3,400
GDP	$18bn	GDP per head in purchasing	
Av. ann. growth in real		power parity (USA=100)	27
GDP 1990–96	-1.0%		

Origins of GDP

	% of total
Agriculture	5.2
Industry, of which:	31.0
manufacturing	...
Services	63.8

Components of GDP

	% of total
Private consumption	49.3
Public consumption	23.7
Investment	38.1
Exports	57.4
Imports	-68.4

Structure of employment[a]

	% of total		% of labour force
Agriculture	9	Unemployed 1996	12.6
Industry	37	Av. ann. rate 1993–96	13.8
Services	54		

Energy

	m TCE		
Total output	6.629	% output exported	35.8
Total consumption	22.755	% consumption imported	87.5
Consumption per head,			
kg coal equivalent	4,263		

Inflation and finance

		av. ann. increase 1994–96	
Consumer price			
inflation 1997	6.1%	Narrow money (M1)	14.1%
Av. ann. inflation 1991–97	16.5%	Broad money	17.3%
Deposit rate, 1997	13.44%		

Exchange rates

	end 1997		December 1997
Kc per $	34.78	Effective rates	1990 = 100
Kc per SDR	46.93	– nominal	...
Kc per Ecu	38.26	– real	...

Principal exports

	$bn fob		$bn fob
Machinery & industrial		Manufactured goods	1.1
equipment	2.0	Raw materials	0.4
Chemicals	1.1	Total incl. others	**8.8**

Main export destinations

	% of total		% of total
Czech Republic	30.6	EU15	41.3
Germany	20.9		

Principal imports

	$bn fob		$bn fob
Machinery & transport		Intermediate manufactured	
equipment	3.9	goods	1.7
Fuels	1.9	Total incl. others	**11.1**

Main origins of imports

	% of total		% of total
Czech Republic	24.8	EU15	36.9

Balance of payments, reserves and debt, $bn

Visible exports fob	8.8	Overall balance	0.4
Visible imports fob	-11.1	Change in reserves	0.0
Trade balance	-2.3	Level of reserves	
Invisibles inflows	2.3	end Dec.	3.9
Invisibles outflows	-2.3	No. months of import cover	3.5
Net transfers	0.2	Foreign debt	7.7
Current account balance	-2.1	– as % of GDP	42.8
– as % of GDP	-11.5	Debt service paid	1.3
Capital balance	2.2	Debt service ratio	11.9

Family life

No. of households	1.8m	Divorces per 1,000 pop.	1.7
Av. no. per household	2.8	Cost of living, Dec. 1997	
Marriages per 1,000 pop.	6.4	New York = 100	...

a   1995

SOUTH AFRICA

Area	1,225,815 sq km	Currency	Rand (R)
Capital	Pretoria		

People

Population	42.4m	Life expectancy: men	62.3 yrs
Pop. per sq km	35	women	68.3 yrs
Av. ann. growth		Adult literacy	81.4%
in pop. 1990–2000	2.22%	Fertility rate (per woman)	3.8
Pop. under 15	37.3%	Urban population	51%
Pop. over 65	4.4%		*per 1,000 pop.*
No. of men per 100 women	98.7	Crude birth rate	29.7
Human Development Index	71.6	Crude death rate	8

The economy

GDP	R543bn	GDP per head	$3,130
GDP	$133bn	GDP per head in purchasing	
Av. ann. growth in real		power parity (USA=100)	24
GDP 1990–96	1.2%		

Origins of GDP		**Components of GDP**	
	% of total		*% of total*
Agriculture	4.7	Private consumption	59.3
Industry, of which:	34.9	Public consumption	20.8
manufacturing	23.8	Investment	18.7
Services	60.4	Exports	30.5
		Imports	-30.5

Structure of employment[a]

	% of total		*% of labour force*
Agriculture	11	Unemployed 1996	5.1
Industry	25	Av. ann. rate 1994–96	4.7
Services	64		

Energy

	m TCE		
Total output	168.238	% output exported	32.2
Total consumption	124.847	% consumption imported	11.0
Consumption per head,			
kg coal equivalent	2,638		

Inflation and finance

Consumer price		*av. ann. increase 1993–96*	
inflation 1997	8.6%	Narrow money (M1)	20.2%
Av. ann. inflation 1990–97	10.8%	Broad money	13.6%
Money market rate, 1997	15.59%		

Exchange rates

	end 1997		*December 1997*
R per $	4.87	Effective rates	1990 = 100
R per SDR	6.57	– nominal	68.2
R per Ecu	5.36	– real	94.6

Principal exports[b]

	$bn fob		$bn fob
Gold	6.4	Food, drink & tobacco	2.1
Base metals	3.1		
Diamonds	2.7	Total incl. others	**25.1**

Main export destinations

	% of total		% of total
Japan	6.8	Germany	4.9
United States	5.9	United Kingdom	4.6
Italy	5.8		

Principal imports[b]

	$bn cif		$bn cif
Machinery & transport		Chemicals	2.7
equipment	10.2	Food, drink & tobacco	1.0
Manufactured goods	2.8	Total incl. others	**23.4**

Main origins of imports

	% of total		% of total
Germany	12.9	Japan	7.3
United States	11.0	Italy	4.2
United Kingdom	10.4		

Balance of payments, reserves and debt, $bn

Visible exports fob	29.1	Overall balance	-0.8
Visible imports fob	-27.0	Change in reserves	-2.1
Trade balance	2.0	Level of reserves	
Invisibles inflows	5.1	end Dec.	2.3
Invisibles outflows	-9.1	No. months of import cover	0.8
Net transfers	-0.1	Foreign debt	23.6
Current account balance	-2.0	– as % of GDP	17.7
– as % of GDP	-1.5	Debt service	3.8
Capital balance	2.6	Debt service ratio	11.1

Family life

No. of households	8.2m	Divorces per 1,000 pop.	0.4
Av. no. per household	4.9	Cost of living, Dec. 1997	
Marriages per 1,000 pop.	3.3	New York = 100	60

a 1991
b 1994

SOUTH KOREA

Area	99,274 sq km	Currency	Won (W)
Capital	Seoul		

People

Population	45.3m	Life expectancy: men	68.8 yrs
Pop. per sq km	458	women	76.0 yrs
Av. ann. growth		Adult literacy	97.9%
in pop. 1990–2000	0.90%	Fertility rate (per woman)	1.7
Pop. under 15	23.3%	Urban population	81%
Pop. over 65	5.6%		*per 1,000 pop.*
No. of men per 100 women	101.6	Crude birth rate	15.0
Human Development Index	89.0	Crude death rate	6

The economy

GDP	W389,813bn	GDP per head	$10,660
GDP	$483bn	GDP per head in purchasing	
Av. ann. growth in real		power parity (USA=100)	48
GDP 1990–96	7.3%		

Origins of GDP		Components of GDP	
	% of total		*% of total*
Agriculture	6.4	Private consumption	52.9
Industry, of which:	44.1	Public consumption	8.9
manufacturing	30.0	Investment	38.7
Services	49.5	Exports	44.1
		Imports	-45.0

Structure of employment

	% of total		*% of labour force*
Agriculture	12	Unemployed 1996	2.0
Industry	32	Av. ann. rate 1990–96	2.3
Services	56		

Energy

	m TCE		
Total output	29.251	% output exported	63.8
Total consumption	186.002	% consumption imported	108.3
Consumption per head,			
kg coal equivalent	4,142		

Inflation and finance

		av. ann. increase 1989–96	
Consumer price			
inflation 1997	4.4%	Narrow money (M1)	15.9%
Av. ann. inflation 1990–97	6.1%	Broad money	17.5%
Money market rate, 1997	13.2%		

Exchange rates

	end 1997		*December 1997*
W per $	1,696	Effective rates	*1990 = 100*
W per SDR	2,288	– nominal	...
W per Ecu	1,866	– real	...

Principal exports

	$bn fob		$bn fob
Electronic components	17.3	Ships	7.1
Textiles	10.2	Clothing & accessories	4.2
Cars	9.1	Total incl. others	**129.8**

Main export destinations

	% of total		% of total
United States	16.7	Hong Kong	8.6
Japan	12.2	Singapore	5.0
China	8.8		

Principal imports

	$bn cif		$bn cif
Machinery & transport equipment	54.7	Raw materials	11.0
		Food & live animals	7.3
Mineral fuels & lubricants	24.3		
Chemicals	13.2	Total incl. others	**150.2**

Main origins of imports

	% of total		% of total
United States	22.2	Germany	4.8
Japan	20.9	Saudi Arabia	4.4
China	5.7		

Balance of payments, reserves and debt[a], $bn

Visible exports fob	128.3	Overall balance	1.4
Visible imports fob	-143.6	Change in reserves	1.4
Trade balance	-15.3	Level of reserves	
Invisibles inflows	29.6	end Dec.	34.2
Invisibles outflows	-37.5	No. months of import cover	2.3
Net transfers	0.1	Foreign debt	74.6
Current account balance	-23.1	– as % of GDP	16.4
– as % of GDP	-4.8	Debt service paid	10.6
Capital balance	24.4	Debt service ratio	7.0

Family life

No. of households	13.3m	Divorces per 1,000 pop.	1.2
Av. no. per household	3.3	Cost of living, Dec. 1997	
Marriages per 1,000 pop.	7.5	New York = 100	101

a 1995

SPAIN

Area	504,782 sq km	Currency	Peseta (Pta)
Capital	Madrid		

People

Population	39.7m	Life expectancy: men	74.5 yrs
Pop. per sq km	79	women	81.5 yrs
Av. ann. growth		Adult literacy	91.7%
in pop. 1990–2000	0.14%	Fertility rate (per woman)	1.2
Pop. under 15	16.6%	Urban population	76%
Pop. over 65	15.0%		per 1,000 pop.
No. of men per 100 women	96.3	Crude birth rate	9.7
Human Development Index	93.4	Crude death rate	9

The economy

GDP	Pta73,572bn	GDP per head	$14,200
GDP	$563bn	GDP per head in purchasing	
Av. ann. growth in real		power parity (USA=100)	55
GDP 1990–96	1.3%		

Origins of GDP

	% of total
Agriculture	3.7
Industry, of which:	33.5
manufacturing	...
Services	62.8

Components of GDP

	% of total
Private consumption	62.0
Public consumption	16.2
Investment	20.6
Exports	25.5
Imports	-24.2

Structure of employment

	% of total		% of labour force
Agriculture	9	Unemployed 1996	22.2
Industry	30	Av. ann. rate 1990–96	20.4
Services	61		

Energy

	m TCE		
Total output	38.977	% output exported[a]	22.9
Total consumption	125.122	% consumption imported[a]	92.3
Consumption per head,			
kg coal equivalent	3,157		

Inflation and finance

Consumer price		av. ann. increase 1989–96	
inflation 1997	2.0%	Narrow money (M1)	8.0%
Av. ann. inflation 1990–97	4.7%	Broad money	9.1%
Money market rate, 1997	5.49%		

Exchange rates

	end 1997		December 1997
Pta per $	151.7	Effective rates	1990 = 100
Pta per SDR	204.7	– nominal	76.9
Pta per Ecu	166.9	– real	88.7

Principal exports

	$bn fob		$bn fob
Raw materials & intermediate products	43.5	Capital goods	14.2
Consumer goods	41.9	Total incl. others	**102.1**

Main export destinations

	% of total		% of total
France	20.1	Portugal	8.6
Germany	14.5	United Kingdom	8.5
Italy	8.7	EU15	71.4

Principal imports

	$bn cif		$bn cif
Raw materials & intermediate products (excl. fuels)	60.8	Capital goods	20.4
		Energy products	11.1
Consumer goods	29.8	Total incl. others	**121.3**

Main origins of imports

	% of total		% of total
France	17.8	United Kingdom	8.3
Germany	14.8	United States	6.3
Italy	9.5	EU15	66.3

Balance of payments, reserves and aid, $bn

Visible exports fob	102.0	Capital balance	26.1
Visible imports fob	-117.0	Overall balance	24.3
Trade balance	-14.9	Change in reserves	23.2
Invisibles inflows	58.5	Level of reserves	
Invisibles outflows	-44.4	end Dec.	63.7
Net transfers	2.6	No. months of import cover	4.7
Current account balance	1.8	Aid given	1.25
– as % of GDP	0.3	– as % of GDP	0.22

Family life

No. of households	15.2m	Divorces per 1,000 pop.	0.7
Av. no. per household	2.6	Cost of living, Dec. 1997	
Marriages per 1,000 pop.	5.0	New York = 100	82

SWEDEN

Area	449,964 sq km	Currency	Swedish krona (Skr)
Capital	Stockholm		

People

Population	8.8m	Life expectancy: men		76.2 yrs
Pop. per sq km	20		women	80.8 yrs
Av. ann. growth		Adult literacy		99.0%
in pop. 1990–2000	0.39%	Fertility rate (per woman)		1.8
Pop. under 15	18.8%	Urban population		83%
Pop. over 65	17.3%			per 1,000 pop.
No. of men per 100 women	97.9	Crude birth rate		11.9
Human Development Index	93.6	Crude death rate		11

The economy

GDP	Skr1,688bn	GDP per head	$25,770
GDP	$227bn	GDP per head in purchasing	
Av. ann. growth in real		power parity (USA=100)	68
GDP 1990–96	0.6%		

Origins of GDP		Components of GDP	
	% of total		% of total
Agriculture	2.2	Private consumption	50.9
Industry, of which:	27.0	Public consumption	25.3
manufacturing	21.6	Investment	16.0
Services	70.8	Exports	40.0
		Imports	-32.0

Structure of employment

	% of total		% of labour force
Agriculture	3	Unemployed 1996	8.0
Industry	26	Av. ann. rate 1993–96	8.0
Services	71		

Energy

	m TCE		
Total output	34.575	% output exported	45.8
Total consumption	59.194	% consumption imported	68.0
Consumption per head,			
kg coal equivalent	6,736		

Inflation and finance

Consumer price			av. ann. increase 1989–96
inflation 1997	0.5%	Narrow money (M1)	...
Av. ann. inflation 1990–97	3.9%	Broad money	4.3%
Money market rate, 1997	4.21%		

Exchange rates

	end 1997		December 1997
			1990 = 100
Skr per $	7.88	Effective rates	
Skr per SDR	10.63	– nominal	85.3
Skr per Ecu	8.67	– real	74.6

Principal exports

	$bn fob		$bn fob
Machinery incl.		Transport equipment	11.8
electricals	28.0	Chemicals	7.9
Wood products, pulp &		Iron & steel	4.6
paper	12.6	Total incl. others	**84.5**

Main export destinations

	% of total		% of total
Germany	11.7	United States	8.3
United Kingdom	9.5	Denmark	6.1
Norway	8.4	EU15	54.9

Principal imports

	$bn cif		$bn cif
Machinery incl.		Food, beverages & tobacco	4.6
electricals	20.2	Mineral fuels	4.4
Chemicals	7.8	Clothing, footwear & textiles	2.8
Transport equipment	6.5	Total incl. others	**66.7**

Main origins of imports

	% of total		% of total
Germany	18.7	Denmark	7.5
United Kingdom	10.0	United States	5.8
Norway	7.8	EU15	66.2

Balance of payments, reserves and aid, $bn

Visible exports fob	84.7	Capital balance	-10.0
Visible imports fob	-66.1	Overall balance	-6.4
Trade balance	18.6	Change in reserves	-5.0
Invisibles inflows	31.3	Level of reserves	
Invisibles outflows	-41.4	end Dec.	20.8
Net transfers	-2.6	No. months of import cover	2.3
Current account balance	5.9	Aid given	2.00
– as % of GDP	2.6	– as % of GDP	0.84

Family life

No. of households	3.9m	Divorces per 1,000 pop.	2.5
Av. no. per household	2.3	Cost of living, Dec. 1997	
Marriages per 1,000 pop.	3.8	New York = 100	105

SWITZERLAND

Area	41,293 sq km	Currency	Swiss franc (SFr)
Capital	Berne		

People

Population	7.2m	Life expectancy: men	75.3 yrs
Pop. per sq km	175	women	81.8 yrs
Av. ann. growth		Adult literacy	99.0%
in pop. 1990–2000	0.81%	Fertility rate (per woman)	1.5
Pop. under 15	17.4%	Urban population	61%
Pop. over 65	14.3%		per 1,000 pop.
No. of men per 100 women	98.3	Crude birth rate	10.9
Human Development Index	93.0	Crude death rate	9

The economy

GDP	SFr364bn	GDP per head	$43,420
GDP	$314bn	GDP per head in purchasing	
Av. ann. growth in real		power parity (USA=100)	94
GDP 1990–96	-0.1%		

Origins of GDP[a]		Components of GDP	
	% of total		% of total
Agriculture	2.6	Private consumption	60.8
Industry, of which:	32.1	Public consumption	15.2
manufacturing	...	Investment	19.9
Services	65.3	Exports	36.1
		Imports	-32.0

Structure of employment

	% of total		% of labour force
Agriculture	4	Unemployed 1996	3.7
Industry	28	Av. ann. rate 1991–96	3.2
Services	68		

Energy

	m TCE		
Total output	13.666	% output exported	28.7
Total consumption	31.672	% consumption imported	73.2
Consumption per head,			
kg coal equivalent	4,401		

Inflation and finance

Consumer price		av. ann. increase 1989–96	
inflation 1997	0.5%	Narrow money (M1)	2.6%
Av. ann. inflation 1990–97	2.8%	Broad money	4.7%
Money market rate, 1997	1.35%		

Exchange rates

	end 1997		December 1997
SFr per $	1.46	Effective rates	1990 = 100
SFr per SDR	1.96	– nominal	108.3
SFr per Ecu	1.61	– real	111.3

Principal exports

	$bn fob		$bn fob
Machinery	22.6	Metals & metal manufactures	6.6
Chemicals	20.9	Textiles & clothing	3.0
Precision instruments, watches & jewellery	11.8	Total incl. others	**75.9**

Main export destinations

	% of total		% of total
Germany	23.3	Italy	7.7
France	9.4	United Kingdom	5.7
United States	9.0	Japan	4.1

Principal imports

	$bn cif		$bn cif
Machinery	16.7	Metals & metals manufactures	6.5
Chemicals	10.9	Textiles, clothing & shoes	6.3
Motor vehicles	9.0		
Agricultural products	6.7	Total incl. others	**74.2**

Main origins of imports

	% of total		% of total
Germany	32.8	United States	6.6
France	12.0	Netherlands	5.0
Italy	11.3	Japan	2.8

Balance of payments, reserves and aid, $bn

Visible exports fob	95.5	Capital balance	-23.4
Visible imports fob	-93.7	Overall balance	2.7
Trade balance	1.8	Change in reserves	0.6
Invisibles inflows	58.1	Level of reserves	
Invisibles outflows	-35.6	end Dec.	69.2
Net transfers	-3.8	No. months of import cover	6.4
Current account balance	20.5	Aid given	1.03
– as % of GDP	6.5	– as % of GDP	0.34

Family life

No. of households	3.0m	Divorces per 1,000 pop.	2.2
Av. no. per household	2.5	Cost of living, Dec. 1997	
Marriages per 1,000 pop.	5.7	New York = 100	117

a 1994

TAIWAN

Area	36,179 sq km	Currency	Taiwan dollar (T$)
Capital	Taipei		

People

Population	21.5m	Life expectancy: men	...
Pop. per sq km	596	women	...
Av. ann. growth		Adult literacy	...
in pop. 1985–95	1.14%	Fertility rate (per woman)	1.8
Pop. under 15	24.0%	Urban population	...
Pop. over 65	7.7%		per 1,000 pop.
No. of men per 100 women	105.8	Crude birth rate	15.1
Human Development Index	...	Crude death rate	5.7

The economy

GDP	T$7,498bn	GDP per head	$12,800
GDP	$273bn	GDP per head in purchasing	
Av. ann. growth in real		power parity (USA=100)	64
GDP 1985–95	6.6%		

Origins of GDP		Components of GDP	
	% of total		% of total
Agriculture	3.3	Private consumption	59.8
Industry, of which:	35.8	Public consumption	14.2
manufacturing	28.2	Investment	21.3
Services	60.9	Exports	48.0
		Imports	-44.0

Structure of employment

	% of total		% of labour force
Agriculture	10	Unemployed 1996	2.6
Industry	37	Av. ann. rate 1990–96	1.7
Services	53		

Energy

	m TCE		
Total output	...	% output exported	3.3
Total consumption	...	% consumption imported	76.7
Consumption per head,			
kg coal equivalent	...		

Inflation and finance

Consumer price		av. ann. increase 1989–96	
inflation 1997	0.9%	Narrow money (M1)	7.3%
Av. ann. inflation 1990–97	3.1%	Broad money	14.5%

Exchange rates

	end 1997		December 1997
T$ per $	32.67	Effective rates	1990 = 100
T$ per SDR	44.10	– nominal	...
T$ per Ecu	35.94	– real	...

Principal exports

	$bn fob		$bn fob
Machinery & electrical		Plastic & rubber articles	7.7
equipment	53.7	Vehicles, aircraft & ships	5.2
Textiles & clothing	15.7		
Base metals & manufactures	10.3	Total incl. others	**114.8**

Main export destinations

	% of total		% of total
United States	23.3	Netherlands	3.3
Hong Kong	23.1	Germany	3.1
Japan	11.8	Malaysia	2.5
Singapore	3.9	United Kingdom	2.4

Principal imports

	$bn cif		$bn cif
Machinery & electrical		Precision instruments, clocks	
equipment	36.0	& watches	5.3
Chemicals	10.4	Crude petroleum	4.9
Metals	10.9	Total incl. others	**96.6**

Main origins of imports

	% of total		% of total
Japan	27.2	Malaysia	3.5
United States	19.7	France	2.9
Germany	5.0	Australia	2.8
South Korea	4.1	Indonesia	1.9

Balance of payments, reserves and debt[a], $bn

Visible exports fob	114.8	Overall balance	1.1
Visible imports fob	-96.6	Change in reserves	-2.3
Trade balance	18.1	Level of reserves	
Invisibles inflows	24.3	end Dec.	88.7
Invisibles outflows	-29.6	No. months of import cover	8.4
Net transfers	-2.3	Foreign debt	27.0
Current account balance	10.5	– as % of GDP	10.4
– as % of GDP	3.8	Debt service	2.1
Capital balance	-8.9	Debt service ratio	1.6

Family life

No. of households	5.7m	Divorces per 1,000 pop.	...
Av. no. per household	3.1	Cost of living, Dec. 1997	
Marriages per 1,000 pop.	7.9	New York = 100	106

a 1995

THAILAND

Area	513,115 sq km	Currency	Baht (Bt)
Capital	Bangkok		

People

Population	58.7m	Life expectancy: men	66.3 yrs
Pop. per sq km	114	women	72.3 yrs
Av. ann. growth		Adult literacy	93.5%
in pop. 1990–2000	0.85%	Fertility rate (per woman)	1.7
Pop. under 15	27.9%	Urban population	20%
Pop. over 65	5.0%		per 1,000 pop.
No. of men per 100 women	99.9	Crude birth rate	16.7
Human Development Index	83.3	Crude death rate	6

The economy

GDP	Bt4,598bn	GDP per head	$3,020
GDP	$178bn	GDP per head in purchasing	
Av. ann. growth in real		power parity (USA=100)	25
GDP 1990–96	8.3%		

Origins of GDP		Components of GDP	
	% of total		% of total
Agriculture	11.8	Private consumption	54.5
Industry, of which:	38.6	Public consumption	9.7
manufacturing	29.3	Investment	42.9
Services	49.6	Exports	41.1
		Imports	-48.0

Structure of employment

	% of total		% of labour force
Agriculture	53	Unemployed 1993	1.5
Industry }	47	Av. ann. rate 1990–93	2.0
Services }			

Energy

	m TCE		
Total output	29.662	% output exported	5.4
Total consumption	73.204	% consumption imported	65.6
Consumption per head,			
kg coal equivalent	1,257		

Inflation and finance

Consumer price		*av. ann. increase 1989–96*	
inflation 1996	5.8%	Narrow money (M1)	14.0%
Av. ann. inflation 1990–96	5.1%	Broad money	18.5%
Money market rate, 1996	9.16%		

Exchange rates

	end 1997		December 1997
			1990 = 100
Bt per $	47.25	Effective rates	
Bt per SDR	63.75	– nominal	...
Bt per Ecu	51.98	– real	...

Principal exports

	$bn fob		$bn fob
Computers & parts	6.5	Rice	2.0
Textiles & clothing	5.4	Footwear	1.3
Integrated circuits	2.3	Total incl. others	**55.7**

Main export destinations

	% of total		% of total
United States	18.0	Hong Kong	5.8
Japan	16.8	China	3.6
Singapore	12.9		

Principal imports

	$bn cif		$bn cif
Capital goods	33.3	Petroleum & products	6.2
Raw materials & intermediates	18.7		
Consumer goods	7.6	Total incl. others	**72.3**

Main origins of imports

	% of total		% of total
Japan	28.3	Germany	5.1
United States	12.5	Taiwan	5.0
Singapore	5.5		

Balance of payments, reserves and debt, $bn

Visible exports fob	54.4	Overall balance	2.2
Visible imports fob	-63.9	Change in reserves	1.7
Trade balance	-9.5	Level of reserves	
Invisibles inflows	21.0	end Dec.	38.6
Invisibles outflows	-26.9	No. months of import cover	5.1
Net transfers	0.8	Foreign debt	95.8
Current account balance	-14.7	– as % of GDP	51.0
– as % of GDP	-8.3	Debt service paid	8.7
Capital balance	19.5	Debt service ratio	11.5

Family life

No. of households	13.0m	Divorces per 1,000 pop.	0.7
Av. no. per household	4.3	Cost of living, Dec. 1997	
Marriages per 1,000 pop.	8.3	New York = 100	58

TURKEY

Area	779,452 sq km	Currency	Turkish Lira (L)
Capital	Ankara		

People

Population	61.8m	Life expectancy: men	66.5 yrs
Pop. per sq km	79	women	71.7 yrs
Av. ann. growth		Adult literacy	81.6%
in pop. 1990–2000	1.59%	Fertility rate (per woman)	2.5
Pop. under 15	31.2%	Urban population	69%
Pop. over 65	5.1%		per 1,000 pop.
No. of men per 100 women	102.3	Crude birth rate	21.9
Human Development Index	77.2	Crude death rate	7

The economy

GDP	L14,320trn	GDP per head	$2,870
GDP	$178bn	GDP per head in purchasing	
Av. ann. growth in real		power parity (USA=100)	22
GDP 1990–96	3.6%		

Origins of GDP		Components of GDP	
	% of total		% of total
Agriculture	17.6	Private consumption	69.7
Industry, of which:	29.3	Public consumption	11.9
manufacturing	…	Investment	24.5
Services	53.1	Exports	22.2
		Imports	-28.3

Structure of employment

	% of total		% of labour force
Agriculture	46	Unemployed 1996	5.8
Industry	22	Av. ann. rate 1990–96	7.5
Services	32		

Energy

	m TCE		
Total output	26.882	% output exported	8.2
Total consumption	72.708	% consumption imported	72.2
Consumption per head,			
kg coal equivalent	1,195		

Inflation and finance

Consumer price		av. ann. increase 1989–96	
inflation 1997	85.7%	Narrow money (M1)	73.0%
Av. ann. inflation 1990–97	77.3%	Broad money	87.2%
Money market rate, 1997	70.32%		

Exchange rates

	end 1997		December 1997
L per $	205,605	Effective rates	1990 = 100
L per SDR	277,413	– nominal	…
L per Ecu	226,166	– real	…

Principal exports[a]

	$bn fob		$bn fob
Clothing & textiles	8.3	Processed food & tobacco	1.6
Iron, steel & metals	2.7		
Vegetables, fruit & nuts	2.0	Total incl. others	**21.6**

Main export destinations

	% of total		% of total
Germany	23.6	United Kingdom	6.0
United States	7.9	France	5.0
Italy	6.5	Russia	4.3

Principal imports[a]

	$bn cif		$bn cif
Machinery	8.0	Chemicals	4.3
Minerals	4.9	Vehicles	3.6
Metals	4.5	Total incl. others	**35.7**

Main origins of imports

	% of total		% of total
Germany	18.9	France	6.8
Italy	10.6	United Kingdom	6.3
United States	7.8	Saudi Arabia	3.7

Balance of payments, reserves and debt, $bn

Visible exports fob	32.3	Overall balance	4.5
Visible imports fob	-41.9	Change in reserves	3.9
Trade balance	-9.6	Level of reserves	
Invisibles inflows	14.6	end Dec.	17.8
Invisibles outflows	-10.9	No. months of import cover	4.0
Net transfers	4.4	Foreign debt	79.8
Current account balance	-1.5	– as % of GDP	44.8
– as % of GDP	-0.8	Debt service paid	10.9
Capital balance	8.7	Debt service ratio	21.7

Family life

No. of households	14.4m	Divorces per 1,000 pop.	0.5
Av. no. per household	4.0	Cost of living, Dec. 1997	
Marriages per 1,000 pop.	8.0	New York = 100	63

a 1995

UKRAINE

Area	603,700 sq km	Currency	Hryvna
Capital	Kiev		

People

Population	51.6m	Life expectancy: men	63.6 yrs
Pop. per sq km	85	women	74.0 yrs
Av. ann. growth		Adult literacy	98.8%
in pop. 1990–2000	-0.21%	Fertility rate (per woman)	1.4
No. of men per 100 women	86.8		per 1,000 pop.
Human Development Index	68.9	Crude birth rate[a]	9.7
		Crude death rate[a]	14

The economy

GDP	$61bn	GDP per head	$1,200
Av. ann. growth in real		GDP per head in purchasing	
GDP 1989–95	-11.9%	power parity (USA=100)	8

Origins of GDP		Components of GDP	
	% of total		% of total
Agriculture	13.4	Private consumption	57.8
Industry	32.5	Public consumption	21.7
Construction	6.1	Net investment	22.9
Other	48.0	Net exports	-2.4

Inflation and exchange rates

Consumer price			end 1997
inflation 1997	15.9%	Hryvna per $	1.89
Av. ann. inflation 1991–97	454.7%	Hryvna per Ecu	2.08

Principal exports

	$ bn		$ bn
Metals	5.0	Machinery	1.6
Chemicals	1.9	Food industry	1.5
Agricultural produce	1.6	Total incl. others	**15.5**

Main export destinations

	% of total		% of total
Russia	38.7	Germany	2.9
China	5.4	United States	2.9
Belarus	5.1		

Principal imports

	$ bn		$ bn
Mineral products	11.0	Chemicals	1.1
Machinery & equipment	2.9	Total incl. others	**19.8**

Main origins of imports

	% of total		% of total
Russia	48.0	Germany	5.5
Turkmenistan	8.8	United States	3.0

EX-SOVIET REPUBLICS

	Area '000 sq km	Population m	Population[a] per sq km	Capital	Currency
Armenia	29.8	3.64	122	Yerevan	Dram
Azerbaijan	86.6	7.59	88	Baku	Manat
Belarus	207.6	10.35	50	Minsk	Rouble
Estonia	45.2	1.47	33	Tallinn	Kroon
Georgia	69.7	5.44	78	Tbilisi	Lari
Kazakhstan	2,717.3	16.82	6	Alma-Ata	Tenge
Kirgizstan	198.5	4.47	23	Bishkek	Som
Latvia	63.7	2.50	39	Riga	Lat
Lithuania	65.2	3.73	57	Vilnius	Lit
Moldova	33.7	4.44	132	Kishinev	Leu
Tajikistan	143.1	5.94	41	Dushanbe	Rouble
Turkmenistan	488.1	4.16	9	Ashkhabad	Manat
Uzbekistan	447.4	23.21	52	Tashkent	Som

People

	Av. ann. pop. growth 1990–2000	Pop. under 15 %	Male life expect.[a] yrs	Birth rate[a]	Death rate	Human Dev. Index
Armenia	0.33	28.6	67.2	13	7	65
Azerbaijan	0.89	32.2	66.5	19	7	64
Belarus	0.03	21.7	64.4	10	12	81
Estonia	-1.03	20.5	63.9	9	13	78
Georgia	-0.08	23.7	68.5	14	9	64
Kazakhstan	0.11	29.8	62.8	18	8	71
Kirgizstan	0.33	36.9	63.4	26	7	64
Latvia	-1.13	20.6	62.5	10	14	71
Lithuania	-0.13	21.7	64.9	11	12	76
Moldova	0.21	26.4	63.5	14	11	61
Tajikistan	1.88	42.0	64.2	30	7	58
Turkmenistan	2.00	39.4	61.2	29	8	72
Uzbekistan	1.99	39.9	64.3	28	7	66

The economy

	GDP $bn	GDP Per head $	GDP PPP USA=100	Agric. as % of GDP	Exports of goods $m	Imports of goods $m	Foreign debt $m
Armenia	2.4	630	8	44	290	760	552
Azerbaijan	3.6	480	5	23	789	1,338	435
Belarus	22.5	2,070	16	16	5,652	6,939	1,071
Estonia	4.5	3,080	17	7	2,064	3,122	405
Georgia	4.6	850	6	35	415	710	1,356
Kazakhstan	22.2	1,350	12	13	6,292	6,618	2,920
Kirgizstan	2.5	550	7	52	529	902	789
Latvia	5.7	2,300	13	9	1,488	2,256	472
Lithuania	8.5	2,280	16	13	3,413	4,309	1,286
Moldova	2.5	590	5	50	828	1,113	834
Tajikistan	2.0	340	3	19	503	553	707
Turkmenistan	4.3	940	7	11	1,692	1,532	825
Uzbekistan	23.5	1,010	9	26	3,781	4,712	2,319

a 1995–2000.

UNITED KINGDOM

Area	242,534 sq km	Currency	Pound (£)
Capital	London		

People

Population	58.1m	Life expectancy: men	74.5 yrs
Pop. per sq km	238	women	79.8 yrs
Av. ann. growth		Adult literacy	99.0%
in pop. 1990–2000	0.14%	Fertility rate (per woman)	1.7
Pop. under 15	19.3%	Urban population	89%
Pop. over 65	15.8%		per 1,000 pop.
No. of men per 100 women	96.2	Crude birth rate	12
Human Development Index	93.1	Crude death rate	11

The economy

GDP	£788bn	GDP per head	$19,810
GDP	$1,152bn	GDP per head in purchasing	
Av. ann. growth in real		power parity (USA=100)	73
GDP 1990–96	1.6%		

Origins of GDP

Components of GDP

	% of total		% of total
Agriculture	1.8	Private consumption	63.9
Industry, of which:	26.5	Public consumption	20.9
manufacturing	21.3	Investment	15.9
Services	71.7	Exports	29.3
		Imports	-30.0

Structure of employment

	% of total		% of labour force
Agriculture	2	Unemployed 1996	8.2
Industry	27	Av. ann. rate 1990–96	8.8
Services	78		

Energy

	m TCE		
Total output	364.154	% output exported	40.2
Total consumption	309.871	% consumption imported	32.4
Consumption per head,			
kg coal equivalent	5,315		

Inflation and finance

		av. ann. increase 1989–96	
Consumer price			
inflation 1997	3.1%	Narrow money (M0)	4.8%
Av. ann. inflation 1990–97	4.0%	Broad money	9.1%
Money market rate, 1997	6.56%		

Exchange rates

	end 1997		December 1997
£ per $	0.60	Effective rates	1990 = 100
£ per SDR	0.81	– nominal	104.7
£ per Ecu	0.67	– real	117.8

Principal exports

	$bn fob		$bn fob
Finished manufactured		Fuels	17.1
products	147.5	Basic materials	4.4
Semi-manufactured products	70.9		
Food, beverages & tobacco	17.8	Total incl. others	**260.6**

Main export destinations

	% of total		% of total
Germany	12.0	Netherlands	7.7
United States	10.6	Belgium/Luxembourg	4.9
France	9.8	EU15	56.9

Principal imports

	$bn cif		$bn cif
Finished manufactured		Basic materials	10.3
products	157.9	Fuels	10.2
Semi-manufactured products	73.1		
Food, beverages & tobacco	26.2	Total incl. others	**280.4**

Main origins of imports

	% of total		% of total
Germany	14.1	Netherlands	6.5
United States	12.5	Japan	4.9
France	9.2	EU15	54.0

Balance of payments, reserves and aid, $bn

Visible exports fob	261.9	Capital balance	-1.2
Visible imports fob	-281.5	Overall balance	-0.0
Trade balance	-19.6	Change in reserves	-2.4
Invisibles inflows	227.9	Level of reserves	
Invisibles outflows	-203.7	end Dec.	46.7
Net transfers	-7.4	No. months of import cover	1.2
Current account balance	-2.9	Aid given	3.20
– as % of GDP	-0.3	– as % of GDP	0.27

Family life

No. of households	21.3m	Divorces per 1,000 pop.	3.0
Av. no. per household	2.7	Cost of living, Dec. 1997	
Marriages per 1,000 pop.	6.4	New York = 100	107

UNITED STATES

Area	9,372,610 sq km	Currency	US dollar ($)
Capital	Washington DC		

People

Population	269.4m	Life expectancy: men	73.4 yrs
Pop. per sq km	29	women	80.1 yrs
Av. ann. growth		Adult literacy	99.0%
in pop. 1990–2000	0.90%	Fertility rate (per woman)	2.0
Pop. under 15	22.0%	Urban population	76%
Pop. over 65	12.6%		per 1,000 pop.
No. of men per 100 women	97.1	Crude birth rate	13.8
Human Development Index	94.2	Crude death rate	9

The economy

GDP	$7,434bn	GDP per head	$27,590
Av. ann. growth in real		GDP per head in purchasing	
GDP 1990–96	2.4%	power parity (USA=100)	100

Origins of GDP

Components of GDP

	% of total		% of total
Agriculture	1.7	Private consumption	68.2
Industry, of which:	22.9	Public consumption	18.4
manufacturing	17.4	Investment	14.5
Services[a]	75.4	Exports	11.4
		Imports	-12.6

Structure of employment

	% of total		% of labour force
Agriculture	3	Unemployed 1996	5.4
Industry	24	Av. ann. rate 1994–96	5.7
Services	73		

Energy

	m TCE		
Total output	2,444.217	% output exported	5.3
Total consumption	3,021.575	% consumption imported	24.8
Consumption per head,			
kg coal equivalent	11,312		

Inflation and finance

Consumer price		av. ann. increase 1989–96	
inflation 1997	2.3%	Narrow money (M1)	4.5%
Av. ann. inflation 1990–97	3.3%	Broad money	3.6%
Treasury bill rate, 1997	5.07%		

Exchange rates

	end 1997		December 1997
$ per SDR	1.35	Effective rates	1990 = 100
$ per Ecu	1.10	– nominal	108.2
		– real	111.8

Principal exports

	$bn fob		*$bn fob*
Capital goods, excl. vehicles	253.1	Vehicles & products	65.0
Industrial supplies	148.0	Food & beverages	55.5
Consumer goods, excl. vehicles	70.1	Total incl. others	**613.6**

Main export destinations

	% of total		*% of total*
Canada	22.0	South Korea	4.2
Japan	10.8	Germany	3.8
Mexico	9.3	Taiwan	2.9
United Kingdom	4.9		

Principal imports

	$bn fob		*$bn fob*
Capital goods, excl. vehicles	229.0	Vehicles & products	128.9
Industrial supplies	209.5	Food & beverages	35.7
Consumer goods, excl. vehicles	171.0	Total incl. others	**799.8**

Main origins of imports

	% of total		*% of total*
Canada	19.8	Germany	4.8
Japan	14.3	Taiwan	3.7
Mexico	9.4	United Kingdom	3.6
China	6.4		

Balance of payments, reserves and aid, $bn

Visible exports fob	614.0	Capital balance	189.0
Visible imports fob	-803.2	Overall balance	-6.7
Trade balance	-189.3	Change in reserves	-15.3
Invisibles inflows	441.3	Level of reserves	
Invisibles outflows	-360.2	end Dec.	160.7
Net transfers	-40.5	No. months of import cover	1.7
Current account balance	-148.7	Aid given	9.38
– as % of GDP	-2.0	– as % of GDP	0.12

Family life

No. of households	100.3m	Divorces per 1,000 pop.	4.6
Av. no. per household	2.6	Cost of living, Dec. 1997	
Marriages per 1,000 pop.	8.9	New York = 100	100

a Including utilities.

VENEZUELA

Area	912,050 sq km	Currency	Bolivar (Bs)
Capital	Caracas		

People

Population	22.3m	Life expectancy: men		70.0 yrs
Pop. per sq km	24		women	75.7 yrs
Av. ann. growth		Adult literacy		91.0%
in pop. 1990–2000	2.15%	Fertility rate (per woman)		3.0
Pop. under 15	36.2%	Urban population		93%
Pop. over 65	4.1%			per 1,000 pop.
No. of men per 100 women	101.4	Crude birth rate		24.9
Human Development Index	86.1	Crude death rate		5

The economy

GDP	Bs29,333bn	GDP per head	$3,020
GDP	$67bn	GDP per head in purchasing	
Av. ann. growth in real		power parity (USA=100)	30
GDP 1990–96	1.9%		

Origins of GDP		Components of GDP	
	% of total		% of total
Agriculture	5.5	Private consumption	62.9
Industry, of which:	40.8	Public consumption	10.2
manufacturing	16.2	Investment	20.2
Services	53.7	Exports	29.3
		Imports	-22.6

Structure of employment[a]

	% of total		% of labour force
Agriculture	13	Unemployed 1995	10.3
Industry	24	Av. ann. rate 1990–95	8.8
Services	63		

Energy

	m TCE		
Total output	284.511	% output exported	65.3
Total consumption	97.616	% consumption imported	0.1
Consumption per head,			
kg coal equivalent	4,469		

Inflation and finance

Consumer price		av. ann. increase 1989–96	
inflation 1997	50.0%	Narrow money (M1)	48.0%
Av. ann. inflation 1990–96	89.2%	Broad money	45.3%
Deposit rate, 1997	14.70%		

Exchange rates

	end 1997		December 1997
Bs per $	504	Effective rates	1990 = 100
Bs per SDR	680	– nominal	16.0
Bs per Ecu	554	– real	179.1

Principal exports[a]

	$bn fob		$bn fob
Petroleum & products	14.4		
Metals	1.5	Total incl. others	**18.9**

Main export destinations

	% of total		% of total
United States	53.2	Brazil	4.2
Colombia	5.2	Germany	1.7

Principal imports[a]

	$bn fob		$bn fob
Machinery & transport equipment	4.0	Agricultural products	1.3
Chemicals	1.8	Total incl. others	**10.8**

Main origins of imports

	% of total		% of total
United States	43.8	Germany	4.7
Colombia	7.2	Italy	4.6

Balance of payments, reserves and debt, $bn

Visible exports fob	23.7	Overall balance	7.0
Visible imports fob	-9.9	Change in reserves	5.3
Trade balance	13.8	Level of reserves	
Invisibles inflows	3.1	end Dec.	16.0
Invisibles outflows	-8.2	No. months of import cover	10.6
Net transfers	0.1	Foreign debt	35.3
Current account balance	8.8	– as % of GDP	49.0
– as % of GDP	13.1	Debt service paid	4.5
Capital balance	-1.7	Debt service ratio	16.8

Family life

No. households	3.9m	Divorces per 1,000 pop.	1.0
Av. no. per household	5.4	Cost of living, Dec. 1997	
Marriages per 1,000 pop.	5.4	New York = 100	68

a 1995

ZIMBABWE

Area	390,759 sq km	Currency	Zimbabwe dollar (Z$)
Capital	Harare		

People

Population	11.4m	Life expectancy: men	47.6 yrs
Pop. per sq km	29	women	49.4 yrs
Av. ann. growth		Adult literacy	84.7%
in pop. 1990–2000	2.32%	Fertility rate (per woman)	4.7
Pop. under 15	44.3%	Urban population	32%
Pop. over 65	2.7%		*per 1,000 pop.*
No. of men per 100 women	98.5	Crude birth rate	37.1
Human Development Index	51.3	Crude death rate	14

The economy

GDP	Z$86bn	GDP per head	$610
GDP	$6.8bn	GDP per head in purchasing	
Av. ann. growth in real		power parity (USA=100)	8
GDP 1990–96	1.3%		

Origins of GDP		Components of GDP	
	% of total		*% of total*
Agriculture	17.5	Private consumption	52.1
Industry, of which:	22.2	Public consumption	20.0
manufacturing	17.9	Investment	20.8
Services	60.3	Exports	36.1
		Imports	-35.9

Structure of employment[a]

	% of total		*% of labour force*
Agriculture	68	Unemployed 1996	…
Industry	8	Av. ann. rate 1990–96	…
Services	24		

Energy

	m TCE		
Total output	2.412	% output exported	2.2
Total consumption	4.382	% consumption imported	46.2
Consumption per head,			
kg coal equivalent	392		

Inflation and finance

Consumer price		*av. ann. increase 1989–96*	
inflation 1996	21.4%	Narrow money (M1)	30.8%
Av. ann. inflation 1990–96	24.7%	Broad money	25.9%
Money market rate, 1997	25.15%		

Exchange rates

	end 1997		*December 1997*
Z$ per $	18.62	Effective rates	*1990 = 100*
Z$ per SDR	25.13	– nominal	…
Z$ per Ecu	20.48	– real	…

Principal exports

	$m fob		$m fob
Tobacco	730	Nickel	78
Gold	300		
Ferro-alloys	170	Total incl. others	**2,305**

Main export destinations[b]

	% of total		% of total
United Kingdom	10.1	Germany	7.9
South Africa	9.6	United States	6.7

Principal imports

	$m fob		$m fob
Machinery & transport equipment	1,126	Petroleum products & electricity	239
Manufactured products	455		
Chemicals	366	Total incl. others	**2,571**

Main origins of imports

	% of total		% of total
South Africa	38.3	Japan	5.1
United Kingdom	7.9	United States	5.0

Balance of payments[c], reserves and debt, $bn

Visible exports fob	2.2	Overall balance[d]	-0.1
Visible imports fob	-2.1	Change in reserves	-0.1
Trade balance	0.1	Level of reserves	
Invisibles inflows	0.5	end Dec.	0.8
Invisibles outflows	-1.1	No. months of import cover	2.9
Net transfers	0.3	Foreign debt	5.0
Current account balance	-0.2	– as % of GDP	73.5
– as % of GDP	-3.4	Debt service paid	0.6
Capital balance[d]	0.3	Debt service ratio	9.3

Family life

No. of households	0.1m	Divorces per 1,000 pop.	...
Av. no. per household	...	Cost of living, Dec. 1997	
Marriages per 1,000 pop.	...	New York = 100	52

a 1990
b Excluding gold.
c 1995
d 1994

Glossary

Balance of payments The record of a country's transactions with the rest of the world. The **current account** of the balance of payments consists of: visible trade (goods); "invisible" trade (services and income); private transfer payments (eg, remittances from those working abroad); official transfers (eg, payments to international organisations, famine relief). Visible imports and exports are normally compiled on rather different definitions to those used in the trade statistics (shown in principal imports and exports) and therefore the statistics do not match. The **capital account** consists of long- and short-term transactions relating to a country's assets and liabilities (eg, loans and borrowings). Adding the current to the capital account gives the **overall balance**. This is compensated by net monetary movements and changes in reserves. In practice methods of statistical recording are neither complete nor accurate and an errors and omissions item, sometimes quite large, will appear. In the country pages of this book this item is included in the overall balance. **Changes in reserves** exclude revaluation effects and are shown without the practice often followed in balance of payments presentations of reversing the sign.

CFA Communauté Financière Africaine. Its members, most of the francophone African nations, share a common currency, the CFA franc, which is maintained at a fixed rate of 1FFr = 100 CFAfr by the French treasury.

Cif/fob Measures of the value of merchandise trade. Imports include the cost of "carriage, insurance and freight" (cif) from the exporting country to the importing. The value of exports des not include these elements and is recorded 'free on board' (fob). Balance of payments statistics are generally adjusted so that both exports and imports are shown fob; the cif elements are included in invisibles.

Commonwealth of Independent States All former Soviet Union Republics, excluding Estonia, Latvia and Lithuania. It was established January 1 1992; Azerbaijan joined in September 1993 and Georgia in December 1993.

Crude birth rate The number of live births in a year per 1,000 population. The crude rate will automatically be relatively high if a large proportion of the population is of childbearing age.

Crude death rate The number of deaths in a year per 1,000 population. Also affected by the population's age structure.

Debt, foreign Financial obligations owed by a country to the rest of the world and repayable in foreign currency. **Debt service paid** is the sum of principal repayments and interest payments actually made. **The debt service ratio** is debt service expressed as a percentage of the country's earnings from exports of goods and services.

EU European Union. Members are: Belgium, Denmark, France, Germany, Greece, Ireland, Italy, Luxembourg, Netherlands, Portugal, Spain and the United Kingdom and, since January 1 1995, Austria, Finland and Sweden.

Ecu European currency unit. An accounting measure used within the EU and composed of a weighted basket of the currencies of 12 EU members.

Effective exchange rate This measures a currency's depreciation (figures below 100) or appreciation (figures over 100) from a base date against a trade weighted basket of the currencies of the country's main trading partners.

Fertility rate The average number of children born to a woman who completes her childbearing years.

GDP Gross domestic product. The sum of all output produced by economic activity within a country. GNP (gross national product) includes net income from abroad eg, rent, profits.

Import cover The number of months of imports covered by reserves, ie reserves $\div \frac{1}{12}$ annual imports (visibles and invisibles).

Inflation The annual rate at which prices are increasing. The most common measure and the one shown here is the increase in the consumer price index.

Life expectancy The average length of time a baby born today can expect to live.

Literacy is defined by UNESCO as the ability to read and write a simple sentence, but definitions can vary from country to country.

Money supply A measure of the "money" available to buy goods and services. Various definitions exist. The measures shown here are based on definitions used by the IMF and may differ from measures used nationally. Narrow money (M1) consists of cash in circulation and demand deposits (bank deposits that can be withdrawn on demand). "Quasi-money" (time, savings and foreign currency deposits) is added to this to create broad money.

OECD Organisation for Economic Co-operation and Development. The "rich countries" club was established in 1961 to promote economic growth and the expansion of world trade. It is based in Paris and now has 29 members.

Opec Organisation of Petroleum Exporting Countries. Set up in 1960 and based in Vienna, Opec is mainly concerned with oil pricing and production issues. Members are; Algeria, Ecuador, Gabon, Indonesia, Iran, Iraq, Kuwait, Libya, Nigeria, Qatar, Saudi Arabia, UAE and Venezuela.

PPP Purchasing power parity. PPP statistics adjust for cost of living differences by replacing normal exchange rates with rates designed to equalise the prices of a standard "basket" of goods and services. These are used to obtain PPP estimates of GDP per head. PPP estimates are normally shown on a scale of 1 to 100, taking the United States, where the average standard of living is highest, as 100.

Real terms Figures adjusted to exclude the effect of inflation.

Reserves The stock of gold and foreign currency held by a country to finance any calls that may be made for the settlement of foreign debt.

SDR Special drawing right. The reserve currency, introduced by the IMF in 1970, was intended to replace gold and national currencies in settling international transactions. The IMF uses SDRs for book-keeping purposes and issues them to member countries. Their value is based on a basket of the five most widely traded currencies: the US dollar, Deutschemark, pound sterling, Japanese yen and French franc.

Sources

Airports Council International, *Worldwide Airport Traffic Report*

Alan Guttmacher Institute

BP, *Statistical Review of World Energy*

British Mountaineering Council

Corporate Resources Group, *Quality of Living Report*

Council of Europe

The Economist Intelligence Unit, *Cost of Living Survey; Country Forecasts; Country Reports; Country Risk Service; Global Outlook – Business Environment Rankings*

ERC Statistics International, *World Cigarette Report*

Euromonitor, *International Marketing Data and Statistics; European Marketing Data and Statistics; World Consumer Markets 1997–98 on CD-ROM*

Europa Publications, *The Europa World Yearbook*

European Bank for Reconstruction and Development, *Transition Report*

FAO, *Production Yearbook*

Financial Times Business Information, *The Banker*

Gold Fields Mineral Services Ltd.

The Heritage Foundation, *The 1998 Index of Economic Freedom*

The Howard League for Penal Reform

ILO, *Year Book of Labour Statistics*

IMD, *World Competitiveness Yearbook*

IMF, *Balance of Payments Statistics Yearbook; Direction of Trade; International Financial Statistics*

Information Please Almanac

International Cocoa Organisation, *Quarterly Bulletin of Cocoa Statistics*

International Civil Aviation Organisation, *Civil Aviation Statistics of the World*

International Coffee Organisation

International Cotton Advisory Committee, *Bulletin*

International Criminal Police Organisation (Interpol), *International Crime Statistics*

International Finance Corporation, *Emerging Stock Markets Factbook*

International Road Federation, *World Road Statistics*

International Rubber Study Group, *Rubber Statistical Bulletin*

International Federation of the Phonographic Industry

International Grains Council, *The Grain Market Report*

International Sugar Organisation, *Sugar Yearbook*

International Tea Committee, *Annual Bulletin of Statistics*

International Wool Textile Organisation

Lloyd's Register, *Statistical Tables*

Network Wizards

Nobel Foundation

OECD, *Development Assistance Committee Report; Environmental Data*

ISTA Mielke, *Oil World*

Taiwan Statistical Data Book

The Times, *Atlas of the World*

Time Inc Magazines, *Fortune International*

UK Home Office

UN, *Energy Statistics Yearbook; State of World Population Report; Statistical Chart on World Families; Urban Agglomerations; World Population; World Population Prospects*

UN Development Programme, *Human Development Report*

UNICEF, *The State of the World's Children Report*

Union International des Chemins de Fer, *Statistiques Internationales des Chemins de Fer*

US Department of Agriculture, *Rice Report*

WHO, *Weekly Epidemiological Record; World Health Report; World Health Statistics Annual*

World Bank, *Atlas; Global Development Finance; World Development Indicators; World Development Report*

World Bureau of Metal Statistics, *World Metal Statistics*

World Drink Trends in association with NTC Publications

World Resources Institute, *World Resources*

World Tourist Organisation, *Yearbook of Tourism Statistics*

World Trade Organisation, *Annual Report*

Zenith Media

List of countries

Whenever data is available, the world rankings consider 171 countries: all those which had, in 1995, a population of at least 1m or a GDP/GNP of at least $1bn. Here is a list of them.

	Population	GDP		Population	GDP
	m	$bn		m	$bn
Afghanistan	20.9	ab 12.8	Egypt	63.3	64.3
Albania	3.4	2.7	El Salvador	5.8	9.9
Algeria	28.8	43.7	Eritrea	3.3	0.8
Angola	11.2	3.0	Estonia	1.5	4.5
Argentina	35.2	295.1	Ethiopia	58.2	6.0
Armenia	3.6	2.4	Fiji	0.8	2.0
Australia	18.1	367.8	Finland	5.1	119.1
Austria	8.1	226.5	France	58.3	1,533.6
Azerbaijan	7.6	3.6	Gabon	1.1	4.4
Bahamas	0.3	3.5	Gambia, The	1.1	0.4
Bahrain	0.6	5.7	Georgia	5.4	4.6
Bangladesh	120.1	31.2	Germany	81.9	2,364.6
Barbados	0.3	2.0	Ghana	17.8	6.2
Belarus	10.3	22.5	Greece	10.5	120.0
Belgium	10.2	268.6	Guadeloupe	0.4	ab 3.7
Benin	5.6	2.0	Guatemala	10.9	16.0
Bermuda	0.1	2.1	Guinea	7.5	3.8
Bhutan	1.8	0.3	Guinea-Bissau	1.1	0.3
Bolivia	7.6	6.3	Haiti	7.3	2.3
Bosnia	3.6	3.3	Honduras	5.8	4.0
Botswana	1.5	4.8	Hong Kong	6.2	153.3
Brazil	161.1	709.6	Hungary	10.0	44.3
Brunei	0.3	ab 4.6	Iceland	0.3	7.2
Bulgaria	8.5	9.9	India	944.6	357.8
Burkina Faso	10.8	2.4	Indonesia	200.5	213.4
Burundi	3.2	1.1	Iran	70.0	132.9
Cambodia	10.3	3.1	Iraq	20.6	21.9
Cameroon	13.6	8.4	Ireland	3.6	62.0
Canada	29.7	569.9	Israel	5.7	90.3
Central African			Italy	57.2	1,140.5
Republic	3.3	1.0	Jamaica	2.5	4.1
Chad	6.5	1.0	Japan	125.4	5,149.2
Chile	14.4	70.1	Jordan	5.6	7.1
China	1,232.1	906.1	Kazakhstan	16.8	22.2
Colombia	36.4	80.2	Kenya	27.8	8.7
Congo	46.8	5.7	Kirgizstan	4.5	2.5
Congo-Brazzaville	2.7	1.8	Kuwait	1.7	31.0
Costa Rica	3.5	9.1	Laos	5.0	1.9
Côte d'Ivoire	14.0	9.4	Latvia	2.5	5.7
Croatia	4.5	18.1	Lebanon	3.1	12.1
Cuba	11.0	a 18.0	Lesotho	2.1	1.3
Cyprus	0.8	8.9	Liberia	2.2	ac 2.3
Czech Republic	10.3	48.9	Libya	5.6	23.1
Denmark	5.2	168.9	Lithuania	3.7	8.5
Dominican Republic	8.0	12.8	Luxembourg	0.4	18.9
Ecuador	11.7	17.5	Macau	0.4	7.4

	Population	GDP		Population	GDP
	m	*$bn*		*m*	*$bn*
Macedonia, FYR	2.2	2.0	Senegal	8.5	4.9
Madagascar	15.4	3.4	Serbia,		
Malawi	9.8	1.8	Montenegro	10.3	15.7
Malaysia	20.6	89.8	Sierra Leone	4.3	0.9
Mali	11.1	2.4	Singapore	3.4	93.0
Malta	0.4	3.3	Slovakia	5.3	18.2
Martinique	0.4	ad 3.9	Slovenia	1.9	18.4
Mauritania	2.3	1.1	Somalia	9.8	ab 3.6
Mauritius	1.1	4.2	South Africa	42.4	132.5
Mexico	92.7	341.7	South Korea	45.3	483.1
Moldova	4.4	2.5	Spain	39.7	563.2
Mongolia	2.5	0.9	Sri Lanka	18.1	13.5
Morocco	27.0	34.9	Sudan	27.3	10.7
Mozambique	17.8	1.5	Suriname	0.4	a 1.3
Myanmar	45.9	63.4	Swaziland	0.9	1.1
Namibia	1.6	3.6	Sweden	8.8	227.3
Nepal	22.0	4.7	Switzerland	7.2	313.7
Netherlands	15.6	402.6	Syria	14.6	16.8
Netherlands			Taiwan	21.5	275.0
Antilles	0.2	ac 1.9	Tajikistan	5.9	2.0
New Zealand	3.6	57.1	Tanzania	30.8	5.2
Nicaragua	4.2	1.7	Thailand	58.7	177.5
Niger	9.5	1.9	Togo	4.2	1.3
Nigeria	115.0	27.6	Trinidad & Tobago	1.3	5.0
North Korea	22.5	ab 21.5	Tunisia	9.2	17.6
Norway	4.3	151.2	Turkey	61.8	177.5
Oman	2.3	15.3	Turkmenistan	4.2	4.3
Pakistan	140.0	63.6	Uganda	20.3	5.8
Panama	2.7	8.2	Ukraine	51.6	60.9
Papua New Guinea	4.4	5.0	United Arab		
Paraguay	5.0	9.2	Emirates	2.3	44.6
Peru	23.9	58.7	United Kingdom	58.1	1,152.1
Philippines	69.3	83.3	United States	269.4	7,433.5
Poland	38.6	124.7	Uruguay	3.2	18.5
Portugal	9.8	100.9	Uzbekistan	23.2	23.5
Puerto Rico	3.7	30.3	Venezuela	22.3	67.3
Qatar	0.6	7.5	Vietnam	75.2	21.9
Réunion	0.7	ab 2.9	West Bank and		
Romania	22.7	36.2	Gaza	0.8	3.9
Russia	148.1	356.0	Yemen	15.7	6.0
Rwanda	5.4	1.3	Zambia	8.3	3.4
Saudi Arabia	18.8	125.3	Zimbabwe	11.4	6.8

a Estimate.
b 1995
c 1994
d 1993